STUPID
WARS

★ ★ ★

STUPID WARS

A Citizen's Guide to Botched Putsches,
Failed Coups, Inane Invasions, and
Ridiculous Revolutions

★ ★ ★

ED STROSSER

AND

MICHAEL PRINCE

 Collins
An Imprint of HarperCollinsPublishers

FIRST EDITION

Designed by Level C

Library of Congress Cataloging-in-Publication Data

Strosser, Edward.
    Stupid wars : a citizen's guide to botched putsches, failed coups, inane invasions,
and ridiculous revolutions / Ed Strosser and Michael Prince.—1st ed.
        p.   cm.
    Includes bibliographical references.
    ISBN 978-0-06-125847-3
    1. Europe—History, Military. 2. America—History, Military. I. Prince, Michael,
1964- II. Title.
D25.5.S84 2008
355.02—dc22
2007039706

14.95

08 09 10 11 12   OV/RRD   10 9 8 7 6 5 4 3 2 1

This book is dedicated to all the GIs, Tommies, poilus, and other dogfaces of the world's armies who have suffered the mindless and generally fatal consequences of war.

CONTENTS

★ ★ ★

Introduction   ix

ONE Valens and the End of
     the Roman Empire: AD 377   1

TWO The Fourth Crusade: 1198   17

THREE The Whiskey Rebellion: 1794   44

FOUR The War of the Triple Alliance: 1865   63

FIVE The War of the Pacific: 1879   81

SIX The U.S. Invasion of Russia: 1918   102

SEVEN Hitler's Beer Hall Putsch: 1923   116

EIGHT The Chaco War: 1932   137

NINE The Winter War between
      Russia and Finland: 1939   154

TEN Romania Fights Both Sides in
     World War II: 1941   174

ELEVEN The Generals' Coup against Hitler: 1944   189

TWELVE The Bay of Pigs Invasion: 1961   205

THIRTEEN The Soviet Invasion of
          Afghanistan: 1979   224

FOURTEEN The Falkland Islands War: 1982   242

 FIFTEEN The U.S. Invasion of Grenada: 1983   258

 SIXTEEN The Soviet Coup against
          Gorbachev: 1991   281

          Acknowledgments   299

          Sources   301

          About the Authors   307

          Index   309

INTRODUCTION

Wars happen. Frequently. A quick survey of human history reveals only the briefest of periods where someone hasn't been shooting or hacking away at other humans. Periods of calm have been few and far between, and are usually reserved for planning the next conflict. Often as not, that planning is half-baked, off the mark, out of touch with reality, and potentially terminal for the planner. In some cases, this type of planning actually gets put into action. The results have not been pretty. A wise person once said, "If you want to know the future, study the past." We salute that wisdom with our study of the most foolish military endeavors man has ever thrown his boundless energy and brilliance into.

A chronicle of man's dumbest conflicts represents history at its spiciest: utterly stupid, pointless, and morbidly curious collisions where—driven blindly by greed, ignorance, ego, boredom, or some other incomprehensible credo—we have committed and continue to commit mistakes on a grand scale. How can we not marvel at these individuals who gambled so recklessly with history itself—with staggering costs in blood and treasure—that readers must shake their heads in disbelief while turning each page?

Most wars are bad. A very, very few seem to have actually been good. And then there are the conflicts that should never

have been undertaken in the first place, that should have remained no more than the fevered little dreams of disturbed
men. As any student of history knows, a smattering of these
conflicts garner much of the attention. These are the "good
wars," such as World War II, which were fought for the right
reasons and ended with a ringing moral victory. Library
shelves groan with books about these rare but clear winners:
the Greeks, the Romans, Napoleon, the British Empire, and
the Allies in the two world wars. All winners. Because winners write history. And no one likes to give himself a bad
review.

It is also extremely hard to write a book when you've been
starved, shot, or marched to death, which is the fate of many
war-losers. And there has always been a certain amount of
shame in losing a war no matter how many of the "enemy"
you may have vainly succeeded in shooting, stabbing, or
bombing from an airplane. Therefore, in a historical Catch-
22 we keep learning the lessons of history's winners, which is
that winning wars is good.

As we delved into the martial history of our pugnacious
little race, a few outstanding examples of really stupid wars
leapt out. We limited ourselves to Europe and the Americas,
although we are highly confident that Asia, Africa, Australia,
and perhaps even the polar nether regions have also shared
in the bounty of stupid wars.

Each stupid war offers useful lessons for the average citizen. Everyone needs to learn these lessons because the barri-
ers of entry to politics, the army, or becoming a dictator are
extremely low, and you may someday find yourself the head
of a large country or army.

For example, if you've been handed the reins to a mighty
empire such as the Roman only because your big brother is
emperor, as happened to a young farmer named Valens, it is
imperative that you first read the emperor's handbook, espe-

cially the chapter on never, ever showing mercy to the barbarians clamoring to get in.

Or you might find yourself on a religious military expedition, such as the Fourth Crusade, in 1198. Consider skipping it entirely if it is launched under the specter of crushing debt, despite the obvious attractions of killing lots of Muslims and sacking Jerusalem for Christianity. The Fourth Crusade did just that and went seriously awry, as the debt-laden crusaders were forced to make a few unplanned stops and ended up sacking, raping, and pillaging Constantinople, the greatest city in Christendom. Oops.

As we studied the stupid wars, we discovered that there has been an understandable but dangerous tendency for politicians to play general—and vice versa—and thus end up in very hot water. Even the most creative and visionary of politicians can fall prey to this danger. During the Whiskey Rebellion of 1794 in the infant United States, Secretary of the Treasury Alexander Hamilton (yes, the founding father with his face on the ten-dollar bill) headed up his own massive army to invade Pennsylvania to slap down some frontier settlers dodging Hamilton's tax on whiskey. In this stupid war against his own country, Hamilton clearly demonstrated the maxim that if you need to raise a huge army to force your democratic citizens to obey a tax law, you should seriously consider changing the law.

Dictators, sporting the zesty combo platter of unlimited political and unlimited military power, topped with unrestrained egomania, are usually the most egregious transgressors. For example, during the 1865–70 War of the Triple Alliance, Paraguay plunged into a war with three of its bigger, stronger, and richer neighbors, largely due to the warped decision of its dictator Francisco Solano López to make his top military strategist the former Parisian whore he shared the palace with. The result was so bad that López blamed his mother for the disastrous results, something not even Hitler was tempted to do.

Dictators also can make terrible allies as the Peruvians discovered during the War of the Pacific in 1879, when Bolivia started a war with Chile over birdshit, and dragged in Peru through a secret treaty to share their pain as its hapless ally. Peru was then forced to learn a basic lesson: when your ally drops out of the war, your army is destroyed, your leader has fled, your capital is occupied, an admiral is running your army, and your only source of wealth has been captured, it's time to surrender. An important corollary for stupid wars was also established by the Bolivians during this affair: if you have a coastline you would like to defend, get a navy.

Even the most educated politicians can find themselves losing their bearings completely when surrounded by the fog of war. Bespectacled, smarty-pants President Woodrow Wilson ordered the invasion of newly Communist Russia in 1918 while World War I was still going on, but Wilson gave the general in charge explicit orders *not* to cause trouble. As the American general was soon to find out, if you're going to invade to overthrow a government, you should expect that the owners of the country you're invading may notice your presence, become upset, and try to shoot you.

The most brutal and devious dictators can even find themselves having trouble getting a stupid revolution up and running, let alone an entire war. During Hitler's 1923 Beer Hall Putsch the leaders of the Bavarian army, police, and government were practically begging for somebody to start a revolution and rescue them from the democracy that was rampant throughout Germany at the time. Hitler, with an all-star staff of evildoers that would later achieve stunning success in starting World War II, threw a coup that seemed like a can't-miss affair. But his clumsy attempt at grabbing power collapsed in less than a day, a grim reminder of the challenges of starting a coup from a cozy spot like a beer hall, especially in a country where most of the populace are highly armed war veterans.

Unfortunately for some countries, war making becomes an end in itself, a sure prescription for spectacularly stupid wars. The Chaco War between Bolivia and Paraguay in 1932 was just such a war. Each country vied to escape the losers' bracket of history by beating the other loser. The result was one of the bloodiest wars, per capita, ever seen. They proved the maxim that even the champion of the losers' bracket is a loser. Medals are not handed out for eightieth place.

It's no surprise that when stupid wars get started, many countries keep making ever more colossal mistakes. Soviet Russia, a repeat offender in this respect, invaded Finland in the middle of the winter in 1939 but neglected to dress their troops in winter clothing. The warmly dressed Finns skied circles around the frozen Soviet troops and cut them to pieces, dealing a harsh lesson to the Soviets and to the watching Nazis that no matter how numerically inferior your army, when fighting the Soviets victory is always an option, if you can produce more bullets than the Russians have men.

Some countries simply don't know how to choose friends and stick with them. Romania proved this truism with flying colors when it ended up fighting everyone on both sides of World War II, first accepting an invitation from superfriend Hitler to invade Russia, then two-facedly turning on its Nazi friends and joining hands with the Soviet bear to attack the Germans.

On the other hand, even the world's best generals make great mistakes. Some of Hitler's horde of Prussian generals, trained for war like no others, finally worked up the gumption to get rid of the severely off-track dictator in 1944. Now they were faced with the inevitable choice between killing the greatest mass murderer in history, or upsetting the comfortable order of the German high command. Obviously, they made the wrong choice, and their abject failure of strategy, execution, and guts—while the world literally burned around them and thousands died daily as a direct result of their actions—is a virtual primer on what *not* to do when taking out a murderous dictator. The first lesson: bring a gun.

Some leaders, usually of the self-styled "advanced democracies" go ahead and invade even when they know it's a bad idea. During the 1961 Bay of Pigs invasion, John F. Kennedy figured the United States could invade Cuba without anyone knowing he was behind it. Unfortunately for Kennedy, the CIA had organized it, and this perfect little fiasco became the first invasion that press flacks tried to spin away.

Most dictatorships and superempires don't know a bad idea even when it smacks them in the face. When multiple-offender Soviet Russia invaded Afghanistan in 1979, they didn't realize that invading Afghanistan is usually the first stop on the route toward post–superpower status for an empire. The United States got carried away and forgot this fact when they began waging a proxy war to try to cleverly outflank the Soviets. The inevitable result was double-blowback for both empires at the hands of the wily warlords of the impenetrable mountains.

Another stunning miscalculation happened during the Falkland Islands War of 1982 when the cadre of Argentinian juntos, who were running their country into the ground, severely underestimated the willingness of Battleship Maggie Thatcher to fight to the death for crumbs of the British Empire. They inadvertently signed the death warrant on their little junta. Seasoned dictators should take to heart the lesson that killing civilians does not automatically make an army battle-tested. The main takeaway for rich empires from this confused little struggle was that the use of sophisticated radar and ship defenses to protect your massive fleet from cheap, French-made cruise missiles should be encouraged.

Even when all the legalistic guideposts for making war are flashing green, leaders are smart to tread warily. When the United States invaded Grenada in 1983, their difficulties in crushing the micro-Stalinist tourist state demonstrated the dangers of one-day wars. Their problems could have been boiled down to a handy invasion checklist, perhaps tacked to the front door of the Pentagon:

1. Confirm if enemy country has a military. If so, do not assume they can be defeated in one day.

2. Find accurate maps of proposed country to be invaded.

3. Bring working radios.

4. Make sure your Special Forces are really special.

5. If you're trying to rescue hostages, do you know where they are located? If possible call the hostages and ask them where they are.

6. Will the invasion start on a weekend? If yes, please coordinate with president's appended golf tee-time schedule.

7. Is your proposed invasion target an island or mainland? If an island, notify the navy.

8. Are sufficient supplies of medals on hand?

The end of empire presents challenges no less stiff either at the beginning or middle of a regime. During the 1991 Russia coup against Gorbachev, the coupsters were generally drunk, sweaty, and unprepared. They had forgotten that successful coups are works of art and must be highly organized, combining a whiff of menace and a hint of overwhelming force. Also, it is not advisable to hold televised press conferences where everyone has bloodshot eyes from a night of confidence-boosting vodka shots.

Our book is dedicated to a study of the wisdom lurking in these outstanding examples of martial stupidity. Clearly, the studying of successful wars has not prevented new wars, let alone the stupid ones. As we studied the stupid wars we discovered what is perhaps the most disturbing trend of all: stupid wars are hard to end. Once started, usually by the actions of inscrutable idiots saddled with unrealistic and heinous goals, the players on each side become reluctant to end the slaughter because they don't want to admit to the stupid reasons that launched the war in the first place. So the war continues, and the goal becomes simply to keep the war going.

With all this in mind, it behooves all of us to do everything we can to avoid the next stupid war before it gets started.

★ ★ ★

ONE

VALENS AND THE END OF THE ROMAN EMPIRE

AD 377

As Roman rule evolved over seven centuries from republic to dictatorship and then to ruin, the only principle held constant by the rulers was that the leaders of Rome should never, ever, show their enemies any mercy.

From its founding in the fifth century BC, when the original Roman gang established itself by tossing the Etruscan kings off the seven hills of Rome and banding together into a republic, the Romans slowly conquered the surrounding tribes and developed the basic template for empire, which served as the model for most of Western civilization down through the ages. The Roman republic trashed the idea of hereditary dynasties and replaced it with two rulers sharing power, known as consuls, chosen from the aristocrats of the conquering class.

The power-sharing model lasted until around 34 BC, when it was replaced by the dictator-like rule of the emperors, starting with Augustus. For centuries the emperors expanded the fascist rule of Pax Romana in a circus of hacked-off limbs. By the fourth century AD, the primary job of the

Roman emperor was to maintain and defend the empire from the hordes of barbarians clamoring at the gates. But by now the real power of the emperor lay with the imperial guard, the cohort of soldiers who protected him.

The Roman imperial guard had been created by the first emperor Augustus around year 1 as his own private army. These were the Praetorian Guards, SS-like in structure, function, and attitude. Over the centuries, the Praetorians were disbanded but replaced by a more brutal cadre of imperial guards who wielded the power to choose any emperor they wanted and assassinate the ones they hated. The imperial guards made their choice of emperors with the main goal of keeping the empire in fighting shape.

The preservation of their power was paramount. Showing no mercy was critical. Revolts and rebellions by dangerous people such as Jesus were squashed brutally, often resulting in the disappearance of entire cities, not to mention most of their unruly inhabitants. Survivors were sold as slaves or dragged home to Rome to be ritually slaughtered in front of the home crowd in the Colosseum as testament to the correctness of the Roman way of life.

The greatest threat to the Roman Empire down through the centuries, amid the wars, famines, and revolts, the greed, bloodlust, stupidity, incompetence, and insanity of its emperors, was mercy toward the barbarians. Mercy, as it were, in the form of Emperor Valens, who was given the job of emperor solely because his big brother was the western emperor. Somebody had to run the eastern part, and Valens opened the crack in the shield that ultimately led to the Roman Empire's downfall.

THE PLAYERS

Emperor Valentinian I—A solid soldier from the imperial guard chosen to be emperor because he posed no threat to the two dynasties vying to control the succession.
Skinny—Hot tempered and noted for his screaming memos.
Props—Favored his eight-year-old son over his brother Valens as next in line for his job.
Pros—Good soldier who served the empire well.
Cons—Ruined the empire by making his brother co-emperor.

Emperor Valens—Valentinian's younger brother, a simple-minded farmer from the sleepy countryside whose sole qualification to be co-emperor was that his brother was forced to share power by the imperial guard.
Skinny—Didn't speak Greek, the lingua franca of the eastern empire, so relied on interpreters.
Props—Built an aqueduct in his capital, Constantinople, which stands to this day.
Pros—Trusted that people were as simple as sheep.
Cons—Often forgot the concept of "show no mercy to barbarians."

THE GENERAL SITUATION

Since the beginning of the Roman Empire in 510 BC, clean-shaven Roman aristocrats were determined to outdo the scope of Alexander's Greek Empire through an unremitting fury of blood-spilling macho aggression. Power and togas mattered to the Romans. Once enemies were subdued by sword or treaty, power kept the peace and filled the coffers with gold. As the empire expanded, the Romans often incorporated the gods of the vanquished people under the big tent of Pax Romana while press-ganging many of their army-eligible men as soldiers and gobbling up their resources as booty and foodstuffs.

Those generals who mastered the rape-and-pillage para-
digm of forcibly welcoming non-Romans (i.e., "barbarians")
into the empire marched into Rome in triumph, trailing gold
and slaves, with the power to stake their claims to be emperor, with the help of the imperial guard.

It didn't matter anymore if the general were a Roman aris-
tocrat, or gods forbid, a Vandal, Goth, or Hun. If the guard
gave you the thumbs-up, you were in. This flexibility allowed
the Roman republic to become the world's first superempire.

By AD 364 the vast size of the Roman superempire required the emperor to spend most of his time battling barbarians on far-flung borders, closely guarded by his cohort of
imperial guards, who traveled with him at all times, in case
of one of those awkward moments when they found themselves with a dead emperor on their hands.

Which happened when Emperor Julian got himself incon-
veniently killed that year in combat against the Romans'
long-standing nemesis, the Persians. Then Julian's replacement died on the way to Rome. The guard huddled yet again
and settled on Valentinian I as the best of a weak field of
blood-soaked soldiers short-listed for the position. He was a
compromise figure, chosen because he was not from one of
the dynastic families of former emperors jousting to regain
power. After appointing Valentinian, the imperial guards,
wise to the challenges and risks of helming the giant war machine, requested in their nonrefusable way that he nominate a
co-emperor to run the eastern half of the empire. Valentinian
shrewdly chose the one person he knew wouldn't outshine
him and whom he could control, his little brother Valens.

The imperial guards accepted Valentinian's choice of
Valens because he was weaker and even more inexperienced
than Valentinian. They arrogantly assumed that even a weak
emperor, not to mention his dumb little brother, was no
threat to the continued existence of the superempire.

Valens was seven years younger than Valentinian and had grown up on his family's farm in the eastern Balkans while his brother was out campaigning in Africa and Gaul with his father, a soldier. Instead of a harsh life in an army camp, Valens was raised in a fairly gentle bucolic environment. He was known for sporting bowed legs and a potbelly, common enough afflictions but apparently unusual enough in a Roman emperor to be duly sniffed at by his contemporaries.

At first, things started off well for Valens and his new empire, which comprised modern-day Turkey, the Balkans, the Middle East, and Egypt. He astutely hired people who spoke the local languages who could explain the incomprehensible bleatings of his new constituents. He married the daughter of a soldier and began treating everyone fairly. But Valens soon ran into problems. Once he attempted anything more than basic administrative tasks, things had a way of backfiring for him. He and his emperor-brother decided to improve the quality of the coins by making them more pure. These new coins helped stabilize the currency in the mind of the average Roman citizen, but by minting new coins with more and finer gold, the ruling brothers were actually robbing themselves. Many of Valens's decisions ended up hurting only himself.

Valens soon had bigger problems, however. The Goths, barbarians out of what is now lower Ukraine and the northeastern Balkans, were up to their old tricks. After being defeated by Emperor Constantine in AD 328 while unifying the empire under his control, Constantine had forced the Goths to contribute troops for the constantly undermanned eastern empire legions.

Now smelling weakness in the plodding new emperor Valens, the Goths invaded the eastern empire in AD 365. As per the emperor handbook, Valens dutifully dispatched legions to start working them over. Now an even bigger problem cropped up. He was facing a revolt in Constantinople, his very own capital. A former imperial secretary named Procopius, a relation of Emperor Julian in the Constantine dynasty, was struck for some reason with the happy thought that he deserved to be emperor. Procopius convinced Valens's two legions to join his coup, made a deal with the invading Goths, and declared himself emperor. He struck new coins and started appointing his people in Constantinople. It was yet another classic Roman power-grab.

Valens sent a distress call to his brother Valentinian, the western emperor. Valentinian was too busy to send help. His excuse was that he was tied down battling Germans in Gaul. Valens, on his own, managed to defeat Procopius in AD 366 with the critical support of a respected general in the army named Arbitio, who defected to Valens after his estates were stolen by Procopius. The smooth-talking Arbitio convinced half of Procopius's army to desert, and the remaining half, sizing up the situation, quickly flipped to Valens's side. Celebrating his first martial victory, Valens gleefully slaughtered Procopius and in time-honored imperial Roman fashion shipped his severed head to big brother Valentinian in Rome. In reality, Valens had dodged only one bullet. There were more soon to follow.

Valens now declared a full-on war against the Goths for supporting Procopius's coup, but he couldn't manage to pin down the slippery barbarians, despite beating Athanaric, the Goth king, in open battle in July 369. But Valens didn't follow the victory up with the coup de grâce. He turned away to rest his troops below the Danube for the winter, and let the moment pass against the reeling Goths, who sent emissaries to Valens and appealed for mercy. Mercy from a Roman emperor? This was an unheard-of proposition, but Valens was willing to try out this shiny, modern idea. He and King Athanaric of the Tervingi Goth tribe signed a peace treaty in mid-Danube, in effect bowing to the barbarian king's refusal to set foot on Roman territory. It was another very un-Roman act, which violated the unwritten Roman law of running the empire as a mercy-free zone. Until then all Roman treaties had been signed in Rome or on the field of battle under Roman standards.

After that three-year slog in the eastern Balkans, Valens was free to return to the more glorious pursuit of reconquering Armenia from the Persians, who had been staying sharp by raping and pillaging the countryside. Kicking around the Goths was not seen by anybody as anything more than day-to-day empire maintenance; crushing the Persians and regaining Armenia would impress his brother much more. So, in 370 Valens set out to attack the Persians.

Valens still suffered from the chronic manpower shortage of the eastern empire. Despite a law that the sons of veterans were compelled to serve, inducements were often handed out to keep up the recruitment numbers, costing the empire's treasury dearly. And Roman soldiers hated serving in the east. Dragooning barbarians was the cheapest way to staff up the legions. Propping up the Armenian king by attacking the hirsute Persians would require all of his forces. Unfortunately, that midriver treaty with the Goths had ended the payment of tribute in gold to the Goths and also ended the requirement of the Goths supplying troops to the Roman emperor, as had been established under their treaty with Constantine. Valens had exacerbated his chronic manpower shortage just when he needed bodies the most. In spite of this, the glory-deficient Valens gave himself the title of *Gothicus Maximus*, or "Top Goth," and emblazoned it on coins to trumpet his mercy-tainted victory around the empire. Still, Valens was getting no love or respect from his big brother in the west. Valentinian had shrewdly used one of the typical Roman-emperor ploys to help solidify his position as the head of a new dynasty of emperors. In 367 he had appointed his eight-year-old son Gratian as emperor-in-waiting, then married him off to the daughter of a former emperor. Valens's young nephew now had more legitimacy as emperor in the eyes of the average Roman than he himself did.

Yet another blow came in 375, when Valentinian dropped dead of a stroke while berating barbarian ambassadors trying to justify their invasion of the superempire. Valens had lost his guiding hand and erstwhile protector, and now found himself competing with his nephew, the teenaged Gratian, now Emperor Gratian.

Valens was now the emperor-weakling. Gratian's regents kicked sand in his face when they elevated Valentinian I's other son Valentinian II, all of three years old, to co-emperor alongside his half-brother Gratian. This was a direct thrust at Valens, whose only son Galatens—consul at the ripe age of three—had died soon after the Procopius rebellion, reportedly bringing Valens to his knees in grief.

Upon the naming of Valentinian II as emperor, the regents handed him chunks of Valens's territory in the Balkans without bothering to consult Valens. Troops from these provinces would have helped solve some of Valens's manpower problems with the Persians and the Goths. But Valens, instead of taking a page from the emperor handbook and murdering the lot of them, consolidating the empire under his rule, labored on like a good farmer.

Facing numerous enemies with few friends, the problems of the empire were starting to overwhelm the farmer-cum-emperor. Preoccupied with his Persian problems, the Goths, who Valens thought he had handled with his mercy-riddled treaty, were turning out to be a problem again.

WHAT HAPPENED:
OPERATION "STUPIDUS MAXIMUS"

In 376 the weakened Goths suddenly found themselves at the mercy of the Huns, a terrifying horde who blitzed out of the eastern steppes, deploying very prescient skills of mobile warfare, and pushed the Goths back up against the Danube, the northeastern border of the empire in the Balkans. The Goths were caught between the Huns, apparently unaware that such a thing as mercy existed, and the Romans, whose survival depended on the maintenance of a mercy-free zone, gods forbid. The Goths were desperately looking for a break.

The mass of Goths—men, women and children—in a group perhaps as large as 200,000, had created a giant refugee crisis for Valens. Always looking for some extra troops, Valens decided to let the barbarians cross the Danube . . . but only those of the clan of chieftain Fritigern, who was an opponent of Athanaric, the king with whom Valens had made his earlier midstream treaty. It was a bad decision, driven by the need to solve his manpower problem against the Persians. The other Goth tribes, unfortunately, would have to stay on the other side and be exterminated by the Huns.

The Goths, welcomed into the empire, imagined themselves not as temporary immigrants or landless refugees but standing on a somewhat equal footing with the Romans, who promised them land and food in exchange for the inevitable draft notices for the young men. But the merciless Roman soldiers knew better how to handle the refugees than did their emperor. Without the usual order to slaughter the hungry barbarians, the frontier troops, headed by General Duke Maximus, created a black market among the impoverished refugees by exchanging dog meat for slaves. So desperate were the Goths they even exchanged their children for moldy bread and wine of a poor vintage. But the Roman legions assigned to the sector were so undermanned that when the refugees revolted over their rough treatment, the Romans pushed them farther into the empire to isolate them. The Romans patted themselves on the back for this clever strategy. But it now left the border undefended, and the Goths of the Greuthungi tribe snuck over.

Meanwhile, the scheming Roman generals, still apparently unconvinced of the wisdom of inviting barbarians into the empire and eager to roll the Goths like every other defenseless barbarian strolling down the via, invited the Goth leaders to a feast in the city of Marcianople. Their plan was to use an old Roman trick of inviting the Goth leaders to a feast, which would also happen to be their last meal on earth. While the restless and hungry Goth masses stuck outside the city gates began to revolt against the Roman overlords, inside the city the wily Romans took out the Goth guards and cornered Fritigern, their leader. The Roman leader of the province, Count Lupicinus, put a knife to Fritigern's throat. They had him. But mercy once again reared its ugly head. Perhaps infected from a recent meeting with Valens, Lupicinus pulled back. The quick-thinking Fritigern convinced the Romans to let him go in order to calm his people. But now Fritigern pulled a fast one and, once among his people outside the gates of Marcianople, flipped on his ungracious hosts. The Romans formed up ranks and came out for what was expected to be a walkover, but they found themselves outmanned and on the business end of a good whipping. Lupicinus retreated into the city with his surviving troops. The Goths were now rampaging inside the empire without constraint, their forces bolstered by other barbarians streaming over the borders and spiced with deserters from the barbarian-riddled Roman legions.

In 376 Valens was stuck on the eastern edge of the empire tangling with the Persians when he got wind of the problems with the Goths. He made a quick truce with the Persians and sent a request to his thankless nephew Gratian, now emperor of the west, for help. Bogged down in Mesopotamia, Valens needed a year to trek back to handle the uprising himself, all the while waiting in desperation for the promised surge from his nephew. In the meantime, Valens ordered his generals on the scene to attack the Goths with the few Roman legions he had in the area. The understaffed Roman legions, many of them poorly trained border guards, were defeated time and time again by the resilient Goths, who continued their rampage.

By the time Valens arrived in 377 the high-stepping Goths stood beneath the gates of Constantinople. Valens, not eager to linger in the despised city that had supported the rebel wannabe Procopius against him, cobbled together enough troops, including some formerly peace-loving monks who had been conscripted into the manpower-short eastern empire army. Valens managed to break out of the city and carve out some room to maneuver for his army on the plains west of the city. His plan was to stop the Goths from occupying the east–west road, where the hoped-for troop surge from Gratian would arrive.

Out in the western empire, meanwhile, Gratian was playing emperor by the book, which included showing no mercy for family who had become rivals, let alone barbarians seeking a warm, dry spot inside the empire. Gratian set out to help his uncle but delayed his march east to take a few whacks at some Germanic invaders who had made the mistake of crossing the Rhine. Gratian's handlers insisted on leisurely slaughtering them to the last man to really make the moment of his first great triumph shine before moving on down the road to help Valens. Gratian's only timely effort was to dispatch a small force down the Danube in boats, which unfortunately landed a few hundred miles away from Valens and his 20,000 troops camped west of Constantinople. Gratian's troops proved to be of no help except to inform Valens that the bulk of long-awaited reinforcements would be late due to his victorious slaughter of the Germanic hordes. Now Valens really was being outshone by his young nephew.

Meanwhile, the Gothic king Fritigern had assembled his forces northwest of Constantinople outside the town of Adrianople in the western spur of modern-day Turkey. Valens, impatient of waiting for reinforcements from the ungrateful teenager Gratian, was eager to conclude his own triumphant campaign with a sound drubbing of the annoying Goths. Valens held a council of war and was encouraged by a report that a Goth force of approximately 10,000 soldiers had been spotted marching south through a mountain pass to take Adrianople. If they succeeded, Valens would be cut off from his supply base.

Valens's commanders were split on their recommendation: some wanted to fight immediately while others advised waiting for the reinforcements to ensure an overwhelming victory. But Valens finally gave in to his anger, jealousy, and impatience. He decided to vent his frustrations as only an emperor can. The surge from Gratian was nowhere in sight. But he didn't care. The time had arrived to punish once and for all the sneaky, border-crossing, backstabbing Goths. Valens's big moment had arrived. With his force of approximately 20,000 troops, he headed out to cut off the Goths at the pass.

The day before the battle Fritigern made an offering of peace in exchange for Thrace, which was a nice chunk of the eastern Balkans bordering the Black Sea. Valens, feeling an emperor level of confidence, turned it down. Perhaps Fritigern's offer of peace was taken as a sign by Valens that he had caught his enemy in a weak position. Valens decided to attack the next day, August 9.

In AD 378 Valens marched his troops seventeen kilometers north through the dusty heat of the countryside outside of Adrianople. The summer heat would have been ferocious. Once he arrived in front of the enemy in the early afternoon, he found the Goth army inside a giant wagon circle, the custom of this mobile tribe. The well-rested Goths seemed to be sitting ducks. They could be destroyed at Valens's leisure.

As the two armies stared each other down Valens rejected another peace offering. One of the previous Goth offers from Fritigern had included a secret letter offering a truce but indicating the necessity of the Romans to show force to the Goths, which would give Fritigern the necessary cover to explain his surrender. Valens, not trusting him, had refused then and anticipating victory, refused now.

One can assume the hot and thirsty legions took a breather, drank water, sought out shade. But now another offer to negotiate was made. This one included an exchange of high-ranking prisoners as a first step in the negotiations, a typical arrangement to keep the two armies facing each other over a few hundred feet of meadow from tangling. Valens accepted it, perhaps now considering the fatigue of his troops and for some reason giving Fritigern the benefit of a doubt about his previous offer of tanking in front of the arrayed might of the Roman legions. As his legions arranged themselves in battle order to finish acting out the surrender ploy, a high-ranking hostage from Valens's entourage prepared to deliver himself to the Goths to start the negotiations.

If it was a trap, it was perfectly laid and sprung on the plodding Valens. He had played into the Goths' hands. The Goth cavalry, which had been roaming the countryside out of sight from the Roman scouts, appeared seemingly out of nowhere and fell against the Roman cavalry, an elite unit of the imperial guard, on Valens's left flank. In all probability they had ridden down one of the almost-dry riverbeds to keep down the dust and hide their approach from the Romans. As they crashed into the left wing, the Roman cavalry was pressed back against the infantry in Valens's center. The Romans were discovering the hard way that the Goth forces comprised probably 30,000 or more fighting men. But the veteran Roman horsemen stabilized themselves and led a thrust forward. The Romans were now winning, with the infantry pushing uphill toward the ring of wagons. But now the cavalry on the left wing was deeply engaged with the more numerous Goth cavalry, and Valens had no cavalry reinforcements to pour into the battle to force the issue. Clearly outmanned by the Goths, the battle soon swung once again to their side as they engulfed the left Roman wing.

The infantry legions were now left unprotected by the decimation of the left cavalry flank. Pressed back in on itself, they collapsed into a protective formation with their wooden shields and battled on. Using their long spears to hold off the enemy cavalry worked as long as the spears lasted, but when they were broken by the cavalry swords of the Goths the Romans were left with only their swords to stave off the swirling mass of Goth horsemen. The Romans were now sitting ducks. The battle continued until the bloodied mass of Roman soldiers finally broke and ran. The rout of the eastern emperor's army was on.

A regiment of soldiers held in reserve joined the panicked flight instead of manning up and trying to rescue the emperor. Other key commanders who had fought before under Valens deserted him in the growing darkness, abandoning their emperor instead of going down fighting. Two-thirds of Valens's army was killed, along with many of the generals.

Perhaps the simple, stubborn emperor, even after watching his generals abandon him and his soldiers massacred, refused

THE GOTHS

The Goths—the very name reverberates through history to the present time. Oddly enough, the people themselves vanished shortly after sacking Rome in 410 under the leadership of their king Alaric. The Goths had originally made their name fighting an endless series of border wars against the Romans and had gained the dubious distinction of serving as slaves to many Roman households. Then the Huns overran them in their Black Sea homelands, and a great mass of Gothic refugees were allowed to enter the Roman Empire by crossing the Danube in 376. After crushing the undermanned legions of eastern emperor Valens at Adrianople, the Goths tried to make peace with the Romans in exchange for a slice of the empire to call their own. But after a series of treaties with the relentless Roman emperors they still didn't have a homeland, and they took out their vengeance by sacking the great imperial capital. After all that they ended up with Visigothic territories in France and Spain as well as a sizable chunk of northern Italy for the Ostrogoths. The Goths who remained in Italy after the sacking of Rome were soon dispersed by more recent Teutonic invaders, and their influence and culture was almost completely washed away. In Spain and southeastern France the Goths soon found themselves at odds with the Roman popes, and the last of the Gothic kingdoms disappeared in the eighth century with the Muslim invasions of Spain.

to flee the field and was left dying on the ground surrounded by enemies. His imperial guard had left him at the mercy of his enemies. But they had been schooled in the Roman way of running an empire better than he. Valens's body was never found.

WHAT HAPPENED AFTER

No Roman ever imagined this could have happened to one of their emperors. There were conflicting reports about what happened to the body of Valens. Some said he was burned alive. In any event, the body was never found, a humbling end for any man, let alone the leader of a superempire. The Romans found themselves suffering their worst defeat since Cannae at the hands of the Carthaginians seven hundred years earlier. The legacy of sacrificing everything to victory, established over the centuries by Roman leaders such as the general who had died spurring on his legions to victory in the climactic battle of the third Samnite War in 291 BC, which solidified Roman control over central Italy and put the Romans firmly on the path to empire, had vanished. And to the Goths no less.

Valens's successor, Theodosius, a general appointed by Gratian as the new eastern emperor, gamely attacked the Goths but wasn't able to defeat them. He was forced to make peace with them on their terms: they had pierced the empire and were there to stay. The Roman Empire was on its last legs—the defeat at Adrianople was overwhelming; the empire was mortally wounded. In 410 Rome was sacked by the Gothic king Alaric, who had been a boy among the refugees crossing the Danube back in 376.

By the end of the fifth century the empire was no more. Valens was committed to the black hole of history, on equal footing with the many others who had succumbed to Roman power. Such are the rewards of mercy when trying to run a superempire.

★ ★ ★

TWO

THE FOURTH CRUSADE
1198

Great debt, like great faith, or heat shimmering on desert sands, can distort reality. Debt can take hold of a person's mind, twisting logic and converting no into yes, wrong into right.

At the dawn of the thirteenth century, religious fervor once again swept through the Christian population of Europe. Rallied by the pope and French nobles, crusaders set out for the fourth time in a century to capture Jerusalem and the Holy Land from the Islamic infidels. Off they marched with the purest of intentions, untainted by the necessity of killing Muslims to achieve their holy goal.

This time out, however, the road to eternal salvation detoured through Venice. The crusaders, eager to avoid the dusty overland route through Constantinople, hired a navy from the Venetians to sail them to the Holy Land. The emerging maritime power was controlled by the doge, a wily, money-loving, deal-making ruler, who had been elected for life by the aristocracy of the city. The doge's sole mission in life was to enrich his beloved city-state. But the crusader army, lacking in gold-laden recruits from the finest families in Europe, quickly piled up a massive debt that the doge refused to forgive—not even for the greater glory of recapturing Jerusalem. His solution for relieving the crusaders of their unfortunate financial burden was to make a series of deals in which the crusaders first attacked a Christian city and then went on to sack, rape, and pillage the biggest, richest, most Christian city in Europe: Constantinople. The doge received his payment in full, but the holy warriors never set foot in the Holy Land.

THE PLAYERS

Prince Alexius—A footloose, wandering prince, the son of the deposed Byzantine emperor, bounced around Europe looking for a spare army to put him atop the throne of the Byzantines.
Skinny—Young and naïve, he nonetheless managed to get himself in the right place at the right time to convince an entire army of desperate crusaders to do his bidding.
Props—Escaped the dungeon that his uncle threw him into, then traipsed around Europe to plead his case for a return to Constantinople.
Pros—Never reneged on his promises, until he did.
Cons—Described by a contemporary as womanish and witless.

Doge Enrico Dandolo—Leader of Venice who wasn't afraid of sacking and pillaging to recover his debts.
Skinny—To spread his own influence he ordered that Venetian coins bear his face on one side and on the other a likeness of the second most important person in his world, Jesus.
Props—Kept his focus on one thing, a successful crusade. Maybe two things . . . making money for Venice.
Pros—Was over ninety years old and blind but still rode into battle to lead the Fourth Crusade.
Cons—Led them everywhere but their destination.

THE GENERAL SITUATION

Jerusalem. Oh, Jerusalem! The small city has the fortune—or is it the misfortune—of being situated at the heart of three major religions. The Jews housed the Temple of Solomon and the Ten Commandments there. Then it became the site of Jesus's Crucifixion. And a few centuries later it was the place where Muhammad ascended to heaven.

Being wanted by three groups of people has turned the city into a battleground for much of its history. Fueled with religious fervor following Muhammad's death in AD 632, Arab armies thundered out of the Arabian Peninsula and captured large swaths of the known world, including Jerusalem. Over the next few hundred years they controlled the Holy City while freely allowing European Christians to make pilgrimages to the cherished site of the Church of the Holy Sepulchre. The Jews had been scattered by the Romans, and the few left in town apparently posed no threat to anyone or anything.

This peaceful coexistence was shattered in the eleventh century when Turks from Central Asia stormed into the Middle East and grabbed large chunks of territory from the reeling Byzantine Empire (made up of the remnants of the eastern part of the Roman Empire). The Byzantines were based in the glorious city of Constantinople (modern day Istanbul), which served as a barrier between the Arabs in the Middle East and the Western Europeans, thus allowing the Europeans to focus much of their medieval energy on killing one another.

The Turks also conquered Jerusalem from the Arabs in 1071. Instead of continuing the Arab policy of allowing the Christians free passage, the Turks ambushed the travelers, throwing them into slavery. The Christians had lost access to their beloved Jerusalem. The Turks had blundered onto the third rail of the nascent international monotheistic scrum over the city.

Tapping into this anger in 1095, an angry Pope Urban II declared that the Christian world must capture Jerusalem, thus creating the First Crusade. The pope declared the Crusade was not only necessary but actually requested by God. He coined a catchy slogan for the venture, "God Wills It," and even came up with a logo, a cross sewn onto the shoulders of the crusaders' clothes. To motivate his troops the pope offered every crusader absolution of their sins, in essence a go-directly-to-heaven ticket upon death. In the Middle Ages, where vast realms of knowledge remained untouched by the geniuses of the age and the average human's life was a constant dodging of an apparently vengeful God, this was a Big One. Eternal happiness, as in forever, was like money in the bank.

In 1097 the crusaders set out, an army of knights on horseback, soldiers on foot, and a vast train of workers to schlep heavy items for thousands of miles. Despite hunger, thirst, disease, and a six-week siege, it worked. Jerusalem fell on July 15, 1099. To celebrate the conquest of the land of the King of Peace, the conquerors raped and killed everyone left alive in the city. Mission accomplished.

The crusaders divided their conquered territory into four regions, fought like caged animals over who would control them, and waged a never-ending series of wars against the Muslims. The crusaders were bolstered by a steady flow of Christians looking for new opportunities and European royals seeking fortune and adventure away from their already royalty-saturated homelands. A Second Crusade poured in yet more troops. Despite a persistent manpower shortage, the Christians hung on to Jerusalem, the jewel of the Holy Land, ruled over by kings, including some children and even a leper or two.

It wasn't enough. Various Islamic peoples united under a fearless leader, Saladin, a great Christian killer. His victories culminated in 1187 with the capture of Jerusalem. Mission unaccomplished. A Third Crusade led by the king of England, Richard the Lionhearted, tangled with Saladin but came up short. Richard returned home to vent his frustration on the more beatable French.

The next pope to catch the crusader bug was Innocent III, who took his seat in 1198 and immediately turned his eye toward rescuing the Holy Land from the Muslims, again. He knew he would need all the help he could get.

But things out east were a mess everywhere, not just in Muslim-occupied Jerusalem. The Byzantine Empire was head-quartered in Constantinople, known to the Greeks as the new Rome. Despite being Christians, the Greeks had significant theological differences with the pope, which resulted in their 1054 mass excommunication, referred to as the Great Schism. Needless to say, that put a damper on the relationship between the Eastern Orthodox Greeks and the Roman Catholics. The Crusades didn't resolve their differences, even though the Greeks provided some help with the first one.

The Greeks had been content to spend most of their time fighting among themselves since the emperor's death in 1180. Various noble families fought to seize control of the prestigious and powerful emperor's crown, considered to be one of the two most powerful of the Christian world. Out of the fighting emerged the Angelos family. Isaac II ruled as emperor from 1185 to 1195 when his older brother, Alexius, perhaps tired of Isaac's fondness for jocular dwarves, gouged out Isaac's eyes and threw him into prison. Alexius took the throne and held Isaac and his teenage son, Prince Alexius, in prison.

In 1201 the young Prince Alexius escaped, with the help of some Italian merchants, by hiding in a barrel. He headed to Germany to enlist the help of his brother-in-law, the king of Germany, to retake the contentious Greek throne. As momentum built for a new Crusade, Prince Alexius was touring Europe looking for anyone who would give him a ride back to his throne in Constantinople. Meanwhile, back in Rome, as the thirteenth century was just gearing up, Pope Innocent III was settling into office, looking to get the new century off to a good start with a nice religious war.

As unlikely as it seemed, their two quests would cross paths with devastating and unintended results.

WHAT HAPPENED: OPERATION "DEBT BOMB"

Enthusiasm for Pope Innocent's Crusade lagged until November 1199 at a tournament of knights in the Champagne region of France: two young, popular, and very rich members of the French royal elite took up the cross and joined the Crusade. After Count Thibault of Champagne and his cousin Count Louis of Blois declared their intentions to march onto Jerusalem, others quickly joined up. Some were inspired by the desire to serve Jesus, some by their family's heritage in leading former Crusades, while others undoubtedly knew that nobody gets the hot babes like a knight back from a Crusade. A third count, Count Baldwin of Flanders, who was Thibault's brother-in-law, joined the mission early in 1200.

Baldwin's family had fought in the three previous Crusades, so the twenty-eight-year-old count looked on crusading as a family rite of passage. The three young nobles took the reins to recruit and lead the new, improved Crusade. God was sure to be on their side since the plan featured as many as 35,000 crusaders, the same size army that had successfully conquered Jerusalem in the First Crusade. The pope admonished the army to conquer based solely on their faith in

Christ and not have their pure feelings sullied by vanity, greed, or pride. As it turned out, however, most of the crusaders' decisions for the next five years were guided by vanity, greed, or pride (and sometimes all three).

Throughout the spring of 1200 the three nobles carefully planned the expedition. They met with former crusaders-turned-crusading-consultants to learn the best routes to the Holy Land, rallied other French nobles to the cause, and discussed the critical question of how to pay the enormous costs of supporting thousands of soldiers for years on end.

They decided to sail. The first choice for a fleet was the merchant powerhouse Venice, one of the largest cities in Europe. Its ships were the top dogs of the Mediterranean due to the expertise gained from the large volume of trade with Muslims, which had been conducted with special permission from the pope. Since 1192 the Venetian Enrico Dandolo had held the leadership position of doge; ninety years old and blind, his dedication to the Church was surpassed only by his love of making money and stockpiling power for his beloved city. Dandolo was the man.

After negotiating with the doge, the crusaders reached a deal in April 1201. The doge agreed to build a navy, transport the army, and feed all of them for nine months. All this for the low, low price of 85,000 marks, about twice the annual income of the king of France. As a special deal, for this Crusade only, the crusaders could pay on the installment plan.

Eager to kill Muslims and recapture Jerusalem, the crusaders signed the deal and headed home to France, unaware that their poor skills in drafting the agreement had planted the seed for their venture's doom. The price was based on transporting an army of 35,000 men plus 4,500 horses, an army bigger than all but that of the First Crusade. No provision was made, however, if fewer troops showed up for the sailing date. The full price would still have to be paid for the half-empty fleet. This meant a higher cost per crusader.

But such trivial details were not in the minds of the crusaders as they made their way home after making their down payment of 5,000 marks to the doge. The Venetians put aside all their business and turned the city into one vast workshop for making ships to meet the June 1202 sailing date.

The deal, like many blockbuster deals, contained a secret clause. The fleet would first sail not to the Holy Land but to Alexandria in Egypt. While this was a sound strategic move as the attack could knock out Egypt as an enemy, making the conquest and holding of Jerusalem easier, it was somewhat controversial. So controversial in fact that the doge kept this detail hidden from crusading troops. For him, this little secret clause was the key to the whole deal. He would get paid to sail to Alexandria, then use the crusaders to capture the city and turn it over to him, further expanding the Venetian trading power into a huge and megarich metropolis. The doge would get a double shot of victory: Jerusalem for the spirit, and Alexandria for the wallet. His grin probably lasted for days.

In May 1201, the first disaster hit the crusaders. Thibault died. Of the three leaders he had been the most dynamic and well liked. Recruitment dropped like a rock. To make up for the loss the crusaders picked up Boniface, the marquis of Montferrat, a city in Northern Italy, as their new leader. Boniface was fifty years old and hailed from a long line of crusaders. He accepted the offer with great enthusiasm.

In early 1202 the crusaders set out for Venice. Upon their arrival they were warmly welcomed by the Venetians, handed their bill, and shown their new home, Lido Beach, a barren sandbar miles from the city. The doge wanted them close, but not close enough to cause trouble. Now the second bit of bad news hit the crusaders. Thousands of crusaders were no-shows. The leaders waited and waited, but as the spring turned to summer on Lido Beach, like a third-rate resort, the crowds simply never materialized.

The doge, Boniface, and the other leaders did a head count, and fingered their worry beads. Only about 12,000 soldiers had shown up, about one-third of the estimated number. This meant that the price per crusader would now be three times as originally planned. Everyone coughed up more coin, but it was not enough to cover the doge's huge tab. The doge refused to lower his price. First, because a deal is a deal, but more important, having spent an entire year building this massive fleet, he needed every promised penny to pay off his bills. To help focus the minds of his crusading brethren he stopped supplying them with food and water until his bill was paid.

As the army slowly wasted away, and desertions started to chip away at their already meager ranks, Boniface and the others dug even deeper and handed over virtually all their valuables to the doge. He counted his booty and told them they were still 35,000 marks short. The army teetered on total dissolution. They didn't even have the food to make the humiliating return home to France where the sum total of their experience would be the equivalent of a cheap beachside T-shirt proclaiming, "I went on a Crusade and only got as far as Venice."

The doge then proposed a way out from under their crushing debt. He asked them to run an errand for him: sail down and recapture the city of Zara (now known as Zadar in Croatia), which had slipped out of Venice's control in 1181. The crusaders would conveniently overlook the fact that Zara was a Catholic city and part of Hungary, a firm supporter of the Crusades. The attack meant postponing the Crusade to Jerusalem in order to fight a war against Christians so that the Venetians could expand their little merchant empire. The move was pure doge.

The crusaders at first resisted but the doge knew that sometimes you have to join them to beat them. He took the crusader's oath in St. Mark's church and the impressionable crusaders were swayed. He was no longer just some money-hungry contractor but a part of the team, on board for the big win. That October the huge fleet sailed down the coast with the deal-making doge in the lead. It was the blind leading the desperate.

Word of the Zara gambit soon filtered back to the pope. He wasn't happy. Coastal raids on Christian cities clearly violated the spirit of "crusading" as the papal world had come to define it. But the pope's emissary, embedded with the army, sensing that the only two realistic options were to crush Zara or go home in failure, gave the crusaders the thumbs-up. The pope had the last word, however, and played the big hand. He wrote a scathing letter declaring that those who attacked Zara would get excommunicated from the church, meaning eternal damnation. As in forever. At this point the crusaders were destined for the fires of hell along with the Greek Christians, the Muslims, and all the other infidels crawling the earth in wretched existence.

On November 11, 1202, the crusader fleet reached Zara just as the pope's letter reached the leaders ordering them not to attack. The leaders split on what to do next. Some—led by the deal-making doge—favored attacking the city; others recoiled from assaulting fellow Christians in flagrant defiance of the pope and the fires of hell. The doge argued that the pope's order was important, but not as important as the crusaders' contract with him. The road to Jerusalem, they convinced themselves, ran through Zara, especially since the alternative was to go home in shame. The pope's letter was slipped into a drawer, never revealed to the soon-to-be-excommunicated army. The crusaders attacked. It was now the doge's army.

Two weeks later Zara fell, and the army surged into the city to reap its booty. But the vaults were empty. After counting up every loose coin, the crusaders still did not have enough money to cover the rest of their trip. The only thing the attack earned them was a one-way ticket to the blistering shores of Hades.

As the crusaders sat in Zara, having committed a massively unholy act that called down the heavy wrath of the pope and still lacking the money to reach Jerusalem, the ambassadors of Prince Alexius showed up. The wandering prince, still cruising the backroads of Europe looking to pick up a ride home, suddenly displayed a level of acuity that had previously escaped him: he presented them with a tantalizing solution to their debt problem and the now-bigger situation of the pope reserving the crusaders a suite in the ninth circle of hell, befitting betrayers of the faith.

Prince Alexius offered to finance the rest of the Crusade and provide additional troops. To top it off, he promised to end the schism between the Romans and the Greeks by recognizing the pope as top man in the Christian world. All the crusaders had to do was escort him to Constantinople and install him, Prince Alexius, as emperor. Then they would be able to easily skip down to Jerusalem and fulfill their crusading destiny. And the pope would achieve one of his top career goals. Prince Alexius had made them an offer they could not refuse.

Still, Byzantine politics being Byzantine politics, the leaders debated. The doge, to no one's surprise, was enthusiastic for the novel Greek caper. The doubting Thomases reminded everyone their job as crusaders was to kill Muslims in Jerusalem on Christ's behalf, not fellow Christians in Constantinople. They could have stayed home and done that. The doge, however, won the debate as usual with a twist of logic that would have made a theologian proud: he convinced the crusaders that restoring a Christian emperor to the throne—through what was surely promised to be a short and easy war—was in fact a very Christlike act.

Some of the troops, however, failed to go along with the doge's impressive reasoning. Killing Christians just was not as fulfilling as killing Muslims. Many soldiers fled. On the bright side, Pope Innocent III had now retreated from his earlier position. He washed away all the crusading sins committed from the Zara gambit but made the crusaders swear they would never again attack a Christian city. The leaders, striving for new heights of duplicity, agreed, knowing that their secret plan to restore Prince Alexius would probably require attacking Constantinople.

In April 1203 the fleet sailed out of Zara after leaving it a smoky wreck. The churches, in the spirit of devotion of men on a high cause such as a Crusade, were spared.

The next month, halfway to their destination, the army stopped on the island of Corfu. Here a chunk of the army, perhaps distracted by the wonderful views, developed second thoughts and refused to sail to Constantinople. They marched to the other side of the island, a sort of self-imposed crusading time-out. Alexius and the crusading leaders confronted the defectors, knowing the loss would cripple their limping army. They begged, groveled, cried, and drooled. The defectors agreed to stay, but in the true spirit of the Fourth Crusade, they wanted to make another deal. They would stay only until Christmas, and then they would be free to advance on Jerusalem. The crusading leaders agreed. Alexius was pleased to report to the doge that the debt-relief plan was still in place.

Jubilant at surviving yet another near-death experience, the army set sail and reached the outskirts of Constantinople by late June 1203. They had never seen anything like it, as they stared in awe at the monstrous walls of the great city before them. With its population of 400,000 people, Constantinople dwarfed anything in Europe. The defending walls were tall and thick, and seemed to go on forever. The crusaders looked at their small force of about 20,000 men and wondered what they had gotten themselves into. Besides its enormous size and wealth attained by being the trading center of the world, the city boasted a powerful military tradition.

The political infighting that ravaged the empire in the previous decades, however, had eaten away at the city's military strength and the fighting spirit of its citizens. Despite knowing for months that the crusaders were coming, the emperor, Alexius III, took few steps to defend the city. The once-mighty Greek fleet was rotting and incapable of any serious naval action; the city's protective walls were actually in need of repair. But perhaps most important, the army lacked any fighting spirit. Its core consisted of thousands of mercenaries, primarily the Star Trek-oid Varangians, who were hard-fighting Scandinavians. The weaknesses of the Greek army were temporarily obscured by its sheer size.

Constantinople sits on the western—European—side of the Bosporus, a narrow channel of water separating Europe from Asia. The crusaders set up camp on the eastern—Asian—side of the Bosporus, where the emperor had allowed huge supplies of food to accumulate, apparently unaware that this might somehow help his enemy. The emperor arrayed his army along the European bank to repel a beach invasion.

To spark a coup against the emperor and avoid a fight, the double-deal-making doge took his young prince Alexius and paraded him on the prow of a ship sailing before the walls of Constantinople. Surely, the doge thought, the people of the city would identify their true leader and quickly rally to him and depose Alexius III, the false emperor. Wrong! No one in the city even recognized the prince. The little expedition returned to camp on the other side of the Bosporus completely deflated. The crusaders gulped hard as this latest stratagem from the doge failed, knowing their only option now was to conquer the massive city. The emperor's army filled the beach below the massive city walls.

On the morning of July 5, 1203, the crusaders, with the blind doge in front, landed on the beach within sword's length of the emperor's massive army. The crusading knights galloped off their state-of-the-art, specially designed ships outfitted with landing ramps. The shocked and awed Greeks turned and fled. The emperor took flight so quickly he was forced to abandon his tent full of personal possessions. Building on this success, the crusaders soon crashed through the chain that protected Constantinople's inner harbor, the Golden Horn, and penetrated the city's weak spot.

Despite some successes at scavenging for supplies, the crusaders were running out of food. Now camped just outside of the city's north wall, they knew they had to act quickly and either capture Constantinople or retreat. On July 17 the crusaders made their move. They split into two groups, with the more numerous French attacking from the land, and the Venetian knights assaulting the city walls from their ships. Time after time the Greeks threw back the attackers on both fronts. Sensing his army's fading chances, the doge ordered his ship to charge toward the city. His reckless charge rallied the crusaders. No one wants to be outbraved by a blind old man. They rushed onto shore, and the Greeks turned and fled into the city through the gates, followed closely on their heels by the Venetians. Emperor Alexius III threw his army against the Venetians inside Constantinople. As the crusaders withdrew toward the gate, they set a fire to protect themselves; it quickly grew to engulf a large swath of the city, shielding the Venetians and allowing them to cling to a section of the city wall.

Finally, the shaky emperor Alexius III suddenly developed some moxie. He poured his army out of the city to crush the French crusader camp. Their numbers dwarfed the small band of crusaders who realized their slim chances to survive; they were running out of food, far from home, and facing ridiculous odds. The two armies closed and waited. A group of the crusading knights, breaking ranks, having endured humiliation, the pope's anger, the fires of hell, and that persistent debt, dashed, forward to attack with desperate élan. There were no more than 500 of them, shining in their armor, including Baldwin of Flanders, one of their founding leaders. On they dashed, almost reaching the Greek lines. They stopped at a small river. Everyone waited. Surely, the Greeks would surge forward and overwhelm the small group of knights, sending the rest of the crusaders in retreat. As the tension mounted and the crusaders pondered their next move, Alexius III turned gutless once again and ordered the Greeks to do what they did best: turn and flee. The crusaders watched in awe as their huge enemy filed back into the city, the knights shadowing close by to drive home the humiliation. Emperor Alexius had blown it.

That night the emperor grabbed some gold, abandoned his wife, and with a coterie of associates fled the city. The Byzantine emperor, one of the two most powerful leaders in the Western world, ran away in disgrace with his army still undefeated and largely untested in battle.

As July 18 dawned, Constantinople found itself emperor free. Fearing the total destruction of the open city, the Greek leaders pulled the former, now blind, emperor Isaac, the father of Prince Alexius (and brother of Alexius III), from his basement prison and installed him as the new emperor, per-

haps the quickest promotion from prisoner to emperor in
history. At the crusader camp they clucked at their great fortune. They could now simply install the young prince to the
throne with his father, collect their money, and put their
murderous skills to better use capturing Jerusalem and killing Muslims.

A delegation of crusaders quickly trooped in to visit Isaac
in his splendid palace, privately informing him of his son's
agreement—the one that brought them to Constantinople.
Although shocked by the debt now owed by his young son,
the new emperor, like fathers forever, had no choice but to
bail out his free-spending son. Refusal would have unleashed
another crusader assault, and with the emperor's political
base so weak, he was unsure how the army would respond.
The Greeks threw open the city's gates, and Alexius strode
in. He was crowned Alexius IV, co-emperor with his father.
The Greeks lavishly supplied food to the crusading army,
which now graciously retired across the Golden Horn. Mission accomplished!

While the crusading nobles wandered the city gawking at
the treasure trove of amazing religious artifacts, the Venetians sized up its profit-making potential. The father-son
rulers started the usual work of a new regime, such as emp-
tying the jails of enemies of the former rulers. This crowd,
unfortunately for them both, included one Alexius Ducas,
known as "Unibrow."

To honor his agreement, the freshly crowned Alexius IV
paid a large chunk of money to the crusaders, and they
started mapping out the last leg of their circuitous trip to the
Holy Land. A subprime borrower with debt management
problems, Alexius could not pay the rest of his debt to the
crusaders. To raise money he desperately ordered sacred religious objects, the envy of the Christian world, stripped from
churches and melted down, a sacrilegious act in the eyes of

the Greeks. Also, he was having problems quickly mustering the army he had promised to the crusaders. And, because the Greeks viewed him as a crusader puppet, he realized that without their army his days in power would be numbered. He needed time and was willing to plunge into a deeper debt hole to buy some.

He made the crusader leaders another offer they couldn't refuse. He would pay the rest of what he owed, plus finance the fleet until September 1204, a year longer than the Venetians had agreed to hang around, and supply the crusader army. All they had to do was hang around until the following spring. By then, the co-emperor reasoned, he would have a firm grip on his empire. His Byzantine mind failed to register that it was perhaps unwise to have the crusaders stay longer when they were the cause of the resentment his people felt toward him.

Like the first deal, this one caused a rift among the crusader leaders. The deal-loving doge—surprise, surprise—said take the deal. The usual dissenters made the picayune point that Alexius still had not paid fully on his first promise. The doge and his crowd thought of the free supplies and the extra money the emperor would pay them. And he pointed out if they sailed right away they would reach the Holy Land at the start of winter, an acknowledged poor time to start killing Muslims. The doge then closed the deal by agreeing to keep his fleet teamed with the French until Christmas 1204. The crusaders doubled-down their investment on the young emperor.

Now fully invested in Alexius IV, the crusaders worked hard to ensure his success, but it was turning into a tough slog. A huge fire torched chunks of the city that hadn't already been burned and which the devastated Greeks blamed on the crusaders. To add to the mix, father and son emperors started fighting among themselves. The aging Isaac, never known for his sharp mind, became even more irrational, inspiring ridicule and hatred from his people. He and Alexius squabbled as each tried to gain the political upper hand. The people, humiliated by defeat, debt, destruction of many of their religious icons, fire, and failed leaders, grew to hate the both of them, nearly as much as they hated the crusaders.

Exploiting this anger was Unibrow, leading the throw-out-the-crusader wing of the Greeks. Bowing to this growing pressure, Alexius stopped payments to the crusaders. In December the crusaders met with Alexius in his palace. Before the city's nobles they harshly demanded he pay his debt or they would attack again. Insulted, Alexius had no choice but to reject the deal. To bow to the crusaders in front of the city's nobles would have meant political suicide and probably assassination. The hostility was so great the crusader delegation fled the city in fear.

Hoping to avoid conflict and restore the flow of funds into his pocket, the now-triple-deal-making doge secretly met with Alexius. For a year the old man had nourished Alexius, carried him to the throne on his own ships, and honored every commitment he made. He simply wanted Alexius to honor his debts in return. But he could not, Alexius told the doge. Angry at the betrayal, and perhaps shamed that he had put so much faith in Alexius, the doge now turned on his protégé and vowed to destroy him.

He had a lot of help. Fed up with Alexius and his inability to stop the crusaders' more frequent armed foraging into the countryside, crowds demanded the city's leaders elect a new emperor. They chose a young noble, Nicholas Kannavos, and appointed him emperor on January 27, 1204. He never wanted the unenviable job.

Desperate, young Alexius, now sharing the throne with a third emperor, turned to his former friends/current enemies— the crusaders—for help. He proposed yet another deal.

If the crusaders drove out Kannavos, he would give them his palace as security that he would honor his second pledge to honor his first pledge to pay them money and raise an army for them. This move to ally with the hated crusaders inflamed his people even further. Unibrow whipped up the anticrusader forces, and now the only option Alexius had to stay in power was pleading for the crusaders' help.

That night it all crashed down on the twenty-two-year-old Alexius. Unibrow secured the treasury and the army, snuck into Alexius's room, and took him prisoner. The next morning Unibrow was crowned the fifth living emperor of the tottering empire and the fourth alive in the city—three of them having recently been in prison. Unibrow then set out to winnow the crowded field of emperors. He sent his minions to Isaac's house; here they either found the blind man dead or helped him along on his journey. One down. Within days Unibrow seized the unlucky Kannavos and threw him into prison, where he quickly died. Alexius IV was the only competitor left. Unibrow then turned his wrath toward the crusaders and stopped the flow of supplies, and locked them out of the city.

Unibrow turned up the pressure a notch on the crusaders by leading raiding parties against them. But the Greeks, as had become their habit, turned and fled when confronted by a group of knights. Being new to the emperorship and not having learned yet how to retreat correctly, Unibrow lost the emperor's standard and one of the leading Christian religious icons he took into battle. The crusaders paraded these precious items before the city to mock Unibrow's failure. Sensing his troops were not equal to the task of facing down the battle-hardened crusaders, Unibrow called a parley with the doge to work out their differences. The doge demanded that Unibrow release Alexius and honor all the young man's commitments.

Unibrow found himself pushed into a corner. If he fought the crusaders it would be an uphill struggle with his underpowered, prone-to-flight army. Within the city he ruled over a divided populace with Alexius still retaining some support. If he eliminated Alexius, however, it would only further provoke the crusaders. He had no winning hand. Still, he had to take some sort of stand, so he took a leap into the unknown: on February 8, 1204, he visited his rival in prison and stabbed him to death. Another emperor bites the dust. Having slain Alexius did not stop Unibrow from mourning sorrowfully at the state funeral he organized to bring the city together in grief under his leadership. But Unibrow's power play had ended all chance of reconciliation with the crusaders. With Alexius alive the crusaders still held out hope he would honor his debts. With his death the money and any hope of finishing the crusade with a happy ending in Jerusalem was gone. Unibrow now had to pay one way or another.

The frustrated crusaders found themselves once again outside the city walls, far from home, unable to reach Jerusalem, and faced with the job of attacking the great city for a second time. They were no closer to Jerusalem than when they started two years earlier. They readily preferred death in combat to eternal humiliation. So they prepared for a war.

As the crusaders spent the next two months preparing their ships and siege machines, they also took the equally important step of splitting in advance the anticipated booty. As might be expected, the triple-deal-making doge walked away with the lion's share of the loot, three-quarters of every cent until they added up to 200,000 marks. Even at this late date the doge was unwilling to relinquish any of his bargained-for money for the good of the crusaders. The invaders also agreed to stay for another year in Constantinople so that the new emperor, to be selected later, would have time to stabilize the security situation in his new prize. Jerusalem would have to wait yet again. They agreed to sack Constantinople, the greatest of all Christian cities, but agreed to not touch the women and churches. Unibrow feverishly built the mighty walls even higher and prepared his army.

On the morning of April 9, 1204, the crusaders launched their assault. They attacked the walls with fury but faced a deadly torrent of rocks from the Greeks. Having made no progress and with casualties mounting, the crusaders turned back. The Greeks celebrated their rare victory over the knights by mooning their enemy.

Dejected from the defeat, Boniface, the doge, and the other crusading leaders turned to the Church leaders to rebuild morale among the shattered troops. They succeeded brilliantly by denouncing the Greeks as worse than Jews. As a final step of purity before God to guarantee victory, the crusaders cast out their prostitutes from the camp. Such self-sacrifice had rarely been endured by crusading armies.

The crusaders launched their second assault on the morning of April 12, from both land and sea. The battle grew in intensity as both sides poured in more troops. The crusaders catapulted pots of flaming liquid at the Greeks, who countered with rocks, arrows, and fire of their own. Despite their determined fury, the crusaders could not penetrate the city's massive walls. Then fortune blessed the crusaders. The wind shifted, pushing the doge's ships flush against the city's walls. Knights, fighting with the fury of the desperately indebted, leapt from the ship's attack bridges, nearly one hundred feet above the water, onto the city's walls. The Greeks slashed to death the first leaping knight. The second one, however, withstood the Greeks' battering, rose to his feet in full armor, and as had become their trademark, the Greeks turned and fled. Other crusaders quickly followed, and a section of the wall was securely in crusading hands. With the same daring the crusaders soon conquered other sections of the great city's wall.

While focused on this threat, the Greeks took their eyes off perhaps their most vulnerable point. Along the water's edge, the city's walls had gates, which in peacetime were used for loading and unloading merchant ships. These gates were sealed when the crusaders first approached the city in 1203. But apparently this work was not as sturdy as the regular sections of the wall. Focusing on this vulnerability, groups of Special Forces knights hacked away at one gate with swords and picks while other knights defended them from barrages of stones and boiling pitch. The ferocious knights now punched a small hole in the wall. They peered through and saw swarms of Greeks awaiting them. Whichever knight dared to go through first was on a sure suicide mission. One of the crusading churchmen, Aleumes, dove through the tiny opening and emerged in the city. He charged at the Greeks, a lone fighter with a sword, not even a knight, and, lo and behold, what surely has become an enshrined custom by this time, the Greeks turned and fled. More knights seeped through the opening, and soon nearly three dozen crusaders were inside the city. Unibrow led a charge to throw them out, but as he approached the knights he stopped, carefully considered the situation and—can it be true?—turned and fled. A handful of crusading knights had scattered the mighty Greek emperor and his troops.

Knights now flooded into the city. They fanned out and headed to Unibrow's headquarters. His loyal guard caught one glimpse of the bloodthirsty crusaders . . . and turned and fled. In fact, with the wholesale flooding of knights into the city, the Greek custom of turning and fleeing reached an impressive scale.

That night, realizing that his position was untenable, Unibrow followed the well-trod path of prior emperors and fled the city. As the city's elite awoke the next morning, April 13, they heard the news of the emperor's defection. To organize resistance, they drew lots to select the new emperor because no clearheaded person was even willing to volunteer for the job. The unfortunate winner was Constantine Lascaris. He urged everyone to resist the crusaders. But at the first sight of the knights just limbering up for the day's fight, the Greeks turned and fled. Their new emperor joined them in hastily abandoning the city, the second emperor in a day to flee and the third in under a year. As the knights prepared to fight their way through the rest of the city they found themselves confronted with an open city. No one opposed them. A contingent of Church leaders approached them and begged for mercy. While Boniface pondered the proposal, his army flowed into Constantinople like a river at high tide. The plunder began.

To sack a city as large and rich as Constantinople required the efforts of not just untamed soldiers, revengeful knights, or greedy leaders. All three segments of the army needed to unite in the crusader-like cause of killing, raping, stealing, destroying, and violating six or seven other commandments. To pillage a massive city like Constantinople indeed required all hands to participate. And all did.

Lathered into an uncontrollable and unholy horde, the crusaders descended into one of the bloodiest and most grotesque sprees in history. The nobles invaded palaces, headed straight to the treasure room, and ran their bloody hands through the loot. Knights and soldiers raped women, slashed the heads off children, and pillaged artifacts from churches. Many treasures were simply destroyed; others were carefully packed up for shipment back to the West. Even the priests got into the action and stripped religious artifacts to carry home to adorn their churches in France. They viciously assaulted the holiest place in the Eastern Church, the Hagia

LEPER KING OF JERUSALEM

Of all the crusader kings who ruled over the Holy Land none perhaps was as unusual as the Leper King of Jerusalem. Either as a testament to their egalitarian spirit or sign of their desperation, the crusader leaders in 1174 appointed a thirteen-year-old leper as king.

Known as Baldwin IV, he was extolled for his bravery, intelligence, and foresight. While his eyes still worked, he led the Christian forces against the legendary Muslim leader Saladin and fought him to a draw.

As the king's body parts withered, his battlefield victories piled up, temporarily restoring the power of the Kingdom of Jerusalem. At age twenty-four, in 1185, after having summoned his strength to do battle against Saladin's army, he died of leprosy not long after his final battle. Like his face and body eaten away by the disease, his legend has been lost down through the centuries.

Sophia, destroying or stealing virtually any item of value, leaving mounds of animal excrement on the floors. For the crusaders' amusement a prostitute danced on the great church's altar.

When the plunder stopped days later, or perhaps when they ran out of targets, the crusader leaders collected their booty and divvied it up. They had hit the jackpot. The triple-deal-making doge got his share plus more. The French got enough to spread a handsome purse to everyone. All that remained was to appoint a new emperor. And now the winner, who would become the seventh emperor of the Greeks in the ten months since the crusaders arrived, was Baldwin of Flanders, who by chance happened to be the doge's choice. The old man always seemed to get his way. In an elaborate ceremony in the Hagia Sophia, presumably now cleaned of mule dung and dancing prostitutes, Baldwin received the crown, ushering in what became known as the

Latin Empire. He had the unenviable job of restoring a city depleted of money and filled with ruined churches and angry people, in addition to half the city having been burned to the ground. To raise money for his new government, Baldwin resorted to pillaging the tombs of long-dead emperors, ensuring the dead received equal sacking treatment as the living.

In a series of letters explaining how the crusaders set out to kill Muslims and free the Holy Land and instead ended up deeply in debt, joyriding with a Greek prince, defeating six Greek emperors, and raping and killing defenseless Christians, Baldwin proclaimed that because they had succeeded in conquering Constantinople, their actions must have received God's blessing.

WHAT HAPPENED AFTER

While Baldwin wrestled with governing a city he helped destroy, three other emperors still roamed the countryside. Two of them, Alexius III—the original emperor when the crusaders showed up—and Unibrow—the emperor next to flee—agreed to ex-emperor-to-ex-emperor talks and possibly join forces to fight Baldwin. Alexius III also agreed to set up Unibrow with one of his beautiful daughters. Alexius III tricked Unibrow into meeting with him privately, and at this point some of Alexius's men grabbed Unibrow and blinded him. That November, Baldwin captured Unibrow, brought him back to Constantinople, and forced the now-blind ex-emperor to leap to his death from the city's tallest column. Around the same time Alexius III was also captured. Baldwin spared him for no apparent reason and packed him off to lifetime exile in Italy. And with that, calm descended upon the new Latin Empire. A short-lived calm, but a calm nonetheless.

By the spring of 1205 the crusader army began to break up. Some went to the Holy Land, most went home. That summer, the pope's man with the crusaders released them all from their vow to reach the Holy Land. The crusade had ended leaving this less than admirable scorecard:

Christian cities sacked: two
Greek emperors defeated during the crusade: six
Times the Greeks turned and fled: thousands
Muslims killed: zero

In the spring of 1205 Baldwin, the adventure-addicted doge, and other leading crusaders, such as Louis of Blois, one of the three founding nobles, took off with a small army to quell a rebellion around the inland city of Adrianople. On April 14, one year after the sack of Constantinople, the crusaders tangled with a larger force under King Johanitza of Bulgaria. Separated from the bulk of his army, Baldwin and some knights were overrun by vastly superior numbers. Louis was cut down; Baldwin, fighting like a savage, was dragged to Johanitza's prison in the Balkan Mountains and was never seen again.

The triple-deal-making doge and the bulk of the army survived and returned to Constantinople. The blind Venetian leader died of old age in June of 1205. He was buried in the Hagia Sophia, never having reached the Holy Land or returned to Venice. He magnificently channeled the energies of the crusading spirit into profits for his beloved Venice and the city-state flourished for centuries afterward.

Pope Innocent III was livid when he heard the crusade had ended without Jerusalem having entered his realm. When he learned of the full extent of the destruction of Constantinople he blanched in horror. He cheered up, however, when he realized his Catholics were now in charge of the Greek empire. He issued no further excommunications because of the massive deaths his own army caused.

The Latin Empire lasted until 1261 when the Greeks retook the city. Constantinople underwent resurgence but never regained its former glory, and it eventually fell to the Turks in 1453, ending the Byzantine Empire. The Catholics held out in the Holy Land, buttressed by a series of further crusades, until 1291. Europeans didn't make it back to Jerusalem until 1917 when the British captured it.

The Greeks never forgave the crusaders and the pope for unleashing their hellacious army on their city and pillaging their holy places. The break between the Catholics and Eastern Orthodox had become too great to fix. The Great Schism was complete. The two wings of the Christian Church would never reunite.

In 2001 Pope John Paul II issued a formal apology for the odious deeds of the Fourth Crusade.

★ ★ ★

THREE

THE WHISKEY REBELLION

1794

Life, liberty, and the pursuit of happiness make for warm and fuzzy reading in declarations of independence. But when push comes to shove, what really matters is money. The glorious new American republic was no different. Shortly after birth its essential character had already been formed: financial matters took precedence over everything else, including the continued enslavement of an entire race, the slow-motion holocaust of Native Americans, and the disenfranchisement of half of the population based on sex.

The Whiskey Rebellion was a haphazard, unorganized, poorly armed struggle by frontiersmen in western Pennsylvania against what they felt to be unfair taxes, the very philosophy upon which the United States of America had been founded in its struggle against the British Crown just a few short decades earlier. Most of the rebels were newly minted white Americans who depended upon only one handout from the government to sustain themselves on the edge of the new nation: freedom.

To these hardy souls freedom meant the freedom from taxation; in a nation whose focus was making money, tax-free status was the highest blessing that could be bestowed upon a citizen. But Alexander Hamilton had other ideas. The treasury secretary, super busy building the financial bedrock of the new country, felt that the tax base needed to be diversified beyond a dependency on taxing British imports. Thus was born his whiskey tax, an excise tax. It was the country's first tax on internally made products.

It drove the frontiersmen to rebellion. It would take three years of unrest before a cautious George Washington succumbed to Hamilton's pleadings to unleash an army planned, outfitted, and headed by Hamilton himself into western Pennsylvania to crush the resistance to his diversified excise tax-funding scheme.

THE PLAYERS

Alexander Hamilton—The quintessential New Yorker, an ambitious, foreign-born, mercantile-minded, highly efficient multitasker and pioneer Thomas Jefferson–hater.

Skinny—Since he was born on St. Croix he could not become president. But he could become king.

Props—Washington's chief-of-staff during the Revolution, one of the founders of the Bank of New York, first secretary of the treasury, and key drafter of *The Federalist Papers*.

Pros—His far-reaching fiscal genius laid the financial footing of the modern U.S. economy.

Cons—His far-reaching fiscal genius couldn't comprehend why poor frontiersmen wanted to dodge paying a tax on home-brewed whiskey.

George Washington—Western Pennsylvania land speculator, slave owner, first president of the Republic, lousy businessman, father of the country.

Skinny—Started the great American tradition of American president's retiring to make loads of money.

> *Props*—His previous experience running a war against white people made him aware of the political difficulties in seeking a high enemy body count.
>
> *Pros*—Graciously pardoned the two rebels eventually convicted of rebellion.
>
> *Cons*—Unleashed "General" Hamilton on the world.

THE GENERAL SITUATION

Western Pennsylvanians in 1790 faced a daunting existence. The forks of the Ohio River, formed by the Allegheny and Monongahela Rivers, today the site of the city of Pittsburgh, lay at the ragged edge of the American frontier. The main problem for settlers was that marauding bands of Native Americans often emerged from the woods to kill them. The land was sparsely settled and defended by local militias, who occasionally blundered out into the wilderness to attack the shadowy Native Americans, without much success. Government attempts to push back the Native Americans by alternating military ethnic cleansing operations with unfaithful negotiations had not worked very well up to this point. Life was stressful. Whiskey helped.

From Pennsylvania down to Georgia these hardy backwoodsmen, the genesis of the "Daniel Boone" icon, faced attacks on all fronts. Not only did they have to worry about Native Americans and hostile actions from British, Spanish, and French forces, they also suffered from the near constant inattention and underinvestment by their own government as they toiled to clear and farm land for absentee landlords—such as their own president.

Naked of all other aspects of orderly government, hugging the muddy banks of great rivers as they hacked out the new American empire from the sea of forest, the settlers were isolated. Pittsburgh was a village with 376 citizens, according to the 1790 census.

To make ends meet, many small farmers distilled whiskey from excess corn to drink or trade. Bartering was a way of life for these hardy settlers. Home-brewed whiskey was a great product in a frontier economy; it was wanted by nearly everyone and was easy to store and transport.

Washington's government and his frenetic treasury secretary, Alexander Hamilton, had agreed that one of the best ways to bind together the young country was through federal taxation. To get things rolling, Hamilton came up with a blockbuster deal. In July 1790 the federal government agreed it would "assume" the debt that each state had piled up in order to win the Revolutionary War. It was called the "assumption" deal. To close the deal Hamilton had to bargain away to the powerful Virginians the permanent seat of the government, sacrificing his personal goal of making New York City the new country's permanent capital. On the other hand he succeeded in making many of his banker friends very rich. When you help to start a brand-new country, sometimes money just happens.

The federal assumption of the states' war debts resulted in huge profits to New York businessmen. They had bought the state debts from private citizens and former soldiers who had been given IOUs in lieu of actual cash during the underfunded Revolutionary War. When the assumption deal passed, the bonds suddenly became redeemable at face value, and the speculators reaped spectacular profits. Virginia got the capital. New York got the cash.

Hamilton, as the author of the assumption deal, was naturally suspected by many people of having engineered this scheme to enrich his natural constituency, the Tory-sympathizing New York City mercantilists. In late 1790, not long after the federal government had relocated to Philadelphia (the temporary capital chosen to placate the powerful Pennsylvanians who were betting that the swampy new capital would never be built), Hamilton submitted his funding plan to pay for the new government and the newly assumed debt.

In his usual thorough manner, Hamilton was eager to diversify the tax base beyond the import duties of British goods, and he came up with the idea of an excise tax on whiskey. This "internal" tax hit the hardy frontier-types right in their thirsty, mud-bespeckled kissers.

Washington was on board with his treasury secretary. They agreed it was a wonderful device to strengthen the federal government by taxing spirits before the state governments could grab some of that swag. In March 1791 Hamilton's funding bill passed. His band of merry capitalists had won. Or so it appeared.

When frontier settlers heard about the new tax, they howled. "No taxation without representation" had rallied the new country through seven long years of war. The frontier citizens could imagine no reason to abandon that idea now that the war had been won, especially for a power-mad New York moneyman like Hamilton, Founding Father or no. The tax was widely flouted up and down the frontier to the point of invisibility. Resistance to the tax in western Pennsylvania surged like a spring flood.

In response to the law that threatened their way of life, a group of approximately 500 men in western Pennsylvania, with deep ties to the local militias, renamed itself the Mingo Creek Association, after a church where they held meetings. The association became the backbone of the organized resistance to the tax.

Not long after this first meeting, a tax collector happened to get himself tarred and feathered by some citizens who disagreed with his efforts to perform his job. The brave collector recognized two of his assailants and attempted to have them arrested for their assault. The federal marshal who showed up to serve the arrest warrants was too scared to proceed; he was directed by General John Neville, the inspector of revenue for the region, to hire an illiterate cattle driver to perform the job. The cattle driver also managed to get himself tarred and feathered by a mob, all of whom were dressed in one of their typical disguises (blackface, women's dresses, and Indian costume were all standard mob issue). It was a hearty frontier welcome for the tax collectors to the ranks of the massively disenfranchised and actively persecuted.

But not all the rebels delivered their message in hot tar while dressed in drag. Some moderate rebels sent a flow of objecting petitions to Hamilton. The debate became countrywide when the *National Gazette*, a Philadelphia paper secretly owned by a friend of Thomas Jefferson, Hamilton's archfoe in the cabinet, published an article in the spring of 1791 by a western Pennsylvania legislator suggesting changes to the law. The opponents also began a whisper campaign accusing Hamilton of hyping the rebellion in order to justify creating a standing army, which they imagined was another one of his tricks to establish a monarchy.

In fact, Hamilton did want to create a standing army, but he knew not even he could push that law through the fractured Congress. His blunt instrument of power would have to remain the barely-in-control state militias. He hated the idea that some faraway field hands were threatening his entire financing scheme and sensed that a face-off loomed. To prepare for this inevitable showdown, Hamilton broke out his sharpest quill and crafted the Militia Act of 1792, which allowed the president to use the state militias to crush an insurrection while Congress was not in session. The only limit on the power of the Militia Act was that a justice of the Supreme Court had to certify that rebellion was in fact happening. A trifling point to a power broker like Hamilton.

Out west, the mob slowly grew bolder. General John Neville was doing double duty making a small fortune providing stores to the nearby army outposts while also distilling whiskey. In a place where most people were too poor to own slaves, hatred and envy of slave-owning grandees like General Neville, not to mention tax collectors, was intense. Neville, showing a flair for creating an incredibly bad public profile, had voted against a previous state tax on whiskey when he was part of the Pennsylvania legislature, but then flip-flopped when offered the post of inspector of revenue, which featured a nice annual salary and a commission on his collections. A convenient bonus was the opportunity to closely monitor his competing distillers.

Hamilton's agile intellect, perfectly suited for designing systems of government and finance, betrayed him in this lowly matter, where the reality on the ground was a messy mass of conflicting aims that defied logic. His genius at expostulating far-ranging solutions from the germ of a problem led him to spring, in one giant leap, past any modest solutions, such as beefing up protection for the tax agents, and arrive almost instantaneously at the conclusion that this unrest in the woods required the dispatch of an entire army. It was all or nothing with him.

Central to his argument was that the western Pennsylvania unrest, so close to the capital, embarrassed and weakened the infant government. But Washington held back his young protégé and insisted on a more cautious and diplomatic approach. The president had ridden, scouted, and fought in the wilds of western Pennsylvania, first with the Virginia militia and later with British General Braddock, and knew the land well. He owned a big chunk of it (nearly 5,000 acres) for speculation and understood backwoodsmen in a way Hamilton didn't. Washington was understandably tired of war, but the ever-restless Hamilton seemingly had not had his fill. Too valuable as a key staff officer to lose, Washington had kept the superefficient Hamilton off the battlefield throughout the Revolution. But Hamilton was desperate to earn more battle stripes and quit Washington's staff to be on the field of battle at Yorktown in 1781. This small role in the big battle was still not enough for him.

As the mob grew in power out west, Neville tried to get additional military help from Philadelphia, but to no avail. During 1793, Benjamin Wells, one of his county deputy inspectors, kept plugging away at his job while getting repeatedly punched and abused, his office sacked, and his wife threatened when he was away from home. Wells traveled three times in 1793 to Philadelphia to report on the situation, but still Washington held his fire. They had bigger problems.

In 1792 France had launched into its own revolution and demonstrated its commitment to democracy by beheading King Louis XVI in January 1793. Hamilton and many in the government saw the increasingly bloody French revolution, led by Robespierre and his fascistic "Committee of Public Safety," which was soon guillotining enemies of the revolution, as a nightmare that could easily be duplicated by the whiskey-swilling radicals roaming western Pennsylvania. Washington's government was also riven with internal strife as Hamilton and Secretary of State Thomas Jefferson continued their gentlemanly brawl over their competing visions for the country's future. Jefferson and Hamilton had been butting heads for a long time. Jefferson, the aristocratic, hereditary landowner who nurtured a fantasy of agrarian simpleness with states' rights paramount for the country's future, was a deeply indebted Virginia planter who opposed the strong Federalist system that Hamilton was feverishly building. Jefferson, like many other Virginia planters of his class, hated banks in the way that only deeply indebted land-

holders could. Jefferson (who shied away from open confrontation) finally quit his post as secretary of state in 1793
when he failed to convince Washington that Hamilton was
secretly plotting to install a monarchy in the United States.
Indeed, Hamilton stoutly denied any monarchical intentions,
professing a preference for an all-powerful executive, a
president-for-life, surely, but not a monarchy.

Washington himself was also stressed out. His Virginia
plantation was chronically cash poor. His land in western
Pennsylvania was proving to be a bad investment, as it was
difficult to collect rents from the rebel-minded tenant farmers. His grand scheme—the Potomac Company—aimed at
opening up a route from the Potomac River to the Ohio
River, was looking like a loser. To top it off Washington himself was now facing open criticism for the first time, in particular from Jefferson's secret paper, the *National Gazette*,
and from small political groups called democratic societies or
clubs, a novelty springing up everywhere, inspired by the
revolutionary fervor from France. All of this added to the din
of criticism against Washington and his government. In this
inflamed environment, the unrest in western Pennsylvania
suddenly began to assume the specter of a prescient nightmare, with enough tinder to inflame the entire country. And
then in the fall of 1793 an epidemic of yellow fever closed
down Philadelphia for two months and nearly put Hamilton
on his deathbed.

Meanwhile, mob rule continued throughout western Pennsylvania. Rebels burned down barns of anyone who dared to
even register his still. The militia mob of the Mingo Creek
Association had shed its disguises and morphed into the fic-
tional character of mayhem, "Tom the Tinker." The rebellion
was growing bolder.

And still no help came from the east for General Neville
and his dogged deputy tax inspector Benjamin Wells.

WHAT HAPPENED: OPERATION "SELF INVASION"

The rebellion simmered along until the summer of 1794. Washington's moderation was still the order of the day, although there were more than enough other problems to distract him. Coupled with Hamilton's impetuous precocity, Washington's restraint was a key to the powerful partnership. But Washington had his phlegmatic limits. He was finally pushed over the edge when General Neville and a federal marshal were attacked in an attempt to serve writs to recalcitrant distillers, the latest brilliant salvo by Hamilton in his low-grade war.

The obstinate deputy tax inspector Benjamin Wells drew up a list of still owners in early summer. Hamilton took the list and drafted writs to be served, which required the defendants to trek three hundred miles to Philadelphia and appear in court in August, when courts were actually closed. Any small farmer who tried to appear in court would have to spend many weeks away from home and work, risking financial disaster. The writs were a spark, deliberately lit by Hamilton. The always-prepared Hamilton also knew that Congress was out of session and that the Militia Act would give Washington the power to call up federal militia by himself during this time.

Out west, an angry mob quickly confronted Neville and the marshal when they started serving the writs on July 17, 1794. They retreated to Neville's estate, already armed and stocked for defense, with Neville's family still inside. The mob pursued them and attacked the plantation. Neville, who had fought in a real war, drove them off with determined musket fire. The seething rabble retreated to an abandoned French fort nearby to wait for backup from the local militias.

The militia, now a small army of 500 men, marched back up to Neville's plantation and demanded his resignation and surrender of the writs. Neville refused. The rebels attacked the plantation, now defended by a dozen or so soldiers from the nearby government fort. They traded fire for an hour until they set the house aflame, forcing the soldiers to surrender. Neville, who had evacuated his family and was watching the battle from the woods, fled to Pittsburgh. The battle was over, for now. Tom the Tinker had evolved into a gangland army.

The mob now threatened to turn its wrath on Pittsburgh, where the marshal and Neville had holed up, unless Neville resigned and handed over the writs. Fearful that the army was looming just outside the town and with his home in ruins, Neville finally relented. But the stubborn marshal refused to surrender the writs.

Enter a Pittsburgh lawyer named Hugh Brackenridge. He stepped forward, perilously placing himself between the two forces in an attempt to defuse the situation. He stalled the rebels long enough for Neville and the marshal to jump on a boat and escape down the Ohio River like Huckleberry Finn and Big Jim. Neville and the marshal eventually made it to Philadelphia three weeks later to report to Washington and Hamilton.

Tom the Tinker's army went back to angry debating. Brackenridge the peacemaker went to a meeting of the Mingo Creek Association around July 22 and urged them to appeal for amnesty to avoid the inevitable violent suppression of the rebellion. He warned them that the Militia Act gave the president the power to crush them, and he possessed the foresight to see that Hamilton would do it.

But a rich lawyer named David Bradford, whose courage under fire was left untested when he declined to join the attack on Neville's plantation, now stepped forward and bravely called for continued resistance. Bradford was under the delusion that he could turn the ragged rebellion into a real revolution in the manner of Robespierre and his trusty guillotine. Bradford called for a congress of delegates from the region to take place in two weeks and urged an attack on the government fort near Pittsburgh to steal arms. At the last second, he backed off when he realized that the soldiers were actually there not to suppress the settlers but defend them from those murderous Native Americans. The overzealous Bradford realized that even in the midst of a rebellion, keeping the woods clear of those pesky Native Americans was mission critical.

Bradford then had the mail to Philadelphia robbed to find out who was plotting against his revolution. When they realized Neville's son was still in Pittsburgh trying to organize resistance, Bradford and other rebel leaders called for a grand muster of all militia leaders and their troops outside Pittsburgh. It would be a show of force to denounce the muddy little village of Pittsburgh as the hated center of government intransigence, whiskey taxation, and perfidy.

When the mob finally assembled outside Pittsburgh at Braddock's field on August 1, 1794—the scene of the French and Indian defeat of British General Braddock in 1755—it was seven thousand strong. Bradford, all doubts about the revolution he was leading and former cowardice safely banished from his mind, now sported a self-crowned general's rank and a flashy uniform. His demands on the citizens of Pittsburgh had increased, on pain of the torch: Neville's son, the army major who had led the defense of Neville's estate, and a list of others must be banished from the town. And the militiamen of Pittsburgh defending the city had to march out to join the rebels and prove their loyalty to the revolution. Frightened Pittsburghers began to board up their little houses to repel the invasion.

But once again the brave Brackenridge stepped into the breach. He was performing a delicate and perilous dance.

When Bradford finally got around to ordering the march on Pittsburgh after a day of drunken speeches and a whole lot of riding around firing random shots into the air, Bracken- ridge recklessly inserted himself at the head of the rebel column. He knew he would be vulnerable to accusations of being a rebel himself but hoped he could defuse the impend- ing bloodshed.

The Pittsburgh militia played their role perfectly. They marched out and pretended to be on the rebels' side, then quickly turned around and marched back into Pittsburgh with the rebel army led by Brackenridge. As they passed through, the townspeople served them free, untaxed, whis- key (fully warned that the thirsty rebels were on the way) and gently guided them toward ferries to send them back across the river. They had hit the backwoods army right in their weak spot: free liquor.

Back in Philadelphia, Hamilton was eager to march. The rebels had proved to be beyond control of the power of his prodigious pen, and now they must finally submit to the sword. The governor of Pennsylvania caused trouble by re- fusing to call out the militia against his own citizens, but this was a trifling inconvenience to Hamilton. He pulled out the Militia Act, found a willing Supreme Court Justice to verify that a rebellion was taking place, without actually conduct- ing an independent investigation, and since Congress was not in session, Hamilton finally had his war.

Secretary of War Henry Knox dutifully called up the mili- tias on August 7 but suddenly found himself with some land problems in Maine, where he had been speculating. Knox faced an important decision: he could leave office and tend to his personal financial situation, or he could lead a large army in attacking fellow Americans in Pennsylvania. At Hamilton's urging, Knox begged off and Washington let him go. Casting about for a substitute Hamilton found the perfect candidate, himself. Surprise! Hamilton took the job as acting secretary of war and drew up postdated orders for his very own, brand-new army while Washington attempted one last peace gambit—a presidential commission.

The commission (including Washington's soon-to-be land agent in western Pennsylvania) galloped west over the Alleghenies to negotiate with the congress of 226 rebel delegates and the hundreds of armed men on August 14 at Parkinson's Ferry. One sight of the armed gathering convinced the commission that their situation was hopeless. They opened negotiations with the rebel leaders and took the hard line Hamilton had laid down, knowing full well that war plans were being drafted back in Philadelphia. They had the rebels up against the wall, although the rebels didn't realize it. The rebels would escape Hamilton's wrath only if everyone in the region signed an oath of submission to the law, starting with the standing negotiating committee of sixty rebels.

Brackenridge-the-peacemaker and the other moderate rebels on the committee were eager to cave in to the commission's demands. They sensed the strength and unalterable determination of the institutional forces gathered by the invisible hand of Hamilton to crush them all should any serious resistance continue. The moderates tried to convince the radical rebel leaders to yield, but they were as divided and ornery as ever. The cockeyed rebels saw it for what it was, total surrender. Bradford was in no mood to surrender. He was out to conquer.

At first, the standing rebel committee of sixty voted to not vote, in a classic example of evasive leadership (all votes in the rebellion had usually been open-vote affairs, the better to intimidate any weak links, of course). But the moderates pressed on, determined to make their final stand, and they convinced the radicals to take a secret vote. The stark choice

was between signing an oath of submission and facing trea-
son charges pressed at the point of a bayonet.

The vote was 34 to 23 in favor of capitulation. But even
one dissenter was too much for Hamilton, who had ordained
that only total submission could forestall the invasion. Despite the charges of imperialism that were already flying from
his political foes, who saw this as yet another power-
grabbing attempt by the monarchically minded Hamilton, he
eagerly pressed on. The army would march. Hamilton would
lead.

On September 30 Washington and Hamilton rode out
from Philadelphia in a carriage. Four days later they met up
with the army at Carlisle, Pennsylvania, where Washington
reviewed the troops, gravely nodded his approval, and left
them in the all-too-eager hands of Hamilton. Militia from
Virginia, Maryland, and New Jersey had been added to
Pennsylvania militiamen, making a grand total of 13,000
troops. It was an army larger than the American forces at the
battle of Yorktown. Hamilton led the northern wing of the
army concentrated in eastern Pennsylvania. "Light-Horse"
Harry Lee led the southern wing coming up from Maryland.
Lee, the father of Robert E., was a stout Federalist and a
revolutionary hero from Virginia. He had once lusted after
the command of the western army tasked to crush the Native
Americans but had been passed over due to his propensity to
be an optimistic overreacher, especially in financial matters.
He was happy to swing back into the saddle.

And so was Hamilton, finally in his glory at the head of an
army, fighting a war completely of his own making. As secretary of war he had ordered the supplies, even down to the
details of the uniforms for his troops. He had whipped
the eastern populace into a patriotic frenzy, writing under
the pseudonym "Tully" in public papers over the summer of
1794 in order to stir patriotism against what he felt was a

LIGHT-HORSE ("LIGHT-WALLET") HARRY LEE

When Light-Horse Harry Lee returned from doing his duty leading the troops during the Whiskey Rebellion, he learned he had been relieved of the governorship of Virginia by citizens who viewed his partnership with the Federalist Hamilton in a very different light. Scion of a famous Virginia family, Lee's revolutionary career never reached the heights of his own ambition, despite a distinguished war record as a leader of his own free-ranging cavalry legion. The Whiskey Rebellion was the beginning of the end for him as the ensuing years saw his encroaching bankruptcy (he was invested in Washington's ill-fated Potomac Company, and bought some of Washington's unpromising land as well). In an abortive attempt to defend Federalism on the eve of the war of 1812, he caught a beating by a mob in Baltimore and retired to the Caribbean to nurse his wounds.

rebellion—not against the tax but against the entire governmental structure he himself had created. Hamilton, the brilliant young man of the Revolution, only thirty-nine, and a long way from his lowborn roots in the Caribbean, was prepared to sacrifice everything to lead this hastily called-up army, including his own life and that of his pregnant wife and seriously ill child.

Unfortunately, the army he led was barely an army, derisively called the "watermelon army" by its detractors. Once on the march Hamilton was forced to upbraid sentries for their lax behavior and found the general state of the militiamen to be bad enough to cement his opinion that the government needed a standing army. Even the frenetic Hamilton hadn't been able to work fast enough to entirely provision the bloated force gathered to crush the rebellion. As the long columns strung out over the Alleghenies in the depths of a cold fall season, the supply situation became a problem, and the hungry soldiers were forced to rob local farms, despite a flogging order for anyone caught stealing laid down by Washington.

Hamilton, not about to let the bad supply situation slow his march, countermanded Washington's flogging order and authorized the quartermaster corps to impress whatever supplies the army needed from the local populace, without restitution. The government's army was legally stealing from the citizens they were supposedly protecting. The New Jersey horse troop was particularly effective, fitted out in glorious uniforms atop big chargers and intimidating the locals.

The law-abiding citizens of Pennsylvania couldn't hide from Hamilton's army, but the rebels could. When Hamilton arrived on the western side of the Alleghenies during the first week of November, there were no rebels to fight. They had simply melted away. There was no rebel army spoiling for a showdown in a field, no revolutionary terror à la France, no peasant uprisings. Nothing. Many leaders who hadn't signed the amnesty apparently floated away down the Ohio to escape. Of course, the phantom war didn't stop young officers of Hamilton's army from comparing their exploits to Hannibal's crossing the Alps.

With no fighting, the army milled aimlessly while Hamilton flung himself into action, determined to crush something, anything. Until Hamilton was convinced a citizen had signed the amnesty resolution, he was fair game for arrest. A midnight sweep of suspects at bayonet point resulted in a raft of indiscriminate arrests where everyone was tossed into makeshift jails to await interrogation. A federal judge had been dragged along to aid the judicial process, but since they were in a war zone, (although there was actually no war) grand juries were conveniently ignored. There were charges of rough treatment and nights spent in freezing barns as suspects waited to be interrogated, many of whom Hamilton questioned personally. The master multitasker easily donned the extra role of inquisitor in chief.

The peacemaker Hugh Brackenridge was put under extreme scrutiny due to his position at the head of the rebel march into Pittsburgh. But Brackenridge managed to convince Hamilton after two days of desperate pleading that he wasn't actually a rebel and was released, cleared of all charges. Eventually just about everyone arrested was cleared and released.

The same governmental momentum that had decreed the useless invasion demanded a show trial back in Philadelphia. On Christmas morning 1794, Hamilton paraded the rebels through the streets of Philadelphia and into jail cells after a long, brutal trudge over the mountains. He prepared cases against twenty prisoners. Twelve cases were finally brought, and two were found guilty. The ever-reticent President Washington then pardoned the pair. It all wrapped up over a year later.

Federal armed suppression of the rebellion had worked. The rule of law would no longer be widely flouted, at least in Pittsburgh. Taxes and rents would be paid. Land values rose. Absentee landlords had nothing to fear. The whip had been cracked. The federal government was here to stay.

WHAT HAPPENED AFTER

When Washington left office in 1797, Hamilton returned to New York to practice law and assume the role of political big shot. In 1801 Thomas Jefferson became ascendant and was elected president, placed there by Hamilton, who chose him over his even-more bitter enemy Aaron Burr, who was relegated to the vice presidency, even in those early days firmly established as a stupid and useless office. Hamilton and Burr worked themselves into a gentlemanly lather and met in 1804 in Weehawken, New Jersey, to settle their differences. Burr shot Hamilton during the duel and the would-be king died a few days later. As a consolation for his early death he got his face on the $10 bill. Jefferson ranked only the ever-elusive $2 bill.

As the first former president, George Washington retired to make money. Long after his death he got a monument, a university, a city, and a state named after him. Despite that, he could get his face only on the $1 bill, plus the quarter thrown in.

David Bradford fled into the wilderness to avoid Hamilton's soldiers, floated down the Ohio to the Mississippi, and eventually surfaced in Spanish-controlled Louisiana. In 1799 President John Adams pardoned him for his role in the rebellion. In 1959 his house in Pennsylvania was converted into a museum.

For the most part, the rebels fled Pennsylvania and moved farther out into the frontier to continue making their whiskey, free from government interference. One of the most popular places they landed was Kentucky, turning that state into the whiskey-making center of the United States.

In one of the most ambitious quick-stepping surges of power in American history, Hamilton relocated the U.S. capital, rejiggered the debt for the federal and state governments, created the country's first internal tax, raised its first army to quash opposition to his scheme, and invaded Pennsylvania. All before his fortieth birthday. He achieved a staggering number of accomplishments in a short amount of time, but the whiskey tax was not destined to be one of his lasting legacies.

One of Jefferson's first acts as president in 1801 was to repeal the whiskey tax.

★ ★ ★

FOUR

THE WAR OF THE TRIPLE ALLIANCE

1865

Some dictators work alone. Others need the love of a good woman to fully ripen their true evil.

In the nineteenth century, Francisco Solano López, Paraguay's megalomaniacal, misshapen ruler, provoked a war with the country's three larger, richer, and more powerful neighbors for no reason other than to gain fame and respect for himself and his mistress. Eliza Lynch, a former Parisian prostitute, was his full partner in a tango of craziness that resulted in Paraguay suffering such a beat-down that 150 years later the country still reels from the pounding it endured.

This loving couple tortured, killed, and robbed the entire population of Paraguay. It's one of the most twisted love stories of all time.

THE PLAYERS

Francisco Solano López—The dictator of Paraguay, he started the war to gain respect and somehow convinced his people to fight until more than half of them were dead.

Skinny—Compared himself to Napoleon and Alexander the Great. It would have been true if Napoleon and Alexander had been fat, ignorant failures from obscure countries.

Props—Started the first telegraph line in South America.

Pros—On a Grand Tour to Paris he had a private audience with French Emperor Louis Napoleon and Empress Eugénie.

Cons—When López tried to kiss the empress, she was so disgusted she turned away and threw up.

Eliza Lynch—Dedicated mistress to her man and mother of his seven children, she stayed with her beloved dictator to the bitter, bitter, incredibly bitter end.

Skinny—Parisian prostitute of lowly Irish birth, she slept her way to the middle of Parisian society, snared López, and sailed away to her dream world as the despised mistress of an impoverished and war-wracked South American country.

Props—Wore a gown to López's burial. An odd choice, not least of all because she was forced to dig his grave with her own hands.

Pros—Bounced back well from devastating defeats such as the destruction of her adopted country due largely to her own efforts.

Cons—Robbed the country blind and shipped the booty off to her European bank account.

THE GENERAL SITUATION

Paraguay is a landlocked, isolated, and widely acknowledged unimportant country—half jungle, half desert, and poor all over. It has always been this way. Its isolation has made it a magnet for foreigners looking to disappear from the beaten track. And its isolation forms perhaps the perfect breeding ground for maniacal and homespun dictators, able to prey on an ignorant and secluded people who are largely unaware that life is not always miserable and filled with swarms of ambitious parasites. They consider their country an island in a sea of land.

Originally discovered by Portuguese explorers searching for gold, Paraguay was settled in 1537 by a group of Spanish conquistadores under the leadership of Domingo Martínez de Irala, who stopped beside a hill on the Plate River and fought a short battle with a distressed local band of Guarani Indians. With their leader killed, the natives offered the Spanish a small harem of young women as a sign of peace. The Spanish, horny and quite far from home, readily agreed and snuggled down for two decades of baby making with the locals. Irala is now one of the most common surnames in Paraguay.

The country settled into nearly three centuries of consistently minor-league status within the Spanish Empire. It achieved independence in 1811 during South America's revolts against Spain. Happy times were short-lived, however; in 1814 the country came under the thumb of the ruthless dictator José Gaspar Rodriguez de Francia, known as "The Supreme One." For the next twenty-six years he closed the borders and had his way with his lonely country; killing perceived opponents, seizing church property, dominating all commerce, and treating the people like badly behaved children. The result was a country filled with politically enfeebled citizens with little knowledge of the outside world. After the death of their dear leader in 1840, the people of the pathological country referred to him as "The Defunct One."

He was succeeded by the corpulent Carlos Antonio López in 1840, who added to the miseries of Paraguay by treating the entire country as if it were his own property and bringing into the world his eldest son, Francisco Solano López. Despite the heavy hand of Antonio, life for the docile population was generally good. Antonio opened schools, built railroads, made sure everyone had enough to eat, and the country lived in peace.

To further educate his eldest son, and to recruit foreign talent to work in Paraguay, Antonio López sent Francisco on a whirlwind Grand Tour of Europe in 1853. A secondary goal was to remove his son from Asunción so he would stop raping the virginal daughters of the aristocracy. The trip proved a turning point in South American history as the twenty-six-year-old spent like Michael Jackson on a shopping spree at Disneyland. The prizes the obese, epauletted dictator-in-training dragged home included military costumes, seventy pairs of patent leather boots, and an Irish-born prostitute named Eliza.

While in Paris Solano López met and was instantly smitten by the astounding beauty of Eliza Alicia Lynch, then eighteen and on the prowl for a rich sugar daddy to take her away from her stressful life as a Parisian courtesan. She was a refugee from the Irish famine whose family had married her off as a teenager to a French army officer in 1850. After a few years at African army posts, her marriage dissolved, and Lynch made her way to Paris and became one of the city's leading female companions to the rich. When she heard of the glorious spending by the Paraguayan prince, she arranged to meet him. After a few meetings between the sheets they discussed their future, and he wowed her with stories of rampant illiteracy and hungry ringworms in his home country. She was soon pregnant, and Solano López invited her to live with him in Paraguay. They arrived in Asunción in early 1855; the city turned out to welcome their prince home but were left stunned by the sight of the red-haired, blue-eyed, very pregnant Lynch hauling crates of finery bought on shopping sprees in Europe with her besotted man.

Lynch's impact on the López family was so strong that Solano's father barely spoke to Lynch for the remaining seven years of his life. Loathed instantly by the Paraguayan people, and the wealthy women of Asunción in particular, she was always known as Madame Lynch. López proved his love to his woman by impregnating her seven times, enjoying numerous mistresses, and ensuring the bastardization of her children by never marrying her.

Father Antonio died in 1862; Solano López seized power and started a killing rampage of his many enemies. He also declared that Madame Lynch must be treated as the first lady of Paraguay, requiring the leading ladies of Asunción society—and yes, they did exist—to pay her homage. Whatever she wanted, she got. Even this, however, was grossly insufficient for Madame Lynch. She did not leave Paris to simply rule over Paraguay. She longed for an empire and insisted on reminding López that he was emperor material and destined to conquer.

The first signs of trouble in Eden began in 1863 when López pestered the emperor of Brazil, Dom Pedro II, to marry his daughter. Dom Pedro laughingly refused his request, calling López "licentious, dissolute, and cruel." Angered by this bold statement of the truth, López set out to prove the emperor correct. He swore that he would extract his revenge on the now-hated Brazilians.

At the same time, López imported European engineers to bring the country within hailing distance of the modern age. These men became his favorites and were therefore among the last López executed. The tireless professionals constructed railroads, factories, shipyards, and when the time came, heavily armed fortifications. López had mansions built to house his mistress in splendor. The final flourish to bring Asunción up to European code occurred when Madame Lynch suggested—meaning demanded—López build a glistening replica of the famous La Scala opera house in Milan, even though the Paraguayans had never seen an opera. Roofless for nearly one hundred years, it did not host its first opera until 1955.

It was these European engineers, the first foreigners to enter the country in decades, who described the people of Paraguay as especially happy. They also noted that, perhaps from the years of living under dictators or because in their isolation they didn't know any better, they were incredibly stoic and brave, and held absolute devotion to their leaders.

Add to this mix a dictator's desire to impress his fancy European lady and a dawning realization that maybe, just maybe, he needs to prove himself in war to become the next Napoleon, and you have a recipe for disaster.

Paraguay, of course, did not exist in a vacuum. Since the end of the Spanish Empire in South America, there had been considerable fighting and confusion among the countries in the region. Much of it centered on Uruguay. Originally part of the Spanish viceroyalty of La Plata along with Paraguay and Argentina, it broke away in 1828 and became independent. After years of civil war Uruguay came under strong Brazilian influence. Both Brazil and Argentina wanted an independent Uruguay as a buffer between them, while Paraguay was concerned that this area remain on friendly terms since Uruguay represented its sole access to the sea.

It was amid this constant flow of conflict that López scored his first, and only, political success. After years of civil war in Argentina, in 1859 López volunteered to mediate between the two warring factions. Incredibly, not only was his offer accepted but the fighting actually stopped.

Returning to Paraguay, López was hailed as a diplomatic savant. The reality was that in a country without any hint of a foreign policy, the only thing separating the ordinary person from a diplomatic god was this one success. Madame Lynch, of course, saw that the road to empire—and to empress—had started. She pushed for more. In the volatile region it wasn't long before new conflicts presented opportunities for advancement.

War again flared up in Uruguay in 1863 when a group of unruly Argentines invaded to overthrow the Uruguayan government. The invaders belonged to the Colorado political party, generally more European and urban than the rural and predominantly indigenous people running the Blanco political party in Uruguay. Uruguay, casting about for allies, turned to Paraguay knowing that López was both a fellow Blanco and had the region's strongest standing army. But López instead played coy and waited until the call for help of his special mediating skills became truly desperate.

Meanwhile, Madame Lynch occupied herself by turning the country into a huge party as she prepared herself for the eventual role of empress. She organized an endless stream of balls and festivals during the summer of 1864, paid for by the entire country at a price that left a tidy profit for Lynch. The people poured their hearts into the festivities and the required declarations of love for their venerated/feared leader. But as López coyly waited, partying with Madame Lynch, the opportunity passed; he failed to seize the initiative and unite the Blancos in Uruguay and Argentina against the Colorados in Argentina. His self-congratulatory letters offering his diplomatic services to the warring parties were met with stony silence. With his country rapidly filling with Argentine invaders, the Uruguayan leader—lacking any outside support—was forced to open negotiations with Brazil. López again offered to mediate. When he was officially turned down, he vowed revenge for the dissing and in an abrupt about-face mobilized his army, now about 30,000 strong.

The situation turned dramatically when on October 16, Brazil, led by Colorados, invaded Uruguay to rid themselves of the Blanco leaders. This was too much for Madame Lynch's fragile sense of importance. She instinctively felt that the opportunity to become empress was ebbing. She berated López to strike at the Brazilians. But how? The obvious choice was to send the army south to support Uruguay and rally the region's Blancos under López. But Madame Lynch had other ideas. Paraguay would first strike north—in the opposite direction of the fighting. And thus was launched the bloodiest war in South American history by a woman whose sole military expertise consisted of a few years as teenage bride to a French officer.

WHAT HAPPENED:
OPERATION "LAST WOMAN STANDING"

It should be noted at this point that Paraguay was very small and poor, with the barest whiff of an arms industry. Brazil, on the other hand, had everything that Paraguay lacked: men, wealth, arms, and contacts with the outside world. While exact figures are difficult to achieve, Paraguay had about half a million people. Brazil's population numbered over 10 million. López, however, was not constrained by the logic of simple math. Besides, it would be a quick war, he convinced himself, and the Brazilians would soon tire of pounding at him and sue for peace. Ah yes, the old formula for success—wear out the enemy by dying too frequently before them.

López was still left with the practical question of what to do after suddenly starting a war with a country on whose behalf he had only recently been attempting to negotiate. He first captured a Brazilian ship docked in the Paraguay River at Asunción, grabbing money and arms. But now he was stymied again. He could not send troops to Uruguay by river because he lacked the necessary ships. He could not march through Brazil to help Uruguay because it was too far away. So, in December 1864, according to Madame Lynch's plan, troops commanded by López's brother-in-law grabbed a hunk of poorly protected Brazilian land, hoping it would divert some Brazilian troops from Uruguay. López's troops looted the countryside, grabbing whatever was not nailed down, turning captured women into slaves, and crafting a souvenir for their beloved leader: a necklace of severed ears. López had achieved one of his goals; his neighbors now knew he existed.

Pausing to digest his new role as conqueror of meaningless jungle, López pondered his next step. But he moved too slow: he was enjoying his life as a conqueror. In the meantime, events once again passed him by. In January 1865 a Brazilian army captured a Uruguayan stronghold and executed the Uruguayan officers. The Argentines and Uruguayans were both internally divided between indigenous Blancos and the cosmopolitan European Colorados. Brazil was angry at both Uruguay and Argentina. It was a scrum. López, with his unified country, could have made a move and emerged as the region's power broker. Only an exceptional person could unite all these factions. López was such a person: He succeeded in uniting them all against him.

In a curious move, he asked Argentina for permission to send an army through its country to help Uruguay. When Argentina said no, López beat the drum for war, and his people fell for it. Then on February 20, 1865, the Brazilian forces conquered Uruguay and installed a sympathetic Colorado government. With the Blancos in Uruguay defeated, the entire rationale for López's fight with Brazil had ended, and he no longer needed to send troops across Argentina. To the rational mind this would have ended the entire affair, and a hasty and heartfelt apology along with a large fruit basket from López might have diffused the whole sordid business. López rejected the rational anything. Instead, on March 18 he turned on Argentina, who had rebuffed his request to let

him help the now-defeated Blancos of Uruguay. López was
on his way to a lifetime membership in the rarefied club of
lunatic leaders hell-bent on total destruction.

López launched his forces. On April 13 his navy captured
two Argentine ships docked on the Paraná River outside of
Corrientes, Argentina. The next day the Paraguayans captured the town unopposed. The Argentines were furious, as
they had not yet received the Paraguayan declaration of war.
It was a sucker punch. The reaction was immediate in
Buenos Aires; crowds took to the streets demanding revenge, heaping scorn and bad names on the hated López.
They beseeched President Mitre to take action, and he responded with shouts that he would take Asunción in three
months.

And, perhaps more important, everyone in the region
joined forces against López. The competing parties in Argentina put aside their differences and united. The same happened in Uruguay. Brazil, already gearing up to punish López
for his unprovoked attack on them, gladly accepted help
from its two neighbors. All three countries were united as
never before with one goal, eliminate López from the region.
Through sheer idiotic cunning, López had turned divided
countries into united allies focused on his destruction. He
was truly a diplomatic idiot savant.

At this point, all-out war took hold. Argentina and Brazil
blocked arms from going upriver to Paraguay as the two
countries joined hands. They cemented their relationship
with the May 1 signing of the Treaty of the Triple Alliance,
which, along with Uruguay, bound them to remove López
from power, or from the earth. It was not a war against the
people of Paraguay, or to take the country's wealth or territory, but simply to do away with one man. The war would
end when López was gone. Little did they realize the difficulty of this mission.

That summer, seizing the initiative with its larger army, López invaded south toward Uruguay in a lightning strike to defeat the Brazilian forces. López put most of his crack troops into this thrust. But the grand winning strategy cooked up by Paraguay's dynamic duo hit a speed bump as the combined Uruguayan and Argentine army wiped out the ineptly led Paraguayans, who divided their forces on opposite sides of a Brazilian-controlled river, among other problems. This battle crippled the striking force of López's army, virtually destroying his 37,000 men. Anticipating victory, Madame Lynch had planned a ball requiring the ladies of society to wear all their jewels, so she could inventory their value. Word of the army's defeat reached her just before the ball started. Rather than cancel the "victory" party, news of the crushing loss was kept secret. The party rolled on.

In response to the failure in June 1865 López hustled off to take personal command of the army. Madame Lynch stayed behind as de facto head of the government. Her first act was to confiscate the jewels of Asunción's leading ladies.

Now the allies took the offensive. They marched north and retook the northern Argentine city of Corrientes. At this point, both the Argentines and Uruguayans felt satisfied and were willing to end the fight. They had pushed the invaders out and felt safe that López's men would not return. But Brazil had other ideas. They smelled blood and had one goal: López. By now virtually almost all made up of Brazilians, the allies pushed on.

While their offensive capabilities were severely limited, on the defensive the Paraguayans excelled. Their fighters were fanatical; their officers fought with extra zeal knowing that surrender meant execution of their families by López back home. Despite lack of equipment, shoes, and sporting nothing more than rags for uniforms, the loyal troops fought with tenacious bravery. The effect was exceptionally high casualty

GENERAL BARTHOLOME MITRE

Perhaps no other person was as obsessed with López's defeat as the president of Argentina, General Bartholome Mitre. He took command of the still-evolving country in 1862. But his control was precarious as he faced strong opposition from his internal enemies, the Blancos. His refusal to allow López to march across Argentina provided the final spark that started the war during which he became commander of the allied forces. Despite the country's battlefield losses, the war united the country, and what was once a confederation of different areas became the modern country of Argentina.

rates. The army was soon running out of men. So López started a new draft sweeping up boys over eleven years of age and those up to sixty into the fighting. Women worked the fields to support the war effort.

A safe strategy for López would have been to continue on the defensive and force the allies to fight him around the stronghold of Humaitá, located at the high ground on a sharp bend in the Paraguay River, one of the stoutest and best-defended fortifications in the world. López, however, was not endowed with clear thinking. With the support of Madame Lynch, he suddenly lurched into the offensive with his remaining able forces, including a newly raised unit of Paraguayan nobles. On May 24, 1866, López threw forward about 20,000 soldiers. They suffered ruinous casualties at what became known as the Battle of Tuyuti. The nobleman unit was virtually wiped out. Overall, the Paraguayans suffered 5,000 soldiers dead and another 8,000 wounded.

Rather than follow up with a quick thrust, the allies waited, building up their army. López emptied the hospitals and restocked the defenses with 20,000 of the walking

wounded. And to encourage the others, López executed officers who retreated.

López, with Madame Lynch's blessing, asked for a peace
conference. Argentine president Mitre agreed to talk, and the
two discussed a peace treaty for several hours in July 1866.
Mitre's main condition was that López abdicate and go into
exile. López refused and since neither side would relent, the
meeting adjourned. López left, convinced that all foreigners
were out to get him, and thus began torturing and killing
anyone he suspected of working with Mitre.

The hesitant allies now settled in for a two-year siege of
the Humaitá stronghold. Brazilian ironclads pushed up the
Paraguay River and bombarded the fortress. López countered with heavily armed canoes. Slowly, very slowly, the
allies pushed through swamps and jungle in order to surround Humaitá. And as the allies closed in around his jungle
stronghold, López slipped into madness. He arrested and
tortured to death his brother-in-law for stealing money from
the treasury that Madame Lynch had actually grabbed. He
saw plots everywhere and encouraged Paraguayans to kill
their neighbors if they saw any signs of treachery. Madame
Lynch supported his paranoia; it was clear to her that the
failures obviously stemmed from a well-entrenched conspiracy, not the inevitable outcome of a deeply flawed strategy.

By 1867 Paraguay had descended into total chaos with the
entire economy devoted to supporting the dwindling army.
Epidemics swept the population, farms lacked workers to
harvest the meager crops, and what was harvested was taken
for the army. To continue with the fight, Lynch ordered that
all women between sixteen and forty be drafted into the
army. She lightened their load by relieving them of any remaining valuables and taking their homes.

Finally, on July 26, 1868, the allies conquered Humaitá.
López had long since decamped and set up his headquarters

in the wilderness, starting the next phase of the war, a tenacious, two-year jungle retreat. To mark the occasion of the
defeat, López shot the garrison's commander along with the
wife and mother of the second-in-command. He also took
time out of his busy schedule to torture his little brother for
his role in some fantasy conspiracy with the American ambassador. It took a special visit from a U.S. warship to rescue
the ambassador, held prisoner in his own home, from López's
executioner.

López ordered the evacuation of the entire population, including Asunción. He led a convoy, with Madame Lynch and
the children, and thousands of his troops—by now mostly
children, walking wounded, and women—on a march north
into the hinterlands. He stopped long enough to set up a new
capital, torture and execute some enemies, and have a splendid meal with Lynch. It was less a retreat than a caravan of
lame circus performers heading slowly north, complete with
piano and wine cellar. López, always one to spread family
joy, locked his sisters in a special traveling cage and let them
out long enough to each receive a lashing. Now, López and
Lynch stumbled upon what they decided was the real reason
for their military failures: López's seventy-year-old mother,
who had hid her anti-Paraguayan feelings behind a facade of
age and frailty. She was caged, repeatedly flogged, and added
to López's execution list.

By early 1869, despite the obvious challenges of moving
an insane traveling caravan through the jungle, López and
Lynch had managed to stay one step ahead of the Brazilian
army. Frustrated at their inability to capture López, the Brazilian military leader, the Duke of Caxias, quit in a huff. In a
moment of biting irony, he was replaced by the Comte d'Eu,
the very man who married the Brazilian emperor's daughter.

López and Lynch slipped farther and farther north, their
caravan shrinking in size with each successive month. His

THE SISTERS OF SOLANO LÓPEZ

Few people felt the fully unhinged craziness of Solano López and Madame Lynch as ferociously as his sisters, Dona Rafaela and Dona Juana. Comfortably settled into their roles as beastly leaders of the Asunción jet set, they were suddenly pushed aside with the arrival of Madame Lynch. They immediately teamed with López's mother to embarrass and isolate Lynch from the rest of society. For their troubles they were turned into Lynch's personal whipping girls when she became head lady. First López made them toady to his woman. Then, after war broke out, he killed their husbands, imprisoned and tortured them while dragging the pair along in his caravan of craziness. Before he could finish them off, the Brazilians ended their big brother's reign. They got the last laugh as they saw their big brother turned into a bloody corpse and his mistress thrown out of their wrecked land.

army fought bravely, but their major weapons—stones and clods of earth—were no match for the Brazilians, who were armed with more conventional weapons.

By February 1870 López was down to 500 men and Madame Lynch's last bottles of good champagne. They took up camp at Cerro Cora, his final capital. Realizing the end was near, he spent his remaining weeks composing his final words and designing a medal to commemorate his upcoming victory. To her credit, Madame Lynch stayed with her man, even though she had every opportunity to take off and head to Europe to live off the jewels she had stolen and thoughtfully shipped off to friends for safekeeping.

On the morning of March 1, the Brazilians stormed his camp. López fled alone on horseback. When he got stuck in a river he waded back to shore into the arms of the Brazilian commander and tried to shoot his way out. A Brazilian soldier speared the dictator and he fell. But like a movie villain, he proved hard to kill. López pulled himself up to his knees and tried to escape. But the Brazilians shot him down. He uttered his long-rehearsed words, "I die with my country," before he expired. Little did he understand that his country was already dead.

Meanwhile, the Brazilians surrounded Lynch and her sons in their carriage. The eldest son, Pancho, at age sixteen already one of the older colonels in the army, came out swinging his sword. The Brazilians slashed him down and gave Madame Lynch the honor of burying López and her son. Dressed in a gown, the woman-who-would-be-empress got down on her hands and knees and scratched out a shallow grave for her two fallen men. The Brazilians then protected Lynch from the surviving Paraguayans, including López's mother and two sisters, who would have preferred to show their love for Lynch by removing large sections of her skin, bones, and organs.

When word reached Asunción that López had died and Lynch had been captured, the survivors of society held a ball. And the Tango of Craziness danced no more.

WHAT HAPPENED AFTER

The new government in Asunción demanded Madame Lynch be put on trial for her crimes, but the Brazilians decided to send her away instead, complete with a huge chest of stolen jewels.

Exiled in Paris, Lynch tried to find the money she had so carefully stolen and secreted out of the country. But she found much of it pocketed by her fellow thieves and spent the better part of the next decade trying to win it back in court. In the meantime, she set up a fashionable home in Paris and sent her boys to fancy boarding schools. In 1875 she even had the impudence to return to Paraguay and pursue claims for her stolen land. The president had her kicked out the next day at gunpoint. Back in France the boys flourished while Madame Lynch slowly spent her money on lawyers and champagne. She died, alone and forgotten, on July 27, 1886, and was buried in Paris.

The war, the deadliest in South American history, cost Paraguay almost 60 percent of its population. And more astonishingly, the country had only about 28,000 males at the war's end, most of whom were children and old men. No modern society had ever suffered so much from a war in percentage of population affected. For years thereafter the country was known as the Land of Women.

For their efforts, and about 100,000 Brazilian and 25,000 Argentine dead, the allies claimed about one quarter of Paraguayan territory that turned out to be essentially worthless. Argentina and Paraguay haggled for years over exactly which territory it should take. Finally, in 1878, President Rutherford B. Hayes, chosen as the arbitrator of the dispute, ruled in favor of Paraguay. Out of gratitude the land of López named a town in the president's honor. This minor victory did not prevent Paraguay from being reduced to a state of chaos that endured for decades. For the sixty-six years following the war's end the country had thirty-two presidents, two assassinations, six coups, and eight failed revolutions.

Not surprisingly, Solano López and Madame Lynch became two of the most despised people in Paraguayan history. But then their fortunes turned. Needing a hero at the outset of the Chaco War in the 1930s, the Paraguayan dictator at the time, yes, the country breeds dictators, resurrected López as a national hero. Almost instantly, his portrait appeared everywhere, and books extolling his virtues were turned out by the tens of thousands. His body was exhumed from the shallow, riverside grave and placed in the country's Pantheon of Heroes where he rests today.

Needing a companion for their national hero, the country

next resurrected Madame Lynch and transformed her from a greedy, thieving whore into the Mother Earth martyr of the country. In 1961 her transformation became complete when the ruling dictator, Alfredo Stroessner, had her body exhumed from its Parisian grave and clandestinely shipped to Asunción and installed in her own museum. Finally, in 1970 she was placed in an elaborate mausoleum in Asunción, where the population is free to ignore her to this day.

★ ★ ★

FIVE

THE WAR OF THE PACIFIC
1879

This is a story about birdshit.

Up until the early nineteenth century, birdshit, also known in the trade as guano, was virtually worthless. Birds pooped, end of story. But as the industrial revolution gained steam, the smelly substance was discovered to contain valuable nitrates that could be used in fertilizer and explosives. On the western coast of South America, in what is now Peru and Chile, the mountains of guano that lined the coast suddenly became the object of a very nasty tug of war among three countries that resulted in many, many deaths.

Peru, Bolivia, and Chile, newly freed from their colonial master, Spain, which had conquered the continent at the end of the sixteenth century, were struggling to find their places in the world as independent nations. Each country, led by the European elites inherited from the Spanish overlordship, ruthlessly continued the economic rape of their countries' resources for the benefit of their own tiny ruling class.

Due to the political naïveté of the ruling classes, many mistakes were made. First of all, they had no idea how to run a country. The Spanish had created a greedy empire based solely on their lust for gold and silver. These three countries were left in such an infantile state of development that not only was the war started over birdshit, but the Peruvians, who were dragged into the affair through a secret treaty with their neighbor Bolivia, who had started the war against Chile without asking the Peruvians if they wanted to join, kept fighting long after they had lost the war but didn't even know it.

THE PLAYERS

President Hilarion Daza—The averagely brutal Bolivian dictator took control in a coup in 1876 at the age of thirty-six and broke a treaty by taxing the bird poop exports of neighboring Chile.
Skinny—Raised mainly on the streets, he quickly scaled the ranks of the Bolivian military.
Props—Robbed the treasury to pay off the soldiers who supported him during his coup.
Pros—Never missed a coup.
Cons—Decided to skip the war he had inadvertently started.

Rafael Sotomayor—Chilean "coordinator" of the war for President Anibal Pinto Garmendia, he was appointed to oversee the military heads and political rivals of Pinto.
Skinny—Perhaps the first military spinmaster, he handed out voluminous press releases extolling Pinto's military prowess and disowning his role for any defeats.
Props—Repeatedly pissed off the military commanders without getting himself shot or his boss couped.
Pros—Realized that an army needs a constant flow of food and water, something the generals often overlooked.
Cons—Micromanaged the war to the point where he was countermanding orders of individual military units.

THE GENERAL SITUATION

On the western coast of Chile, Peru (and formerly Bolivia), where the bone-dry Atacama and Tarapacá deserts run up against the sea, the cool Humboldt current sweeps up from the South Pacific. The water is filled with plankton that attracts great schools of fish, which in turn become tasty meals for legions of birds.

The birds feed from the sea and hang out on land, where they defecate prodigiously, mountainously. In this driest part of the planet, decades pass with no rainfall. Lacking water to wash the guano away, towering cliffs of birdshit grow to hundreds of feet all along the coast.

In the middle of the nineteenth century, after the dissolution of the Spanish Empire in South America, it was discovered that bird guano contained nitrogen, a key ingredient for fertilizer and explosives. Along the desert coastline, devoid of roads and visitors, the towering bird guano cliffs, the accumulated droppings of millennia, suddenly became incredibly valuable. They were the gifts of the birds that laid the golden poop.

At first, Chile, Bolivia, and Peru cooperated to mine the guano, with the more economically adroit Chile making most of the investment and sharing the profits with Peru and Bolivia. Treaties established the boundaries between the nations and the tax rates to be paid on the smelly export.

The Bolivian and Peruvian ruling classes of Spanish descent were happy to sit back and reap the rewards of yet another God-given resource like gold, silver, and tin, with most of the nasty work done by foreigners. The guano soon became a major revenue source for Peru, but with British and French companies reaping most of the profits, the locals were unable to create their own mining companies. Even though the bird poop business was booming, Peru was soon going broke because wealthy Peruvians invested their profits outside the country and neglected the rest of their own nation. Nothing was reinvested in Peru. Corruption and debt began to rise.

Bolivia suffered from the same shortsighted complex. Known as Upper Peru in the days of the Spanish Peruvian viceroyalty, Bolivia was the site of Mount Potosi, from which flowed a huge portion of the silver sloshing around the Spanish Empire. After liberation, the Bolivian elite were more than satisfied to do nothing except harvest the wealth generated by the treasure that flowed out of the ground and to fight—almost continuously—over their share of it.

The result was that Bolivia had long been plagued by a seemingly endless series of dictators pretending to be presidents. The long-suffering native populace, huddled in their ancient villages on the high Andean plain, the Altiplano, survived the holocaust that befell their North American counterparts; the devout Spanish Crown had actually felt responsible to provide some measure of protection to the masses of potential new Catholic converts while the continent was stripped of its mineral wealth. The natives were rewarded with survival but at the price of being trapped as second-tier residents in a third-tier nation, subsisting in a slavelike state of economic misery for centuries.

Mariano Malgarejo took over in 1864 and proved to be an outstanding example of the type of bad dictators cycling through the presidential office of Bolivia. Malgarejo earned his stupid stripes by handing over a chunk of valuable Bolivian guanoland to Chile. Malgarejo's giveaway hastened his end by the inevitable coup in 1872 at the hands of a dictator named Morales, who tried to undo some of Malgarejo's mistakes. His well-meaning attempts were frustrated when his own nephew gunned him down, but not before he completed a secret treaty in 1873 with Peru under which each side pledged to support its brother country if invaded by the annoyingly well-organized Chileans.

In 1876 Hilarion Daza seized power from Morales in a coup of his own. Daza was a dumb and fiery soldier who quickly distinguished himself by raiding the treasury to pay his fellow officers of the palace guard, who had supported him loyally, and continued to do so until the next coup.

That same year, Mariano Ignacio Prado became president of Peru, succeeding Manuel Pardo, at a time when all Peruvian presidents apparently were required to share the same letters in their last names. Each successive president unsuccessfully attempted to bail the country out of the economic mess left by his decouped predecessor.

Chile was, by contrast, a paragon of political normalcy, but by the 1870s its economy had started to slip and the country became more volatile.

Borders drawn by the former Spanish Empire were somewhat elastic. Not much thought or effort had been put into defining the actual lines separating the Spanish viceroyalties, especially in desert wastelands like the Atacama and Tarapacá. The mining of the guano proved to be so lucrative that Chile's mining operations kept creeping farther north, to the irritation of the Bolivians. Amid this simmering squabble in 1877, a tsunami devastated the coast and wiped out Antofagasta, the main guano mining port. To rebuild it the Bolivians wanted a tax, which the Chileans duly noted was illegal under their just-inked treaty. But Bolivian President Daza, finding the treasury he had recently raided short of funds, boldly slapped a tax on every shipment of exported birdshit.

The Chileans refused to pay and, to emphasize their point, dispatched their newly purchased ironclads into the area. In response Daza canceled the Chilean mining contracts and ordered all of the Chilean mining equipment impounded and sold at auction. The Chileans showed up on the day of the auction—not with a check but with their military, and snagged a chunk of Bolivia's coast along with the port of Antofagasta for good measure. The war was on. Chile asked Peru to abrogate its treaty with Bolivia. But Peru could not break out of its dictatorial death spiral with Bolivia and spurned the Chilean offer.

On April 5, 1879, Chile declared war on Bolivia and Peru.

WHAT HAPPENED: OPERATION "THUNDERPOOP"

The guano regions were some of the driest and harshest areas on earth. Because no one lived there permanently, the region possessed virtually no roads, and those that did exist ran from the mines straight to the coast. Without any north–south routes, whoever controlled the sea-lanes would have the ability to move troops at will and could easily win the war.

Even though Chile had about half the combined population of Peru and Bolivia, its military was stronger. Its regular army had 3,000 men armed with sixteen new artillery pieces, some machine guns, and repeating rifles. It also had an 18,000-man national guard outfitted with U.S. Civil War–era muskets. The navy boasted precisely two ironclads, the *Cochrane* and *Blanco Encalada*, that possessed the firepower and strength to dominate the Peruvian Navy. The soldiers were poorly paid, however, and the army lacked a medical corps. In addition, the top officers of both the army and navy were political appointees lacking significant military experience. Still, by the standards of South America, Chile stood as a major power.

Chile's President Pinto faced an even bigger problem, however. His top generals also happened to be the leaders of the opposing political party; a resounding victory in the field could catapult any one of them into his office. A defeat, however, would fall on Pinto's head, also turning him from office. It was a classic no-win situation. Pinto cleverly solved the problem by appointing Rafael Sotomayor as the war "coordinator" to oversee the potentially victorious service chiefs, stealing their glory or handing them the blame.

Reflecting their economies, the armies of Peru and Bolivia stank. Peru's standing army of 5,000 men was haphazardly equipped with a hodgepodge of guns. As befitting a dictatorship more concerned with infighting than defending its borders, the regiments were stationed close to the main cities, to lend a hand during any coup action.

Peru's navy sported two English-made ironclads. While solid ships, they paled in comparison to the two Chilean ships. Even more problematic for the Peruvians, their ships had been manned mostly by Chileans. When the war started these sailors got kicked out, leaving the ships thinly staffed by the poorly trained Peruvians.

Bolivia's state-of-war preparedness stank even worse. Despite having a coastline at this point in their history, it had no navy. Their army was just one step better, with slightly more than 2,000 men, principally skilled in overthrowing yesterday's dictators as opposed to facing well-armed soldiers in the field. The best troops were probably the "Colorados" regiment of the palace guard (from which President Daza had ascended), numbering 600 seasoned coupmakers armed with modern repeating rifles. The army was also so top heavy it was a miracle it didn't topple over. Of the 2,000 troops more than 600 were officers, almost all of whom had been promoted for political loyalty. Establishing a pattern of ridiculous missteps, at the war's outset Bolivia promised its Peruvian allies it would field an army of 12,000 soldiers, a figure even casual observers knew was impossible.

Still, in Bolivia's capital, La Paz, war fever ran as high as the Andes. Four thousand or so volunteers, some from Bolivia's best families, raised lavishly funded new regiments, wearing white trousers and jackets of various colors signifying their dandily organized regiment. The paucity of weapons didn't dampen their enthusiasm for what everyone predicted to be a short and victorious war, filled with glory. The feeling seemed to be a cocktail-party war for the La Paz jet set.

To start the land part of the war, a force of Chileans had moved against the tiny Bolivian town of Calama. The town was defended by about 135 citizens with a smattering of soldiers, all armed with a jumble of old and barely functioning guns. On March 22 the Chileans marched across a river into town and scattered the defenders. One holdout remained, a civilian named Eduardo Abaroa. Surrounded, he poured fire from two rifles at the enemy. The Chileans asked for his surrender. He rejected the offer, declaring, "Let your grandmother surrender, dammit," and the Chileans shot him down. For his defiance, generations of Bolivian children would repeat his stout declaration of honor, and a bronze statue of him stands prominently in La Paz. Bolivia had established its approach for the war; defeat followed by martyrdom.

By mid April, Daza gazed upon his poorly equipped, untrained, and untested army and declared them ready to whip the Chileans. He paraded his force before the gushing citizens of La Paz, turned left out of town, and headed to the coast, 250 miles away.

Chilean leaders quickly realized that any large-scale movement of troops in the region must go by sea. The desert was too harsh, few roads existed, and supplying an army was a daunting challenge entirely dependent on control of the coastline. Sotomayor ordered naval commander Rear Admiral Juan Williams Rebolledo to move against the Peruvian navy. But the admiral proved irresolute and refused to attack, despite knowing the Peruvian fleet was a sitting duck, its two ironclads in dry dock in Callao, hundreds of miles to the north, with their boilers dismantled.

Rather than attack his defenseless enemy, Admiral Williams established a blockade off the Peruvian port of Iquique, in the heart of guano territory, where the Peruvian army was assembling. His strategy was to economically squeeze the Peruvians by preventing any of their guano from leaving the country, forcing them to either come out and fight away from the protection of their shore guns, or watch their army wither.

Admiral Williams, after delaying so long, suddenly decided to sail north and attack Callao. His clockworklike plan dissolved along with his element of surprise. By accident Williams now learned from an Italian fishing boat that his prize, the two Peruvian ironclads, had left port four days earlier—the two fleets unknowingly passed each other at sea going in opposite directions. The enemy had done what he was planning—but Williams had missed it. And even worse, the Peruvian ironclads bore down on the two old ships Williams had stationed outside Iquique. The Chilean admiral turned around to rush back to their aid.

But he arrived too late. On May 21, the Peruvian Admiral Grau aggressively attacked the two aging Chilean ships. After much futile firing from his poorly trained sailors, Grau resorted to ramming his ironclad *Huascar* into the Chilean wooden ship *Esmeralda*. Knowing his ship was doomed, the Chilean commander Captain Arturo Prat gave the order to board the enemy, but in the din only one sailor followed. Peruvian sailors cut them down in seconds. After a second ramming failed, another Chilean boarding party leapt onto the deck of the *Huascar*, only to suffer the same fate. Finally, a third ramming put the Chilean ship on the bottom.

The other Peruvian gunship *Independencia* chased after the tiny Chilean ship, the *Covadonga*, whose shallow draft allowed it to hug the shore. The *Independencia* followed in hot chase, unaware of the dangers lurking beneath the water. Suddenly, the ship struck a large rock, tearing a huge hole in her hull, a mortal blow. With his two ironclads, Grau held out hope he could defeat the Chileans, or at least threaten the Chileans' naval dominance enough to keep their troops at port. But now with only one ship, the *Huascar*, those hopes were dashed on the unseen rocks under the Pacific. The war was already over for Peru and Bolivia. Everyone knew it but them.

The disaster pushed Admiral Grau to even greater heights of aggression. He raided up and down the coast with his one remaining ironclad. The Chilean people became noticeably testy over this turn of events. Admiral Williams was fired, and the entire cabinet resigned. Incredibly, Peru seemed to be winning, but this was merely an illusion. Chile, with its new nitrate-rich region safely in hand, stocked up on European arms.

Finally, on October 8 the Chileans caught up with Grau. The Chilean ironclad *Cochrane* locked horns with Grau's *Huascar*, killing the Peruvian admiral with a shell straight into his bridge. The Chileans towed the *Huascar* into Valparaiso as a prize. Now they had almost won the war. Almost. The Bolivians and Peruvians still didn't know.

The following month the Chileans gathered their invasion force to deliver the knockout. The invasion on November 2 did not go as planned, however. The Chileans didn't arrive until after daybreak, and the captain in charge of the landings was, allegedly, drunk. Fortunately, they were fighting the Bolivians, many of whom deserted, apparently led in flight by their generals, and victory was secured.

The inept allies planned a counterstrike with two main forces. Bolivian dictator Daza and 2,400 men, including his prized battalion of Colorados, were poised to swing into action after months of training. On November 10 Daza set out on a desert march south to join forces with General Juan Buendia and his Peruvians in typical haphazard, uninformed style: he didn't bother to check rations and planned to march during the hot daylight hours. Instead of food and water, Daza issued his troops cash, apparently believing they would find a few dozen well-stocked bodegas on the way. After four days of brutal marching, Daza had gotten only halfway to his goal when he stopped at the Camarones River, which means "shrimp" in Spanish. Ten percent of his troops had deserted along the way. Daza hit the panic button. He realized he was taking the huge risk of losing the support of his Colorados with his stupid foray into the desert, opening up the possibility that the troops he had armed for the war could be used against him back home. Defending his power was more important than any coastline to him. Without ever finding out the location of his allies or the enemy, he turned around and marched back. Daza realized the fight was not really worth dying over and became a refusenik in his own war. Bolivians honored him with the nickname of "The Hero of the Shrimps."

General Buendia, with his 9,000-man army of Bolivians and Peruvians, however, refused to quit. The Chileans marched into the interior with 7,000 troops and waited for Buendia. Allied incompetence was still raging unabated. The Chileans sent in reinforcements on the railroad right under the allies' noses; Buendia's column stopped within sight of the enemy in broad daylight, under the brutal sun, in the stinking nitrate fields.

On November 19, both sides waited for the other to start the battle. But some thirsty Peruvian and Bolivian troops wandered out to fetch water from a well right under the Chilean guns and suddenly decided to attack. Without orders. An alarmed Buendia had little choice but to order a general advance. Chilean artillery drove off the attack. Sensing it was safer in the rear, the allied cavalry galloped away from the battle, followed by most of the Bolivian infantry.

A shrouding fog, typical in the area, descended upon the fleeing army and hampered their ability to get as far away from the Chileans as possible. Their leader had not bothered to bring along maps of the area nor a compass, further hampering the army's ability to flee the battle in good order. When the sun rose the next day, the hapless allied troops found themselves still in sight of the enemy on the San Francisco hills—they had simply marched in a circle. Now that they were able to see around them, the troops finally scrambled away from the Chileans, and the parched remnants of Buendia's army staggered into the Peruvian province of Tarapacá on November 22. The map-carrying Chileans shadowed them from a safe distance.

Unable to defend themselves, the Peruvians abandoned the port of Iquique the following day. They had now lost their last remaining guano port and any ability to sell their only valuable export. The allies regrouped in Tarapacá. The Chileans, believing the soldiers were demoralized and ready to topple, launched an attack, but the allies outnumbered them two to one. Each Chilean thrust was thrown back. Fighting died down in the afternoon as the heat rose and the water levels in the canteens fell. Over five hundred Chileans were killed that day. Even though they resumed their retreat, the allies savored this minuscule taste of victory, their first . . . and last.

The loss of all the guanolands rocked both losing countries. Even before the loss President Prado had sniffed defeat in the air. He turned over command of the Peruvian army to Vice Admiral Lizardo Montero and fled to Lima, to "organize" the war effort. There, however, riots over the abysmal state of the war trapped him in the presidential palace. On

December 18 he figured out how to fix the problems: fire his cabinet, take a chunk of government gold, kiss his family good-bye, and hotfoot it over to Europe to "buy more arms." In a letter to Daza, Prado said he was fleeing for the good of the country, personal reputation be damned. He was right—his reputation took a beating.

Now chaos erupted in Peru. Not only was a foreign army camped on its soil, not only had the country suffered a catastrophic defeat, not only had it lost its sole valuable resource, not only was its army commanded by an admiral, but the country now had no leader. Vice President de la Puerta assumed command, but at the age of eighty-four he was in no condition to lead the war. On December 21, into the leadership breach jumped Nicolas Pierola, a former pirate and ever-lurking power grabber. He wrangled the support of some troops and led them against soldiers loyal to de la Puerta, but the aging VP had no stomach for a fight, and the cream of Lima society convinced him it was best for Pierola to take over. Pierola quickly established a much more efficient constitution that handed himself all the power and eliminated potential ambiguities such as the legislature. He also tacked on the unfortunate title of "protector of the indigenous race." To bolster his hold on the country, Pierola created his own army. While he redirected new arms to his favored army, he slowly strangled the regular army under Admiral Montero, his archrival.

Sill locked in the death spiral with its ally, Bolivia dabbled in its own version of political twister. Unearthing a plot by Daza to pull his troops completely out of the fight, the Bolivian army leaders on December 26 appealed to Admiral Montero for help in removing Daza. But the Peruvian did not want to start a mini civil war within the Bolivian army camp based in Peru, so he gracefully declined to lend his troops. He did, however, agree to a sneaky plot.

On December 27, Daza boarded a train to meet Montero. A few hours later Daza's chief of staff and coup leader ordered Daza's Colorado troops to stack their arms in their barracks and head to a river for a relaxing bath. While they splashed in the river, troops loyal to the coup locked up the barracks and took control of army headquarters.

Word reached Daza that he had been double-couped out of his posts of army and government leader. Panicking, he asked Montero to put down the coup. Montero, having lived through his second coup in a week, was now an expert in sidestepping such upsets and declined to get involved. Daza rushed madly about: he jumped on horseback, fled to the coast, and started the well-worn trek to exile in Europe.

As the two former dictators slunk off to their European futures, the leaders in Bolivia appointed General Narcisco Campero as provisional president. Trained at France's military academy at St. Cyr, Campero's new title came with the dubious prize of leading the feeble Bolivian war effort.

To compound its avalanche of problems, the Peruvian economy was officially in shambles. The country had lost its guanolands and virtually all exports were halted by the Chilean blockade. The one bright spot was that it still outclassed Bolivia's economy. Chile had control of the seas, conquered all the guanolands, and signed deals to sell vast quantities of bird poop to them, parlaying the money into fresh arms.

As 1879 closed, the allies had suffered naval, military, political, and economic defeat. But true to their undying spirit of incompetence, they didn't know enough to call it quits.

Chile wanted to end the war but couldn't, at least not until they had a treaty that officially awarded them the conquered guanolands. While the war had achieved more than they could have imagined, Chilean pride was hurt by the defeat at

Tarapacá. They didn't want to end the war on a down note. Sotomayor reorganized the army, pumped up the number of troops, and prepared to attack again.

On February 26, 1880, the Chileans landed at a town called Ilo, one hundred miles north of the Peruvian town of Arica, and sent the defenders fleeing into the desert. The road to Lima lay wide open for a strike to end the war, but the Chilean president Pinto got cute. He wanted to defeat the allied army based in the southern Peruvian city of Tacna, take possession of that region, and exchange it with the Bolivians for agreeing to quit the war. The Chileans struggled with the difficult terrain, searing heat, and lack of water along their long march to Tacna. As they assembled their army outside Tacna, Sotomayor suddenly died of a stroke.

The allied army of 9,000, under the direct command of the new Bolivian dictator, Campero, defended Tacna on a mesa north of the town, holding a strong defensive position. The Chileans scouted them and withdrew to prepare their offensive. The allies, however, mistook this as a sign of Chilean weakness and mounted a surprise predawn attack. But once again, the troops got lost in the dark and struggled back to their positions just in time to absorb the surging Chilean attack at dawn on May 26. They beat off the Chileans successfully until a Peruvian officer decided that a temporary lull by the Chileans to rearm was a retreat, and repositioned his unit on the exposed slopes. A quick Chilean counterattack cut them down, and this blunder snowballed into yet another devastating defeat.

Two thousand Chileans had been killed and wounded, one quarter of their forces, but their allied opposition had been crushed. Campero led one thousand Bolivians on the long march home, through blistering desert and icy mountains, where he learned he had been formally elected president of his beleaguered and defeated nation. Meanwhile, his hard-

marching men died in droves along the way and had to
endure the further humiliation of being disarmed at their
own border to prevent them from rioting when told the government would not pay them for losing the war. The Bolivians had ignominiously quit the war they had started, and
now they let the Peruvians carry the fight for them. Admiral
Montero trudged home to Lima with his victory-challenged
fighters, now smothered in defeat. The Bolivians were done,
never to be heard from again.

The Chileans now focused on the Peruvian town of Arica,
the port that connected La Paz to the Pacific by train. The
defenders installed large guns to defend the town from a
naval invasion; they dug in on the land side to counter the
inevitable attack from the Chileans marching down from
Tacna. The Peruvian defenders planted newfangled land
mines all around the town, which had the unintended effect
of imprisoning the Peruvian troops who feared patrolling
near the minefields. When the Chileans captured the proud
designer of the defenses, he was uninhibited by any sense of
loyalty and happily revealed the exact locations of the mines.
A daylong bombardment by the Chilean fleet signaled the
start of the attack. Two days later, after the Peruvians refused
to surrender, the Chileans easily sidestepped the mines and
stormed the trenches from the land. The Peruvians were decimated, and their inevitable surrender arrived even before the
morning dew had burned off.

Now Chile stood tall. It had conquered the entire Bolivian
coastline along with Peru's nitrate region. They had indeed
cornered the market on bird poop.

The logical move for Bolivia and Peru was to finally give
up. Logic, however, was not an abundant natural resource in
these two countries. While Bolivia watched with waning interest from its distant mountain perch, the Peruvians slogged
it out with the enemy mano a mano.

The Chileans were desperate to get this whole thing over and return to their beloved guano mining. Their navy blockaded Peru's coastline to squeeze the remaining life from Peru's economy. After failing to buy some new warships in Europe to turn the tide of war, Peruvian president Pierola finally agreed to a peace conference. The Chileans demanded they keep the conquered nitrate territories and required the allies to pay them for the privilege of getting smashed. In return they would cede a chunk of Peru's coast to Bolivia as a consolation prize. In essence, Peru would be agreeing to lose money, territory, and prestige. Perhaps still believing they were as important and powerful as in the days when Peru held the seat of the Spanish Empire in the new world, they rejected the deal. Their losing effort would continue.

The Chileans, running dangerously low on victory medals, now planned a march on Lima, the Peruvian capital. Forty-two thousand Chileans landed on the coast and marched toward the Peruvian duct-taped defenses outside the city. The defenders scraped the bottom of the barrel and formed ten reserve divisions of troops grouped by their civilian jobs. Thus the retail merchants, decorators, hairdressers, economists, teachers, and others with normally peaceful jobs all had their own divisions and their share of the city's defense. Even some of the Altiplano natives with blowgun darts and poison arrows pitched in. When you are defending your capital with hairdressers and guys with blowguns, one must begin to realize that hope has fled the field.

The Chileans punched through the Peruvian hairdressers, shrugged off the flesh wounds from the dart guns, and capped their victory with a spree of looting and killing stragglers. Pierola ordered his soldiers to turn in their weapons and go home. Lima was now wide open. As the Chileans moved in to loot on January 16, 1881, Pierola took his government into the hills, becoming the second Peruvian leader to flee in the war. He bugged out so quickly he didn't even have time to cart along the state papers or raid the treasury for some traveling money. A South American dictator actually fleeing and leaving money behind? Yes, indeed. The Peruvian elite, despite complete incompetence from the beginning of this disastrous war, were determined not to give up their ill-gotten lordship over their remnants of the Spanish Empire.

The Chileans occupied Lima and installed a lawyer by the name of Francisco García Calderón as Peru's new president, expecting that he would repay the kindness by surrendering. The Chileans allowed Calderón to raise a small army mainly to protect himself from some of his angrier citizens. The Chileans found out, however, that he was not the pliable puppet he appeared to be. Infected with the illogic of the office, Calderón found a way out of signing a total surrender when the U.S. diplomats insisted that Chile could not keep any conquered territory unless the losers refused to pay war reparations.

Meanwhile, Pierola continued his resistance from the hills and was joined in April 1881 by the recently wounded General Andrés Cáceres, one of his ablest generals. The duo planned to maintain a low-level guerrilla war, hoping the Chileans would tire and offer a face-saving peace. To fight his new war Cáceres gathered sixteen of his finest comrades.

Beyond desperation, the Chileans sent a division into the mountains to chase the rebels. As they plodded high in the Andes, the wily Cáceres, whose forces now numbered about one hundred, easily sidestepped his would-be captors. They never got within smelling distance. The occupation-hating Peruvians flocked to Cáceres and swelled his mountain army by the thousands.

Frustrated by Calderón's refusal to sign the peace treaty, the conquerors tossed him into jail. Easy come, easy go. The imprisonment transformed Calderón into a Peruvian martyr.

On his way to the big house he named Admiral Montero the new president. Peru now boasted two illegitimate leaders. Cáceres, a wily backstabber, abandoned Pierola and threw his support to Montero. The now-dangling Pierola headed out on the well-worn path of exile to Europe.

Despite the march of Chilean victories, the war still refused to end. Cáceres took on the Chileans and even bested them on a few occasions. The occupation was beginning to tear Chile apart. Politicians in Chile raged at each other to handle the occupation. Some favored staying the course until a single, stable dictatorship was established in Peru. Others wanted to pull out and just hold on to the guanolands.

Into this swirling stew of chaos emerged another Peruvian wannabe, General Miguel Iglesias, a former army commander who then called for peace under any terms. Chile had found their man. That December he was elected "Regenerating President" by representatives of northern Peru. Peru now had its third title contender. The Chileans gratefully gave him money and arms so he would survive long enough to sign the articles of surrender.

To bolster Iglesias's rule over Peru, the Chileans needed to take out Cáceres. They set out in April 1883 and crushed his army three months later. But the wily, backstabbing, apparently indefatigable leader fled, atop his wounded mount.

Now down to two rulers, the Chileans moved to pare the list. They sent several columns against Montero, holed up in his freshly declared capital of Arequipa. As the two sides faced off in October, the town's citizens suddenly came to their senses and forced Montero to surrender without firing a shot. Montero, the fifth Peruvian leader they vanquished in the war, fled to, where else, Europe, which now boasted a bulging population of former South American rulers.

After numerous false endings, finally, the war was over. Almost.

True to his word, Iglesias signed a peace treaty with the Chileans ending the war, but he forgot to tell the Bolivians, who were now shocked that their secret alliance had been violated. Of course, the Bolivians had been secretly negotiating with Chile for years, but that didn't prevent them from getting all lathered up by this Peruvian stab in the back. Under the treaty Chile got all the guanolands it conquered and agreed to evacuate Lima, ending their nasty three-year occupation. The two countries agreed to defer ownership of some other territories for at least ten years.

Now Bolivia wanted to sign something. Having rejected out of hand a standing offer of peace in exchange for a slice of Peruvian coast, the Bolivians now decided to take the deal. The Chileans looked at the Bolivians as if they were delusional. Didn't they get it? This sweet deal was offered solely to break up the Peru/Bolivia marriage from hell. Once Peru had capitulated, the deal was dead. The Chileans wanted to legalize their conquests, not dicker with the broken Bolivians. The Bolivians had proved equally inept as diplomats as fighters. Finally, the two sides collapsed into a truce; the Chileans administered the conquered territories, and a final peace treaty was worked out.

First, the war wouldn't end. Then peace negotiations wouldn't end. After years of talks, in 1904 Bolivia and Chile signed a deal ending the war and legalizing Bolivia's status as a landlocked nanopower.

Peru and Chile haggled for years over the disputed territories. Finally, they wrapped up the paperwork in 1929 with Peru salvaging an infinitesimal grain of honor by retrieving one of the lost territories.

After losing its coastline, Bolivia decided to create a navy. With admirals.

WHAT HAPPENED AFTER

Bolivia has been landlocked ever since losing the war. Every year, on March 23, people gather in downtown La Paz to hurl invective at the Chileans. The country's leaders speechify about how they plan to regain the lost territories. When the rally breaks up, the people make plans to renew their passports so they can visit the beach.

Peru has continued its slide from keystone of the vast Spanish Empire to also-ran. General Cáceres resisted the lure of European exile and instead hunkered down and continued to lead his small band of mountain rebels. In 1884 he declared himself president of Peru aiming to oust the traitorous Iglesias. The next year Cáceres marched his army over freezing mountain passes to bypass Iglesias's army and stormed Lima. Iglesias surrendered and Cáceres took over. Widely viewed as the true hero of the resistance to Chile, he was elected president the following year in a wave of patriotic fervor. Cáceres, perpetuating the dictator revolving door, welcomed Iglesias back into the army as a general.

Daza returned to Bolivia from his exile in Europe in 1894. When he stepped off the train, he was immediately assassinated.

As for the birdshit, during World War I its value plunged as newer explosives didn't require nitrogen and a method of synthesizing ammonia was developed, making the towering cliffs of guano no longer worth fighting over. Chile's economy, totally dependent on poop exports, shuddered. The cliffs of dung have returned to their rightful place among the planet's least valuable and mostly smelly places.

As a bold gesture of reconciliation, in 2007 Chile returned 3,800 books borrowed from Peru's national library more than 125 years before. Peru graciously waived the late fees.

★ ★ ★

SIX

THE U.S. INVASION OF RUSSIA

1918

The United States invaded Russia.

Yes, that is correct. The United States put boots on the ground in Siberian Russia in 1918 in an attempt to overthrow Lenin and his Communist pioneers at the dawn of the Soviet Union. It was a bold, visionary stroke in identifying a future enemy and striking at it in its cradle, the kind of preemptive strategic action rarely attempted by lumbering democracies such as America, for reasons that will become obvious.

This allied adventure, doomed from its inception, had to overcome its lack of an actual plan (not to mention that World War I was still happening). The only actual planning made for the invasion of Russia, the largest country on earth, was a short memo from President Wilson to Major General William S. Graves, who Wilson picked to lead the U.S. troops assigned to this ill-fated caper. Wilson, a former college professor, titled his invasion report the "Aide-Memoire"; unduly influenced by the numerous vague freshman philosophy papers he had graded, Wilson copied their style. Politicians talk theory, generals talk logistics, and Wilson's invasion memo lacked both. Its main features were its brevity and total paucity of detail. Wilson did not seem to have thought through the practical implications of such goals as "Overthrow the Communists," in a country five thousand miles wide, armed with a few brigades of doughboys and a handful of uncontrollable allies.

The invasion of Siberia wounded the Communists to the extent that they managed to rule for only another eighty years.

THE PLAYERS

Woodrow Wilson—Bespectacled and idealistic president of the United States. The former college professor led the United States into World War I a few months after getting reelected by promising to stay out of the war. But once you get an academic fighting mad, watch out. Even a war that cost the United States more than 100,000 killed didn't diminish Woody's fighting mojo: when he saw the chance to take on the Commies, he dashed off a memo and put the gloves on.

Skinny—He was so arrogant even the French hated him.

Props—He took on the Commies when Senator Joseph McCarthy was still in grade school.

Pros—Had a fourteen-point plan for how to run the world.

Cons—It was four more points than God's plan.

Vladimir Lenin—With the invaluable assistance of Kaiser Wilhelm II, he led his Bolsheviks in seizing power in Russia after killing the tsar and his family of threatening young children.

Skinny—Believed in a worldwide workers' revolution in which no one owned anything but were expected to work like hell so that everyone owned everything, or something like that.

Props—Convinced the Kaiser to send him back to Russia to start a revolution even though he hated the Germans and the Germans hated him.

Pros—Kick-started a worldwide revolution featuring a catchy theme song, the "Internationale."
Cons—Formed the Soviet Union.

Admiral Alexander Kolchak—Caught up in the excitement of being headquartered in the city of Omsk, in Western Siberia, 1,500 miles from Moscow, the former admiral promoted himself Supreme Ruler of Russia.
Skinny—He looked good in his admiral's uniform and had the support of the Western countries.
Props—Stole the tsar's entire gold reserve.
Pros—Was devoted to destroying the Bolsheviks.
Cons—Naval tactics don't work well on land.

Major General William Graves—General Graves, having not exactly distinguished himself by defending the San Francisco front during World War I, received the unenviable task of overthrowing the Russian government with a pint-sized infantry division.
Skinny—His final orders from the secretary of war at a train station in Kansas City were "God bless you and good-bye."
Props—In Russia he quickly realized his troops were better off fighting hangovers than Bolsheviks.
Pros—Was not fooled into believing the Siberian adventure was going to turn out well.
Cons—Read Wilson's ridiculous memo, figured the turgid affair would end badly but dutifully went anyway.

THE GENERAL SITUATION

Wars make strange bedfellows, and World War I was no different. The United States, Britain, and France, along with a bunch of small countries that always fight alongside the major allies but no one really pays attention to, joined together against the Kaiser's Germany and Austria. The tsar wasn't really a democratic kind of guy, but because of a series of interlocking treaties that no one really understood, the Russians somehow ended up on the French/British team against the Germans/Austrians/Turks for the first big show of the very bloody twentieth century.

After millions of casualties suffered by the inept Russian armies, the huddled masses back home in Russia revolted and in early 1917 overthrew the tsar, replacing him with the provisional government. This was welcome news for the Allies as the new government featured a much more democratic sounding name than the Kingdom of Russia.

But Russia was weakening. Russian democrats, landless serfs mostly, had finally grown weary of the centuries-long role of cannon fodder for the grandiosely inept Russian officers. The Russian peasant cannon fodder, however, were highly valued by the French, British, and Americans because the vast Russian army tied down equally large numbers of German troops on the eastern front. The Allies feared that if the massive number of German serf-fighting troops became free to hit the western front, they would probably roll right up to the English Channel in about six weeks. The French believed, of course, that this could never, ever happen.

The situation in Russia took a horrifyingly dramatic turn for the Allies in late 1917 when the Bolsheviks, led by Lenin and Trotsky, took over the country in a neatly executed coup (disguised cleverly as a revolution), pushing aside the provisional government, proving that if your goal is to establish a new government, and you call it the provisional government, it probably will be.

For the Allies, having a bunch of Bolsheviks as their new allies in charge of Russia was bad enough. But in February 1918, when they declared they would stop fighting the imperialistic, capitalistic war against Germany and that their soldiers would go home, the Allies suffered the blow of peace heavily. The removal of Russia meant the potential transfer of about seventy German divisions from the eastern to western theater of war.

The Bolsheviks eagerly signed the treaty of Brest Litovsk on March 3, 1918, handing themselves a complete and utter defeat. This happy event for the Kaiser cleared the way for a vast German spring offensive designed to push the beleaguered Allies beyond the breaking point. The Allies were desperate to get the Russians back in the game. If this meant changing its government one more time, so be it. And if changing the government of Russia meant ending the experiment in communism, whose stated goal was to eradicate capitalism and destroy all the Allied governments, well, that's why bonuses are handed out.

The Allies agreed that with a world war already in progress, an invasion made perfect sense. Unfortunately, President Wilson had already whipped out his Fourteen Point Plan for everlasting world peace; it stated emphatically that countries should be allowed to rule themselves, which was what the Russians were doing in spades. Despite his plan for world perfection, he threw his ideals overboard, under pressure from the British and French.

Fortunately, a cover story dropped into Wilson's lap in the form of the lost Czech legion. The legion, nearly 30,000 men strong, had been fighting the Germans and Austrians alongside the tsar's serfs, who kept dying in order to keep themselves in bondage to their dim-witted ruler. Once the Russians pulled out of the war, the Czechs, their ranks filled out by deserters from the Austrian army, became soldiers without a war. The Czechs received permission from the Bolsheviks to ride the Trans-Siberian Railroad to the port of Vladivostok on the Pacific coast, from where the effortlessly feckless French had kindly agreed to transport them safely back to the charnel house of the western front.

The Allies now had their cover story: the Czech troops

needed help. Plus, there was a lot of equipment the Allies had sent the ungrateful Russians, which sat rusting on the docks of Vladivostok as well as the northern Russian ports of Archangel and Murmansk. The Allies owned the equipment, and if the Russians were going to quit playing war, they wanted it back.

When the secretary of war handed Wilson's memo to Graves in the train station in Kansas City on August 3, 1918, he apologized for sending him to Siberia and promised, someday, to tell him the real reason why he had to go. He told Graves, "Watch your step. You will be walking on eggs loaded with dynamite." And then he left.

The Aide-Memoire, as the scholarly Woody Wilson named it, is clearly the contortions of a self-loving politician and not the concrete thinking of a military leader. Nevertheless, it represented the only guidance provided to the U.S. invading force. Wilson's vacuous freshman paper was actually a unique diplomatic soufflé, a noninvasive invasion, and not the gigantic playbook one would expect for conquering the world's largest country. Graves was left to ponder the confusing seven-page invasion memo that contained one unspoken message that rang out like a bell: Invade Russia, but don't cause trouble.

WHAT HAPPENED: OPERATION "SIBERIAN STORM"

Graves, despite being caught in a fantastical situation, remained stubbornly rational and interpreted the confusing memo as an order to maintain total neutrality after invading. Upon landing in Vladivostok (approximately 5,000 miles away from the seat of power in Moscow) on September 1, 1918, General Graves discovered his micro-invasion force surrounded by enemies: hostile Russians, both Bolshevik and anti-Bolshevik (the Whites), as well as the French and British who were openly working to oust the Bolsheviks and trying to trick the Americans into helping them by shooting someone. Vladivostok itself was controlled by a portion of Czech troops apparently trying to figure out how to get their brethren, who were stuck in the middle of Siberia, out to Vladivostok.

In addition, a large force of Japanese troops were hunkered down trying to take advantage of the chaos in Russia to gobble up chunks of Russian territory. Graves quickly deduced that virtually any activity by U.S. troops could cause a confrontation with one of these armed groups. He approved a plan designed to thwart all the threats against the valiant American doughboys: guarding empty buildings for which the U.S. government was also paying the Russian landlords rent, exploring the city, drinking vodka, and chasing women. They bunked in the old tsarist barracks, which had been built without bathing facilities—in the Russian style.

The U.S. troops, highly trained for their mission in the cities and towns of pre-Prohibition America, failed to execute the plan perfectly. As is often the case with large numbers of armed men sharing the same area who don't speak the same language, actual fighting soon broke out, although it was more fisticuffs than large-scale troop maneuvers. The first U.S. casualties took place on September 16, 1918, after an encounter with the Bolsheviks, who had somehow caught wind of the fact that they were being invaded and teamed up with German and Austrian prisoners to take on the Allies.

Any attempts by Graves to help the Czech legion was soon abandoned when he saw that they were in fact in control of Vladivostok, and controlled many points west along the Trans-Siberian Rairoad. A large group still remained west of Omsk, where the Bolsheviks were negotiating with them to try to get the Czechs to leave. They were dragging their feet because they were in fact helping the Whites oust the Bolsheviks in many of the towns along the railroad. Instead of needing to be rescued, the flexible Czechs kept themselves busy fighting the Bolsheviks up and down the railroad line wherever possible. And Graves had noticed that the Allies, despite professing that one of the aims of their mission in Siberia was to evacuate the Czechs, had neglected to send any ships to take them home.

By October more Allied troops had rolled into Vladivostok and spread throughout Siberia. The total now included 9,000 Americans, 1,000 French, 1,600 British, 72,000 Japanese, and the implausible sight of 12,000 Polish soldiers—all invading Russia. The Japanese, perhaps anticipating their Pearl Harbor gambit, glibly told Graves that their troops were there simply to load steel and coal onto ships.

General Graves, his options hampered by his position as the head of an invasion force, continued his desperate battle to not wage a war, against mounting odds. The British and French wanted to exploit the Siberian front to oust the Bolsheviks and replace them with a government that would continue the fight against Germany, as implausible as it was. The Japanese troops continued to occupy land and not give it back.

As one confused U.S. soldier put it, "What in hell are we doing here? After a while, we figured we had come over there to keep the Japanese from taking over, the English came over to keep an eye on us, and the French to check on the English, and so on."

Meanwhile the fighting in the western front took a dramatic turn during 1918. The German high command, General Erich Ludendorff, knew that the German army had only one more shot left to win the war in 1918. The Allied blockade had by 1918 taken its toll on the Germans, who were facing severe food shortages. Ludendorff shifted manpower from the Russian front to the west, but instead of sending all

THE CZECH GOLD

One of the legends that came out of the Siberian affair was this: Of the eight train cars of the tsar's gold nabbed by the Czech legion, only seven were bartered to the Soviets for the legion's freedom (along with Kolchak) and free passage out of Russia. What happened to the other trainload of gold?

No one really knows, of course. The Soviets were not scrupulous record keepers, but it's clear that the amount of gold bullion, inherited by the provisional government from the tsar and which then ended up in Bolshevik hands, was considerably less than the tsar had held. And the Czechs weren't talking except to refute the story, in 1924, by saying that some of it had been stolen under the noses of the Russian guards. It is indisputable that after World War I the Czech Legion Bank was established in Prague. The bank building features relief scenes of the legion's retreat through Russia. In a bit of possible payback, the bank was looted by the Soviets in 1945 when they took over the country after World War II.

available divisions, he kept some back to keep an eye on the chaos in Russia, and his western armies gained approximately forty divisions. Ludendorff also planned to use new shock troop tactics that had been successful against the Russians. Ludendorff rushed to knock out the British by cutting them off from the French. The British would be forced to evacuate before the American reinforcements, which were arriving daily, could make their presence felt. But his first two massive German drives in northern France, in March and then in April, despite achieving impressive breakthroughs in places, soon bogged down due to a lack of reinforcements and matériel.

Ludendorff's third drive in the center of the line toward Paris in May was spectacularly successful at first, but once again the German troops ran ahead of their supplies. Their attacks were blunted at the tip with the help of fresh American troops thrown into melees at Belleau Wood and Château-Thierry. The Germans, at last poised for victory against the disintegrating French army, eagerly rushed their next assault without disguising their intentions particularly well. The still-formidable French artillery caught the German shock troops as they were forming up for their attack, and despite giving ground, prevented the Germans from breaking through.

That summer both armies were attacked by the Spanish influenza, killing thousands, but the hungry German army took the hit harder. Their morale started to crack, made worse by the growing presence of the corn-fed Americans. Ludendorff, still wishing to make one more diversionary thrust against the French before knocking out the British, cranked up his fifth assault on July 15. The French again learned of the hour of attack and scattered the Germans with a well-timed artillery barrage. The Germans, without tanks, were initially successful, but with American, Italian, and British support the French line held; a counterattack, with Americans and French colonial troops in the lead, hit the Germans in the flank. The Germans were forced to retreat, and the Allies, now building momentum, never slowed down.

Ludendorff, stressed by the failure of his last grand offensive, turned on the Kaiser in October 1918 and insisted that he negotiate peace, long after the Kaiser had come to the same conclusion. The Germans skillfully conducted a fighting retreat across their entire western front. Ludendorff quit at the end of October, and by the beginning of November the Kaiser had fled. The fledgling German republic, practically stillborn, signed the Armistice, ending the fighting on November 11, 1918.

A week after the end of the war-to-end-all-wars, things were starting to look up for the Allies in Siberia. On November 17, Admiral Kolchak took over the White Russian government in the landlocked Siberian city of Omsk and appointed himself Supreme Ruler of all the Russias. The Allies, casting about for a strongman to grab power from the Reds, took a liking to the Supreme Ruler and started feeding him supplies down the Trans-Siberian Railroad. While a ruthless reactionary, tsarishly untroubled about ordering the deaths of those who opposed him, the former head of the Russian Black Sea Fleet convinced the Allies he was an enlightened leader, and Wilson was ready to recognize him as the legitimate head of Russia. Despite losing the obvious rationale that had been conveniently provided by the war, the Allies remained stubbornly undeterred in their position—the noninvasion invasion must go on.

Graves pressed on, continuing his brilliant strategy of doing absolutely nothing amid the growing tumult of the Russian Civil War. The White armies, filled with Cossacks, made initial gains against the Bolsheviks. The Czech freelancers, unimpressed with Kolchak and realizing the writing was on the wall for anyone opposing the Bolsheviks, decided to finally take advantage of the fact that the war was over and just go home. Now they found themselves trapped in the growing chaos of the civil war.

In the spring of 1919, the Kolchak government gave its dubious stamp of approval to the Allies's plan to run the decrepit Siberian railroads. Graves, happy to have his soldiers actually doing something that didn't involve boozing and whoring in Vladivostok, moved his forces out of the city and took control of a section of the railroad in support of the Kolchak government. The American troops, however, quickly got into a confrontation with a local White Russian Cossack leader, Grigori Semenov, who was nominally part of Kolchak's forces but was backed by the invasion-practicing Japanese. By this time, Graves had started to receive thousands of rifles meant for the Kolchak forces, but he refused to hand them over to Semenov because his wild Cossacks had been taking potshots at American troops (and anyone else who got in their way) whenever possible.

Semenov stopped a train of weapons bound for Kolchak in Omsk and demanded 15,000 rifles. After a two-day standoff, Semenov backed off and the train chugged on to Omsk. So, in this noninvasion invasion, designed to shorten a war that had already ended, the United States had confronted a friend of a friend that was backed by yet another friend, natch. This was just one of the many scenarios Graves faced in Siberia on which Wilson's memo provided no guidance.

In July 1919 Graves was instructed by Washington to visit Kolchak in Omsk, as the American government and the Allies had the month earlier promised to provide his government with munitions and food. Graves arrived in Omsk after a long train ride through Siberia, past Lake Baikal, deep in the interior . . . in time for the collapse of Kolchak's government. He came away unimpressed with the Land Admiral.

Kolchak, without support of the Czech legion and realizing that the bulk of his army was in fact an unruly gang of Cossacks, concluded that not all Russians felt he was Supreme Ruler material. In November he passed command of the Whites to the pesky Cossack Semenov. The dispirited Kolchak retreated east until captured by the opportunistic Czech legion. Sensing his barter value, the Czechs, in return for their safe passage out of Russia, turned him and his captured gold over to the crafty Reds. General Graves, now firmly in command of the port, bars, and restaurants of Vladivostok harbor, watched over the departure of the Czech soldiers as they finally shipped out home, more than a year after the end of World War I. There were no more cover stories. It was time to go.

The American transport ships soon followed, loaded down with their war booty of eighty Russian wives of servicemen. The official figures put the American losses at 137 killed in action, with an additional 216 deaths from other sources, such as accidents and diseases.

The grabby Japanese stayed, still hoping to add a nice chunk of Russian tundra to their growing empire, but they eventually bowed to Bolshevik pressure and left in 1922.

In his book General Graves summed up his role in this amazingly stupid conflict with typical understatement: "I was in command of the United States troops sent to Siberia and, I must admit, I do not know what the United States was trying to accomplish by military intervention."

WHAT HAPPENED AFTER

One would expect that when two heavyweights such as the United States and Russia go at it, the world would indeed change. And perhaps that may be the most amazing aspect of this madcap affair. It changed absolutely nothing, except to give the world a few more Czech World War I veterans and provide the Bolsheviks propaganda they could use for the next eight decades: America was trying to invade us. No one in the United States remembers, but they do.

Woodrow Wilson suffered a stroke in 1919, and his wife became de facto president until the end of his term. During her time in charge she hid the ailing president from the vice president and the cabinet. She invaded no countries. Wilson died in 1924.

General William Graves retired from the army in 1928 and wrote a book damning the whole experience.

The Bolsheviks held Kolchak in prison for a few weeks and, as expected, placed him up against a wall and shot him on February 7. The gold found its way to the Bolsheviks in

Moscow. On the bright side, a statue of Land Admiral Kolchak now stands in Omsk.

Vladimir Lenin suffered a series of debilitating strokes, starting in 1922, and died two years later. Josef Stalin took control of the Soviet Union and invaded many countries.

The Soviet Union remained communist until 1991.

★ ★ ★

SEVEN

HITLER'S BEER HALL PUTSCH

1923

What makes a good putsch?

Unlike the revolution, its more belligerent cousin, few have possessed the delicate touch to successfully pull off this somewhat subtle affair. Adolf Hitler, as we now know, wasn't known for his delicacy.

A successful putsch is a lighthearted event, the fiesta of government overthrows. The putschists are only "giving the people what they want," which is, of course, a new government run by the putschists. A well-run putsch should seem to magically spring from the streets and encounter light or no resistance, spilling only a soupçon of blood. Nothing dims the gleeful prospects of a good putsch faster than unnecessary bloodshed.

If there ever was a country ready for a putsch, it was Germany in 1923. And Munich was the perfect spot. Munich beerhalls were tailor made for putsch gathering spots: large caverns with food and beer to ply hungry irregular troops, perfect for inflammatory speeches and weapons caches. The political and military leaders of Munich and the entire province of Bavaria all detested anything vaguely resembling democracy and hungered for the security of a dictatorship, although no one could quite agree on what flavor. As the topper, the entire leadership of the region supported the overthrow of, well, themselves. They just had not yet figured out all the details, such as who would lead the new government.

Hitler, his rabble-rousing political skills already in full flower, had by then assembled many of his all-star cast of supporting characters that later successfully waged the largest, most devastating war of all time. The crew was headlined by the jovial World War I fascist hero of the air, Hermann Goering, and backed by the incomparably Prussian General Erich Ludendorff, the former leader of the spectacularly unsuccessful but widely admired German war effort in World War I.

Hitler was ready. Munich was ready. The beer was cold. There were plenty of unemployed former soldiers milling about, eager to put their bitter aggression to good use. It seemed like a slam dunk. But it all ended less than a day later with blood in the streets and short jail terms.

How could it have possibly failed?

THE PLAYERS

Adolf Hitler—A decorated veteran of the German army in World War I, native-born Austrian, nonsmoker, vegan, budding visual artist, uneducated, skill-free weirdo with absolutely no scruples, who somehow came up with the idea that he should be running the world and then convinced a lot of other people this sounded like a really good idea.

Skinny—Joined the nascent Nazi party in 1919 and by an incessant haranguing of the populace took the little party into the big leagues.

Props—Made great use of his odd, blinkless stare by becoming a riveting speaker.

Pros—Knew how to sway a crowd.

Cons—Thought he should be running the world and continually threatened to kill himself if he wasn't given the chance.

General Erich Ludendorff—Hitler's ace-in-the-hole for the putsch. The bumbling Prussian who had blown the once-every-thousand-years opportunity to crush England and France in a one-front war after the Russians bowed out of World War I, had saved his reputation by inventing the "stabbed in the back by the lousy politicians on the home front" excuse, before fleeing to Sweden at the end of the war sporting a false beard.

Skinny—Ludendorff's participation ensured that Hitler's ragtag army of street thugs would get instant street cred and be taken seriously by the average right-wing sympathizing citizen of Munich.

Props—Took advantage of the fact that a uniform ablaze with medals and the too-small-for-his-head spiked helmet remained an oddly comforting image to most Germans.

Pros—Looked every inch what he was, a fantastically violent retired general turned naïve revolutionary.

Cons—Suited up for battle dressed in a tweed suit the first night of the putsch.

THE GENERAL SITUATION

In 1923 Germany was chaos. After losing World War I it suffered every kind of revolution possible—Communist, monarchist and right wing—pretty much everything except democratic. The widely despised legal government, the Weimar Republic, hung on for dear life amid the raging winds of revolution.

The German economy was also a complete disaster. A key reason was that the German government didn't have the money to pay the high amount of reparations demanded by the French, who were feeling quite vindictive that their country had been invaded, fought over for four years, and had lost millions of their citizens and soldiers.

Before the war Germany had been the growing power in Europe, with the largest population of the western countries and the most technically advanced industry. It just didn't make sense to most Germans that they had lost the war, especially to the French, their sagging, democratic, arch-enemy whom Bismarck had so easily manhandled in the Franco-Prussian War of 1870. But now, unemployment in Germany was high, and rampant inflation—at its worst in 1923 when prices doubled every two days—had eroded the currency to the point that a cup of coffee cost billions of marks. Wheelbarrows had replaced wallets.

The Prussian officer corps longed for the inherent stability of a country organized around the codes and traditions of the Prussian military killing machine that they all had come to know, love, and trust. It was an article of faith among the defeated and disgraced Prussian officers of noble birth, who had marched the country into war before inadvertently plunging it into the chaos of revolution, that their glorious army was the crucial backbone of the German nation. They believed it was their duty to make a last stand for unchallengeable, oligarchical rule—or their country might disappear under the converging waves of radical Communism, radical democracy, or an evil and unimaginable combination of both.

The most vehement of these former soldiers were the "Freikorps," groups of former soldiers secretly hired, armed, and silently sanctioned by the legitimate government into illegal paramilitary companies. The Freikorps were tacitly given a free hand in crushing the revolutionaries of the left in exchange for propping up the Social Democratic regime of President Friedrich Ebert, who had inherited the tottering German state after the abdication by the Kaiser.

But the Freikorps were uncontrollable by anyone, including the hard-bitten officers who commanded them. The troops were invariably front-line veterans who had survived years of the unimaginable horror of trench warfare, and could in fact no longer exist in a peaceful society. Many of the German masses agreed with the aim of the Freikorps, if not the jackbooted tactics they had perfected on the rest of Europe.

The revered loser of World War I, Field Marshal Ludendorff—he of the big lie that Germany had been "stabbed in the back by the November criminals" to save his skin—was turning out to be an impatient, naïve putschist. He had been one of the organizers of the Kapp Putsch in 1920, a failed attempt to overthrow the Weimar Republic, and with its collapse was forced to once again flee Germany in disguise. Ludendorff ended up in Munich, where he installed himself in a suburban villa and began to interview candidates for the open position of German dictator.

Adolf Hitler, a complete nobody at the end of the war, with a war record blemished solely by his own survival, also landed in Munich, where his army regiment put him to work haranguing returning soldiers against the evils of Communism. Marked down as a promising intelligence officer, he was assigned to keep tabs on the burgeoning right-wing revolutionary scene, which resulted in his visit to the tiny, nascent Nazi party in a beer hall on September 12, 1919. Impressed by his ability to shout down the half-dozen members of the party, they invited Adolf to join them. A week later he signed up.

Feeling inspired for the first time since the end of the war, Hitler honed his raw haranguing power; through hard work and dedication he grew the party with his message that Germany's woes were due to the Jews and the Communists. Hitler's rhetorical pictures of a racial fantasyland, where honor and order would be restored to the proud Germans, proved much more popular than the bad watercolors he had sold on the streets before the war. The growing masses who attended his beer-hall speeches soon made him a local celebrity.

By 1922 Hitler had attracted two of his main cohorts who were to prove instrumental in bringing him to power and then crashing the world into World War II. Hermann Goering, after a war in which he had taken over the famed Richthofen squadron from the Red Baron in 1918, had moved back into his mom's apartment in Munich. A bigger humiliation, however, was the open contempt he received from the left-wing revolutionaries who often stripped the medals off the chests of soldiers in public.

Goering often vented his anger at beer-hall rallies. He was soon window-shopping for a radical party to join that was as bitter and determined to avenge the defeat as he was. He quickly found Hitler in the fall of 1922. When Goering heard Hitler's harangue about the injustices of the Versailles Treaty, it was love at first rant.

Hitler instinctively knew the dashing, decorated former war ace was a great addition to the still-small party. Goering possessed the rare combination of a common touch covering a ruthless cunning. Shortly after their first meeting, Hitler handed him command of the SA (*Sturmabteilung*), Hitler's street brawlers.

Meanwhile, Heinrich Himmler, the son of a middle-class devoutly Roman Catholic Munich family, joined the team as an anonymous peon. While not the usual background for a grand terrorist-in-the-making, Himmler was overly influenced by his history-obsessed father. He nurtured dreams of the good old days when racially pure Teutonic knights ruled the forests of Prussia with nary a Jew or Communist to mar the vision.

Little Heinrich always strived to be the best in whatever he did, and as a German youth he craved to serve his country by joining the futile slaughter of World War I. But the German army was very strict in denying non-nobles the opportunity to become officers and direct the carnage. The rules changed only when the ranks of young noblemen started to grow thin at the end of the war.

Heinrich finally landed his officer post, but to the dismay of millions of his future victims he missed all the action and failed to achieve the ultimate sacrifice for his country. Back home in one piece he set his hopes on tilling the soil of a far-flung Prussian outpost like a knight from his juvenile Teutonic fantasies. He joined a Freikorps but narrowly missed out on the bloodletting as his unit failed to join the thrashing of the Reds in 1919. After a year of chicken farming in 1921 in preparation for tilling his Prussian fantasyland, he met Ernst Röhm at a weekend Teutonic fantasy camp. Röhm, another embittered veteran, was an active army officer whose main job was to hide weapons from the Allied soldiers who were haplessly trying to control the growing chaos in Germany. Röhm was in a position to help any political group he favored by giving them access to the stashed weapons. He soon took a shining to Hitler's promising little group of Nazis. As the Nazis grew in popularity, they needed brawlers to control their raucous beer-hall meetings, and Röhm nurtured the fledgling SA by providing it with men and weapons. Himmler, part of one of Röhm's groups, tagged along and was soon sucked into the growing vortex of the Nazi party.

After Munich had been brutally cleansed of its Bolshevik-styled government a few years earlier, it became the focal point of a right-wing revolution, its streets and beer halls bubbling with fascistic energy. In the evenings the Freikorps leagues kept themselves in trouble and prepared for the next day of unemployment by battling each other for control of the streets. In their quieter moments, they crowded into the beer halls to discuss the various violent methods of over-throwing the elected government. Like blood and beer mixing in the gutters, the right wingers, Communists, and socialists could agree on only one thing: anything had to be better than the democracy they were suffering under.

The Prussian generals were determined to keep the rowdy Freikorps under their control, and they kept a wary eye on Munich. Gustav von Kahr had installed himself as Bavaria's right-wing dictator in Munich. Kahr was amenable to any right-wing government, but particularly enamored of monarchy, and still pined for the recently scuttled Wittelsbachs, one of the minor royal families who had been tossed back on the monarchical scrap heap after their seven-hundred-year interlude of ruling Bavaria.

By 1923, Hitler was in full control of the Nazi party. He gave his buddy Röhm the task of staffing up the violence bureau, and he brought in the angriest of the Freikorps rowdies. Hitler's first big speech as a politician had been in February 24, 1920, in the Hofbräuhaus before 2,000 people. Now his little party had almost 100,000 members, including 15,000 SA brawlers, and was recognized as a real threat by the government and the Prussian officers who really controlled the country. Determined not to invite retaliation by the French before the German army was slowly rebuilt into its former Europe-stomping glory, the government, still struggling with the obscure limits of democracy, outlawed fringe parties and clamped down. Hitler retreated from the scene that summer and considered his options.

The time for someone to strike was ripe. In January 1923 the French had occupied the industrial Ruhr valley, combining further Gallic humiliation with a crushing economic blow. The German government, backed in a secret and cynical effort by the industrialists, was busy printing marks like so many strudels in order to pay off the reparation debt owed to the Allies. The resulting massive hyperinflation had the unfortunate side effect of wiping out the bank accounts of most ordinary Germans. The despised democratic government took the blame, of course.

In Munich, the protoführer von Kahr and the other right-wing-leaders-to-be had been meeting with Hitler about extending von Kahr's Munich dictatorship over all of Germany. But to Hitler's exasperation, everyone kept dickering over the details, including, most importantly, who would become the Big Leader. Kahr wanted to reinstall the monarchy; Röhm wanted to turn his Freikorps into a real military threat and pined for a replacement dictatorship; von Seisser, the Bavarian police chief, liked Hitler but not as much as the Freikorps and could not decide whom to support; von Lossow, the Bavarian army chief, who supported the dictatorship model of governing, also liked Hitler but knew that supporting the pushy young wannabe dictator would displease his superiors in Berlin. So he also sat on the fence.

Hitler, impatient to start dictating, met with all of them throughout the fall. He had given von Kahr, von Lossow, and von Seisser his word that he would not start the counterrevolution without them. But time, it seemed, was quickly running out for the impatient future führer. When von Kahr announced a big speech in Munich's Bürgerbräukeller, slated for November 8, Hitler panicked and, not wanting to get left behind in the führer race, quickly cooked up a plan and made his move. He met with his minions the night before, and they plotted well past midnight. Their jury-rigged plan depended on the unproven organizational genius of Goering leading the Nazi's SA fighters and the participation of the unassailable General Ludendorff.

WHAT HAPPENED: OPERATION "CAN'T ANYONE HERE THROW A REVOLUTION?"

To Hitler, mesmerized by his own fanatical beliefs, as were his growing army of followers, the organization and planning of the coup had been an afterthought. The plan was simply to pull the leaders of Bavaria aside before von Kahr's speech, convince them to join Hitler's putsch then and there, declare the revolution, and march on Berlin immediately. With Hitler, of course, in the lead.

Hitler got to the beer hall early and conspicuously loitered in the lobby waiting for Goering and his personal bodyguards. As planned, von Lossow and von Seisser, as well as virtually all of the other Munich power figures, arrived at the Bürgerbräukeller to hear von Kahr's speech. While von Kahr was speaking, Goering and the guards drove up in trucks, barged in, and set up a machine gun right in the lobby of the cavernous beer hall. On a signal from Hitler, the door was thrown open; Hitler, at the center of a flying wedge of troopers, pushed through the crowd waving his pistol like the Lone Ranger while Goering indulged his over-the-top flair by dramatically brandishing a sword. They pushed their way onstage, and Hitler quieted the crowd with a pistol shot into the ceiling. The revolution was on.

Angry that Hitler had broken his promise not to putsch without them, the three leaders, Kahr, Lossow, and Seisser, refused to move. Hitler, livid at their intransigence, dragged them into a side room and stuck his pistol in their ears. They still balked. Hitler ranted but was forced to return to the auditorium where Goering was trying to calm the restless crowd by telling them to relax and joking that "after all, you have your beer!"

Hitler strode onstage, announced the lineup of the new

government, including the roles Kahr, Lossow, and Seisser would play, and swayed the crowd to his side. He strutted back into the side room triumphantly, knowing that he had forced their hand. But the balky triumvirate was only warming to the idea. Then Ludendorff, the World War I hero who had lost the war, entered. He was Hitler's closer, but his effect at first was less than fully Prussian because he was dressed for a weekend of hunting in a bad suit instead of his impressive uniform, to preserve the flimsy fiction that his involvement was a spur of the moment kind of thing.

Now the triumvirate realized things were flowing against them. Under Ludendorff's spell, Lossow and Seisser agreed to join up, but Kahr kept holding out for the restoration of his beloved monarchy. He finally caved when Hitler told him the perfect lie: that the putsch is what the Kaiser would have wanted. Hitler would be in charge, of course, with Lossow and Seisser receiving plum roles; the unemployable Ludendorff would get to run the army again, and Kahr would stay on as governor of Bavaria. After taking over Munich, everyone would march on Berlin and complete the revolution.

The deal signed, they all marched back onstage where everyone pledged to join Hitler's revolution. The crowd went wild.

Outside, the night had finally arrived for the rowdy fighters of the SA battalions to prove their worth to the Nazi revolution on the cold streets of Munich. They gathered in the city's beer halls, drinking and awaiting word to pounce on the levers of government and attack anyone who resisted the revolution.

Veteran Freikorps leader Gerhard Rossbach had been given six troopers and tasked to capture the Infantry School. The cadets gladly turned themselves over to the popular Rossbach, a hard-fighting Freikorps legend. Rossbach's new cadets marched out with weapons toward the Marienplatz, the center of town, across the river from Hitler's putsch hall.

Elsewhere in Munich, the putsch was having less success. SA troopers failed to trick soldiers at the Nineteenth Infantry regiment barracks armory into handing over their weapons. Other SA troopers got locked inside another armory by an army officer determined not to get putsched without explicit orders.

Meanwhile, Ernst Röhm, waiting for word that the putsch had launched, had formed up his SA battalion at the upscale Löwenbräukeller under pretense of a fun night out with a brass band and a speech by Hitler. Himmler was there, clutching the Nazi flag, his major accomplishment of the putsch. When they got the call that the revolt was on, Röhm announced it to the crowd and everyone formed up in the street, suddenly sporting firearms, courtesy of the master arms-stasher Röhm. The armed troopers marched off to the Bürgerbräukeller to join forces with Hitler, led by a brass band and picking up hidden arms along the way. Himmler, flag in hand, marched along proudly, finally getting his chance to storm into war.

The plot then started to spring leaks. In the confusion at the Bürgerbräukeller, a police inspector slipped out the side door and sounded the alarm. Word reached senior police officers, who dispatched police to protect the telegraph and phone exchanges. With von Lossow, the head of the army in Munich, trapped at the beer hall, the police called the ranking army officer in the city, Major General von Danner, a monarchist who hated the Nazis. He immediately rushed over to help.

Another police officer, alerted by shouting in the streets that the national revolution had started, rushed out in his house in slippers to quickly secure von Kahr's governmental office. The strutting, disorganized putschists were getting beaten on all sides by a handful of quick-acting middle managers.

Röhm's noisy parade bloodlessly conquered the war ministry for Ludendorff and von Lossow, but inadvertently neglected to secure the telephone exchange inside the building where loyal officers called around and found that Röhm, despite being a top military officer in Munich, should not be trusted.

When Hitler, basking in his glorious moment of newfound dictatorship, learned about the problem at the Nineteenth Infantry barracks, he rushed out of the putsch hall to fix the situation. He left Ludendorff there in charge of the captive Kahr, Lossow, and Seisser. Hitler's convoy then ran into Rossbach with his infantry cadets. He stopped to treat his new recruits to a fiery speech and then swung by the war ministry to congratulate Röhm. His convoy passed citizens out in the streets proudly strutting their officially licensed Nazi wear and the red-black-white of the old German monarchy. The putsch-friendly carnival atmosphere filled the cool night air, which was exhilaratingly free of gunfire. The putsch was succeeding brilliantly it seemed. Hitler beamed.

Hitler finally arrived at the barracks, but the stubborn gatekeeper refused to allow him in. Sensing a glitch in the momentum, Hitler circled back to the putsch hall and delegated the barracks problem to von Lossow to untangle.

While Hitler was away, Ludendorff grew impatient to finally retake his position atop the army and decided to release the triumvirate of vons—Kahr, Lossow, and Seisser. He, of course, received their absolute, Prussian-bound assurance that they would continue to support the putschers. The other putschers disagreed vehemently but couldn't sway the aging general. And so von Kahr, von Lossow, and von Seisser sauntered out, and the putsch unknowingly received a deathblow at the hands of its ace in the hole.

Once freed from the putschers' clutches, the von trio, who controlled virtually all the legal channels of power in the region, decided they didn't want to work for young Adolf. They set off to save their own hides, and if necessary, sink the putsch.

Kahr bolted to his office where a representative from a Freikorps brigade told him that if Kahr declared himself dictator, the brigade's 15,000 troops would invade Bavaria to support him. The cautious Kahr declined the invitation to kick-start a civil war. At the same time Seisser scuttled off to a local police command post and issued orders for the state police to protect themselves. Hedging his bets like almost everyone else at this point—to not move yet against the putsch—Seisser then set out for Kahr's offices.

When Hitler had arrived back at the putsch hall, he didn't realize the seriousness of Ludendorff's blunder in releasing the von trio. He still believed they would support him and could not fathom that anyone did not yearn for him to become dictator. What concerned him more were the SA troopers hanging around the beer hall snacking instead of conquering key government buildings.

Hitler had completely lost the diabolical focus that had brought him to the point of near victory. His head was already swimming in the newfound glory of an apparent victory. When Rossbach and his infantry cadets arrived at the putsch hall and wanted to pass in triumphant review, Hitler obliged and trotted out to treat them to a little speech with Ludendorff watching proudly. Then the soldiers trundled inside for beer and sausages.

Ludendorff, his innate Prussianness awakening, finally left for the war ministry, guarded by Röhm. He sat down in his outer office to wait for von Lossow to show up so they could start planning the march on Berlin. But Lossow never showed: he had headed for the infantry barracks. And it wasn't until another hour or two later that Ludendorff, the naïve revolutionary, started to get suspicious—but not suspicious enough. In other rooms in the war ministry, Röhm's delay in securing the telephones meant that resistance to the putsch was being organized as Röhm and Ludendorff sat waiting for the one man who they thought would control the fate of the putsch. But he had already turned against them.

Ludendorff, cooling his heels in von Lossow's anteroom, finally started thinking like a soldier again and rousted Rossbach's lounging infantry cadets from the putsch hall to take over the state government offices, all of which were now guarded by the state police. It was to be the first clash of the night. The police cordon outside the offices politely informed Rossbach's troops that the trio had switched sides. Rossbach refused to budge. Finally Seisser popped out to tell Rossbach personally. Sides were now being taken. The approximately one hundred police officers were facing down over four hundred armed infantry cadets.

Rossbach, the fiery Freikorps leader, knew that revolutions required blood, and he ordered his troops to open fire. But the soldiers, many of whom knew one another and all wanted a right-wing revolution of some flavor, were reluctant to end the carnival atmosphere by shooting one another. At this point, the confused putsch leadership weighed in to sink their chances even further. Suddenly, a murky message appeared from the putsch hall ordering Rossbach's troops to guard the train station. Once the cadets took off, Kahr and Seisser were free to escape and met up with von Lossow at the infantry barracks. Hitler's opposition was now united.

The night, however, was quickly becoming a comic "who's on first?" scenario, Prussian army style. Nobody wanted to make a move without knowing first what the other guy was going to do. Loyal-but-sympathetic soldiers refused to shoot putschers but also refused to join them. They didn't have orders! A German soldier couldn't be expected to join a revolution without orders!

The SA company that had been frustrated at the barracks had marched back to the putsch hall. The men sat down in the hall, waiting for orders, stuffing their faces with free beer and sausage. Some started to bunk down under the tables, sensing it was going to be a long night. Some of them had to get up in the morning to go to their regular jobs.

The putsch had turned into an uncoordinated circus. Goering was worried about his ailing wife. Instead of occupying the power centers of the city, random attacks on the Nazis's favorite targets became the order of the day. The hotel where the Allied army officers were lodged was attacked; the French and British arms control officers were accosted in their pajamas; the hotel staff was able to convince the Nazis to let them stay in the hotel. Enemies of the Nazis, including the usual Jews and Commies, were attacked and fifty-eight prisoners dragged back to the putsch hall.

By midnight, the alarmed President Ebert in Berlin, by now well versed in crushing challenges to his government from both the left and right, turned to his head coup-crusher, General Hans von Seeckt, and told him to handle it. When nervously asked by the ministers where the army stood, the icy von Seeckt replied "Behind me." Von Seeckt wasn't about to let Germany's rebirth be hijacked by a rookie like Hitler. He ordered the army on a midnight march to Munich to bolster the tiny army force in the city.

From the safety of their secret lair in the barracks, Kahr, Lossow, and Seisser issued a message repudiating the putsch and ordered posters to be printed and circulated. But in actuality they were badly outgunned. There were only a thousand state police and a handful of loyal army troops who could be relied upon to fight against the thousands of SA troopers roaming the streets.

Hitler and Ludendorff still had the upper hand, but it was slipping out of their grasp. Even after waiting in von Lossow's office in vain Ludendorff had wasted yet more time phoning around the various ministries to find him. Lossow's aides put off the dupable Ludendorff by either not picking up the phone or telling him that von Lossow was still en route from somewhere to somewhere else.

When dawn arrived on November 9, the fifth anniversary of the Kaiser's abdication, Hitler and Ludendorff finally realized that the von trio—Kahr, Lossow, and Seisser—had betrayed them. It had taken them almost seven hours to comprehend this fact. Almost all of the key installations were still under the control of the police and army: infantry barracks, telegraph and phone exchanges. Reconvening at the putsch hall they argued bitterly over their next steps while the troopers milled about the smoky, dank beer cellar. Goering's contribution was to find a band to roust the tired troops out of their morning daze while Hitler frantically planned his next moves. The sleepy band played without their breakfast or pay and under threat of a good kicking.

To further boost the troops, Hitler sent two SA commanders, including Ludendorff's stepson, both of whom happened to be experienced bank clerks, and a couple dozen toughs in beer trucks to rob the presses where government officers were up all night printing money to keep up with inflation. The troopers each received a couple trillion marks for their night's service, just enough to cover the night's beer bill.

Then Hitler, in a crazed, desperate gambit, dispatched a drinking buddy of the deposed crown prince of Bavaria to plead with him to join the coup and order monarchy-adoring Kahr to obey Adolf.

The good news for Hitler was that SA battalions were making their way back to the putsch hall, and reinforcements

BARON MICHAEL VON GODIN

Baron Michael von Godin was one of the sensible, moral, and nameless middle managers in the sea of German radicalism who put his life on the line to try to stop Hitler and the fascists. A senior lieutenant in charge of the company of Bavarian state police that faced down Hitler and Ludendorff in the Odeonplatz, he gave the order to fire upon them, ending the putsch. For this act, the Nazis hounded him until he retired in 1926 and was forced to leave the country. When he returned in May 1933, he was captured and tortured by the Nazis for eight months before he was finally allowed to leave again, due to some hiccup in the Nazi horror apparatus. After World War II he became the chief of the Bavarian police.

from outside the city were arriving. Kahr had finally allowed word to leak out about his government's resistance to the coup. But Hitler's finely tuned propaganda machine beat them to the punch. Posters and papers blared headlines that the revolution was on, and Hitler and Ludendorff were leading it.

Around 11 A.M., a detachment of state police was finally sent to guard the bridge that led from the putsch hall into the heart of the city. Their orders were crafted as if for a column of schoolchildren: if confronted by the putschers, they were not to resist actively but only to politely ask them to please take another route. Everyone was still on the fence.

Hitler sent his bodyguards to take the police HQ, but when the leader pounded on the door they were politely but firmly turned away. Instead of attacking the HQ, he decided to check in with the putsch hall. Goering told him to come back—there had been a change in plan. The founding members of the group that was to kill and terrorize millions had packed up their machine guns and meekly marched back to the beer hall, where Hitler had found time in his schedule to fit in an interview. They found him holding his first international press conference with reporters from the *New York Times* and other American newspapers.

Back to Goering. After getting the um-pah band together and needing something more to do, he took the city council hostage and made sure the good citizens of Munich were flying the Nazi flag. But the state police were finally posting themselves on the bridges separating eastern Munich from the western part. It was almost noon, and except for Goering's energetic hostage taking, nothing much was happening. Hitler and Ludendorff realized something had to be done or the putsch would fail. Reports came in that police and army reinforcements had moved out in force to surround Röhm and the flag-clutching Himmler, who were both still holed up at the war ministry where Hitler and Ludendorff had forgotten them.

Ludendorff knew they must immediately attack or retreat. Retreat to the hills was rejected. Hitler wanted to wait until they got an answer from the deposed crown prince, but their messenger was still on the train. Ludendorff chose neither and oddly decided to march peacefully from the beer hall to the center of town in a triumphant procession to try to sway the populace to their side, and presumably lead on to Berlin. Hitler didn't like the idea, most likely because it wasn't his, but Ludendorff, wearing his revolutionary tweed cap instead of his spiked Pickelhaube, commanded "we march." Swept up in revolutionary fervor he blithely abandoned the most basic of infantry tactics, such as attacking your enemy.

Not even Hitler could hold back the bullheaded general when he finally worked up a full head of steam. The band, still unpaid, packed up its instruments and went home. Ludendorff, the Great War hero, Hitler, the ingénue, and his retinue of thousands of desperate soldiers of fortune would have to march to victory unaccompanied by music.

Hitler, Ludendorff, and Goering fronted a column and marched from the putsch hall toward the center of town a few hundred yards away. After presumably declining to take another route when asked by the police, the bridge into downtown Munich was stormed by Hitler's bodyguards who easily pushed aside the police troopers gamely blocking their way. The march moved on.

The morning papers and the posters had done their job: the populace was turning out to cheer them on. At every corner they seemed to be gaining strength. It was the glorious first morning of the Nazi revolution. The confusion of the night before was vanishing in the festive morning air. In the Marienplatz, about a mile west of the river, they came to another line of state police but this time veered around them and kept marching. Singing broke out. Hitler, Ludendorff and the others linked arms. It was just how they dreamed it would be.

Then they turned another corner and confronted a line of police at the entrance to the Odeonplatz, in the heart of Munich. The marchers pushed the police back into the square. The police stiffened. A shot rang out. Hitler's reliably brutal bodyguards attacked with drawn bayonets. More shots rang out as the crowd scattered.

The shooting lasted for almost a minute. The volley of police gunfire had devastated the column, scattering the marchers, except for the implacable Ludendorff, gloriously and stubbornly out of touch now with even his own immediate environment. He picked himself up off the street, stepped over the dead and wounded, and marched straight through the police lines into captivity.

The man marching next to Hitler was shot dead while Hitler's bodyguard, a beefy ex-wrestler named Ulrich Graf, yanked Hitler to the ground and took eight bullets in order to shield the future murderer of millions from death. Hitler suffered a badly strained shoulder before fleeing in a waiting car. Goering, hit badly in the groin, crawled into a nearby house where he was patched up by the wife of a Jewish businessman and her sister, and then smuggled into Austria. (Goering later helped the sisters escape Germany on the eve of World War II.)

Enough of the putschers managed to return fire to kill four state policemen. The rest of them fled like rats, leaving fourteen of their putschmates dead in the street.

The putsch was over, ending ignominiously less than a day after it started.

WHAT HAPPENED AFTER

Hitler fled to a farmhouse outside the city, where he was rounded up a couple days later like a common criminal. Goering's wound at the Odeonplatz led him to a morphine addiction that would plague him to the end of his life. Himmler and his pet flag, along with most of the putschists' troops, were allowed to march out the back door of the War Ministry by sympathetic troops when Röhm surrendered. Röhm was cashiered from the army, sent to prison, and then sailed to Bolivia as a military consultant to its fascist-leaning government.

Ulrich Graf, the bodyguard who saved Hitler's life, was dropped from Hitler's inner circle after he got out of prison.

The whole affair was soft-pedaled by the courts, and Hitler and his coterie were given ten months easy time in Landesberg prison, a cushy castle, where the putative dictator used the time to finally jot down his thoughts about taking over the world in a book titled *Mein Kampf*.

Hitler and his gang finally gained widespread success by using their vile messages to seduce the one power in Germany that could free them to do their evil bidding: the German army high command.

★ ★ ★

EIGHT

THE CHACO WAR

1932

Some countries have never won a war. You might say they inhabit the losers' bracket of history. To them the way out of that bracket is to beat somebody. Anybody. But what they don't understand is beating another loser won't put them in the winners' bracket; it'll just elevate them in the losers' bracket.

Two members of the losers' bracket are Paraguay and Bolivia. Paraguay had fought the disastrous War of the Triple Alliance, while Bolivia suffered a huge defeat during the War of the Pacific, leaving both countries poor and landlocked. Gradually it occurred to them that the only path to the winner's circle of history lay in beating the other. For decades they circled each other and prepared, which in their military traditions meant barely prepared. In 1932 neither was even close to battle-ready, but it seemed as if history itself had doomed them to fight. It became the bloodiest fight of the century in North and South America.

In the end nothing was gained or lost, except for a lot of lives and treasure.

THE PLAYERS

Marshal José Félix Estigarribia—Smart and calm, Estigarribia quickly rose through the officer ranks to lead the Paraguayan troops. As preparation to commanding Paraguay's army he spent three years in France and graduated from the French army's Staff College the year after Charles de Gaulle.

Skinny—As a young man he was recognized as an outstanding officer and sent to Chile for additional training with its professional army.

Props—His victories gained more worthless territory for Paraguay than any other military leader in its history.

Pros—Despite years of French military training, he managed to win a few battles for his country.

Cons—Crowned himself dictator after the war.

General Hans Kundt—Bolivia's secret weapon, known by the clever nickname of "El Aleman"—the German—because he was from Germany. Kundt, a German staff officer, first went to Bolivia in 1911 to help build the army and returned there after World War I to moonlight as army commander. In 1930, however, he fled Bolivia after a coup knocked him and his presidential ally from office. Then, with his adopted land of the perpetual dictator in trouble against Paraguay, he became "Das Ringer" who returned from exile and in 1933 brought Bolivia to the brink of victory.

Skinny—He fought under the Kaiser in World War I, rising to the rank of brigadier general.

Props—He came from Germany where they know how to fight wars.

Pros—Willingly returned to Bolivia. Reason for Bolivians to cheer.

Cons—Often confused Bolivia with Bavaria and vice versa.

THE GENERAL SITUATION

War has been a mixed blessing for both Bolivia and Paraguay. On one hand, both fought bitter and calamitous wars that left them devastated. On the other, the wars are the main reason outsiders read about the two countries. Paraguay, led by its feckless dictator, Francisco Solano López, and his beautiful but venomous mistress, the Irish-born and Parisian-trained lovelady, Eliza Lynch, started a war against Brazil, Argentina, and Uruguay in 1865. The war came to an end in 1870 when the Brazilians shot López on a riverbank and forced Lynch to bury him in a shallow grave. A few years later Bolivia joined Paraguay in the loser's bracket. Bolivia started an ill-advised war over birdshit profits with Chile and resulted in a crushing, smelly defeat outdone in stupidity only by their Peruvian allies, who continued on long after the war was lost. The war left Bolivia landlocked and burning with a deep desire to extract revenge on somebody, anybody, most likely a neighbor it had not yet fought a war against.

By the 1920s, it became clear to both countries' dictators *du jour* that their only chance to drink from the sweet cup of military victory was beating up the other. Each country simultaneously arrived at the same conclusion: *We* can take *them*. To top it off, both countries had found the perfect reason to fight a meaningless war: the same perfectly meaningless piece of land.

This is called the Chaco. Few have heard of it. Fewer have been there. And even fewer stayed. No one has ever reported enjoying it. Located in the center of South America, the Chaco consists of hot, steamy swampland in the summer and dry desert in the winter—and somehow manages to incorporate the worst of both. It's a vast, flat homeland for an army of ants, piranhas, jaguars, snakes, spiders, and horrible-smelling air. Those who've been there nostalgically describe it as a green hell. Its few inhabitants are Indians apparently unaware that other members of the human race spend their days without being surrounded by terrorizing clouds of over-sized flies and belligerent mosquitoes.

Adding to the other charms of the Chaco is its lack of water. Plenty exists to support vast mosquito swarms, but not enough for humans. Water holes are miles apart and are often not sufficient to sustain large numbers of people. To fight in the Chaco, armies needed to first think about water.

Bolivia had a reason to control sections of the Chaco. The landlocked country had no hope of gaining access to the ocean through its archenemy Chile, so it looked east. By taking the Chaco they would obtain access to the Atlantic through a series of rivers. For their part, equally landlocked Paraguay wanted the Chaco to expand its harvest of the quebracho tree, whose bark yielded valuable tannins, one of the country's few exports.

On a deeper level, however, were the feelings held by both countries' leaders that this was a chance they could not afford to lose. Bolivians were tired of being pushed around by their more powerful neighbors and to accept anything less than total control of the Chaco was too much even for them. Getting manhandled by Chile was not fun but understandable. Getting pushed around by Paraguay would be too humiliating to consider. Paraguay held similar but more desperate feelings. After suffering its devastating defeat in the war of the triple beating, the country was on trigger alert for any neighborly aggression. Showing weakness would leave the country vulnerable to attack and dismemberment, ending its extended experiment in isolated poverty. Like a small, wounded animal, Paraguay needed to be tough and vigilant at all times.

The tension between Paraguay and Bolivia escalated over the decades, and by the 1920s the drumbeat of failure in both countries ratcheted up the pressure. Clearly something big was going to happen. Skirmishing broke out. Army raids back and forth kept everyone on edge. Diplomatic relations broke off, only to be reestablished months later. Each held back from attacking only because they lacked any semblance of a functioning military.

On paper, Bolivia held a huge advantage in the coming fight. Its population was about three times Paraguay's and its potential army equally bigger. Plus, Bolivia had a thriving tin exporting business, producing a strong income stream for the country. Paraguay exported only tea and unskilled workers.

To prepare for the coming conflict, the combatants went on buying sprees. In 1926, Bolivia contracted with a British firm for a large shipment of warplanes, artillery, small arms, and mounds of ammunition. But they never got the full shipment of weapons (possibly because they never paid in full), and what they did receive often didn't work. These minor details failed to discourage the wound-up Bolivians. They didn't fully appreciate that unpaid-for weapons sitting in warehouses in Great Britain can't help win wars.

In addition, Bolivia's neighbors had blocked most of the arms shipments, so Bolivia's only option was to ship the arms through the ports of former ally-in-failure Peru, where the sticky-fingered locals helped lessen the Bolivian carrying burden. A trickle of arms flowed through Brazil to the Bolivian town of Puerto Suarez, but the Bolivian transportation system was so primitive there was no way of moving these arms to the fighting troops. Alas, the tricky life of the landlocked and unloved.

The Bolivians went to war without most of the arms they thought would help them win. They had other problems as well, geography being the foremost. Most of the country's population resided much farther to the west in the Altiplano around the capital of La Paz. To move troops and equipment to the front meant a two-day trip by road or rail, then a long walk on unpaved, dusty roads for days and days. Trucks tried to make the route, but they quickly wore out in the extreme heat and dust. A shortage of spare parts and mechanics forced the Bolivians to abandon them. No bridges were ever built over the rivers, and everything had to cross on pontoon bridges. The politicians talked tough in working up the people for war, but they never put in the hard work necessary to make any attack successful. The army broke down and rusted by the side of the road.

Paraguay went on a similar weapons-buying spree but with greater success. Starting in the early 1920s, the Paraguayans devoted a large chunk of their meager national treasure to arms purchases. They sent agents throughout Europe looking for deals and spread the buying over many countries. This enabled them to force arms companies to compete against each other on price and quality. The buyers even snagged two important and first-rate river gunships. In addition, Argentina, concerned with Bolivian aggression, allowed the arms to flow through the country to Paraguay and provided secret arms shipments themselves. Paraguay also had a significant advantage due to its actual working transportation system. Soldiers and equipment traveled by river to the Chaco and then by train to the front.

Leadership ability varied on the two sides as well. Bolivia lurched from one dictator to another. In the hundred years up to 1930 the country had endured forty governments and 187 attempted coups. That's almost two a year for a century. When successful, the coups were usually gentlemanly affairs. The competitors lined up support within the military and at coup time compared lists of supporters, like comparing cards in poker. Whoever held the aces and kings walked away with the office; the loser slouched into well-appointed exile in Europe, the inevitable landing spot for former despots.

Complicating the situation, Bolivia's president Daniel Salamanca led the pro-war party, and his political opponent,

Luis Tejada Sorzano, of the antiwar party, held the post of vice president and chief complainer.

Bolivia's military strategy was daringly brilliant in conception. Given their extremely limited war-fighting capabilities, the best weapon they possessed was the Chaco heat, which would wear down the enemy without firing a shot. The army's plan, therefore, was to retreat, forcing the Paraguayans to fight through the green hell into Bolivia over lengthening supply lines. Then the Bolivians would overrun the worn-out and weakened enemy. But giving up territory would spark an outcry and, of course, a coup. To forestall the inevitable countercoup as long as possible Salamanca rejected the plan and insisted on aggressive attacks.

By 1932 Bolivia chugged steadily toward war, lacking nothing except arms, a strategy, and the ability to transport its army to the front.

Paraguay, in comparison, was a model of rational planning. In the sixty-one years before the war, the country had forty-one presidents. Bloody coups occurred like the changing seasons. But the people inevitably united behind whoever was *presidente* in a desperate attempt to stave off elimination from the tournament of countries. They vowed to fight with the grit and determination that had made Paraguayans famous—and in Estigarribia they had a sturdy and knowledgeable military hand. To Bolivia this was a war for a foreign territory; for Paraguay a fight for survival. Paraguay adopted the same rope-a-dope strategy, i.e., stretching enemy supply lines through continuous retreats. But the fear of coups prevented Paraguay from putting the retreat plan into operation. Politics had trumped strategy on both sides.

Finally, for no apparent reason, it became time to decide the champion of the losers' bracket.

WHAT HAPPENED:
OPERATION "DOUBLE ELIMINATION"

In June 1932, the Bolivians felt bold enough to start the festivities. A small group of their elite fighters attacked a cluster
of mud huts, optimistically called a fort, and drove off the
defenders—all six of them. "Viva Bolivia," the victors cried.

Hearing of the attack, Estigarribia, who was commanding
an army division in the Chaco, ordered a few dozen troops
to retake the mud huts. A few days later the troops attacked
but were repulsed. Both sides gathered more troops. By mid-
July the Paraguayans had obtained the upper hand and attacked. Overwhelmed and scared, the Bolivians retreated.

In Paraguay's capital, Asunción, a grim determination prevailed. Paraguayans were ready to fight, but not eager. For
them it was one more uphill fight against a bigger, richer
enemy, with bleak prospects for victory. President José P.
Guggiari managed to rally the people to the cause by declaring his people would fight with the bravery of the old days of
the Triple Alliance war. "We must repeat history," he thundered. Irony was not his strength.

In Bolivia's capital, La Paz, President Salamanca exhorted
the crowd into a frenzy. Bolivian honor had been stained.
The people wanted blood . . . and Salamanca promised to
deliver. There was also no need to get the country on a war
economy. Its vastly superior size and wealth would make this
a quick war, the leaders convinced themselves. They agreed
to fight it on the cheap.

In a meeting with his army leaders, Salamanca ordered immediate reprisals against the Paraguayans. His officers cau-
tioned patience, however. The army had only 1,400 men in
the Chaco, they told him, and it would be wise to call up reserves and organize an effective force before starting a major
war. Salamanca would have none of that organizing talk. He

wanted action. The troops departed for the front amid a chorus of cheers from the capital's citizens.

In the Chaco, Bolivian troops took two small Paraguayan forts. By August the Bolivian forces had pushed forward and captured Paraguay's Fort Boquerón, yet another fort that was little more than a shack on a hill. Then they paused as President Salamanca pondered the next Bolivian move.

Estigarribia didn't pause. He realized he had to throw all of his country's resources into the fight early or face certain defeat. Paraguay rushed its military-age men into service and through quick training. Bolivia slowly brought its men into service, unwilling to pay for an army. As a result, by September Estigarribia's larger forces besieged the Bolivians at Fort Boquerón. Through weeks of hearty fighting, the garrison slowly melted from lack of food, medicine, water, and constant artillery bombardment. In late September the Bolivians, out of ammunition and nearly all dead of dehydration, surrendered. The Paraguayans themselves had barely hung on to win because the lake they were using for water had almost completely dried up. The harsh Chaco life was taking nearly as many lives as the bullets.

After Fort Boquerón, the Paraguayans pushed forward as the Bolivian army reeled from defeat to defeat. By December the Bolivians stiffened as the Paraguayan surge ended.

The war stalled at the end of 1932, and the Bolivians called in General Hans Kundt—"Das Ringer." Everyone perked up when General Kundt, the former German World War I staff officer, goose-stepped to command of their army. He studied the war during his trip over by reading out-of-date newspaper articles on the fighting, believing this would suffice for a Prussian general to thrash any opponent. Bolivians cheered and greeted the imported Prussian with flowery huzzahs when he entered La Paz. Their hero had returned, and the crowds all agreed he would soon bring the hated

Paraguayans to their knees. After all, the enemy only had Paraguayans in charge, hardly a match for a general from the country that had practically invented modern war. On Christmas Day, Kundt, armed with his half-sketchy knowledge of the fighting and the Chaco terrain, took command of the Bolivian army in the field and began issuing orders as if he were in charge of actual, competent German troops.

But the Bolivians' problems reached deeper than just poor commanders. To reach the battlefields required long marches through hot, dusty trails. The harsh terrain wore down their soldiers faster than the Paraguayans could. Bolivians came from cool, mountainous regions and were incapable of over-turning centuries of logical belief that a quiet life in the hills was better than traipsing around the deadly Chaco. To these mountain dwellers, the heat and humidity turned the trip into sheer agony, and for many it became a death march. To the leathery Paraguayans, however, it was just like home.

Immediately, Das Ringer earned his pay. In a surprise counterstrike he grabbed the initiative and threw his men in a flanking movement against the Paraguayans, standard operating procedure for a Prussian, and it turned the tide against the stunned Paraguayans.

As 1933 began, the war's toll hit home in Bolivia. President Salamanca initiated a draft to boost the army's man-power as volunteers dropped to a trickle. Gangs of wounded veterans dragooned young men into the army, and they often arrived at the front fortified with only hours of training. Kundt, in full western front mode, drove against the Para-guayans at yet another meaningless place. He planned a three-pronged attack—left flank, center, and right flank—the classic double-envelopment. But his left hook bogged down in swamps and never got into the fight on the first day, January 20. Unwilling to change his plan, Kundt pressed ahead, and the two other columns fought without any coordination.

The Paraguayans decimated the densely attacking Bolivians with deadly machine-gun fire, imparting to the Bolivians a valuable lesson learned by millions of unfortunate soldiers destroyed by machine guns in the trenches of World War I. The stuck column finally attacked the next day, but now the two other wings were too exhausted to take part, and the Paraguayans stopped it cold. Kundt ordered wave after wave of attacks over the next few days, none more successful than those on the first day. On January 26 the reinforced Paraguayans counterattacked, and both sides settled into deadly trench warfare. Indeed, Kundt had imported the western front to the Chaco.

For most of 1933, the imported Prussian suffered the same consequences everywhere he went. He threw his troops into brutal frontal assaults against entrenched machine guns that succeeded only by adding to the piles of bodies. It was World War I all over again, but without the French wine and German mustard gas. As the only person in this war who participated in the Great War, you might think Das Ringer would have learned this lesson.

Now Kundt insisted on holding every inch of the front lines, overstretching his army, solely to control territory without any thought to an overall strategy. Military folly again. Bolivia . . . had hired the wrong Prussian. Further adding to the Bolivians' problems was their desire to run the war on the cheap. They had failed to build a larger army than the Paraguayans' despite a much larger population.

In May 1933, again for no apparent reason, Paraguayan president Eusebio Ayala finally declared war on Bolivia. It was the first declaration of war by any country since the founding of the League of Nations. The noble intentions of the League had met head-on with the reality of South American politics.

During September 1933 Estigarribia pushed forward. He thrust ahead in flanking movements, trapping large numbers

ERNST RÖHM

Hans Kundt was not the only German imported by Bolivia. A key military advisor to the Bolivians during the late 1920s was Ernst Röhm, a violent, scar-faced pal of Adolf Hitler. An early member of the Nazi party and a Munich native, Röhm befriended Hitler and stood by his side during the failed Beer Hall Putsch of 1923. In 1925 he became leader of the SA, the Brownshirts, the Nazi's military wing of out-of-work-and-angry street brawlers. But Röhm's soldiers were too aggressive even for Hitler, who wanted to keep a lower street profile while he prepared to take over the world. So that year Hitler drove him away, and Röhm fled to Bolivia where he became a lieutenant colonel. In 1931 Hitler, now on the verge of attaining power in Germany, invited his old buddy back to take the helm of the SA once again. This time around the relationship lasted three years until Hitler, now running Germany, needing to quell the SA and appease the German army, had Röhm arrested and executed. In Bolivia, Röhm left behind one important imprint. His assistant was Germán Busch Becerra, who took control of Bolivia in 1937 and declared himself dictator in 1939. This makes Röhm perhaps the only modern fascist who could claim mentorship to two dictators in two different countries.

of Bolivian troops. Surrounded and waterless, they surrendered rather than die of thirst. The Paraguayans pushed onward again, drilled wells for water, and committed their reserves. Kundt held firm. Too firm, it turns out. He refused to ask for more troops and refused to make any strategic retreats. His subordinates, already upset at being led by a foreigner, could not understand his decision to hold all sectors of the crumbling front. The few planes in the Bolivian air force regularly reported Paraguayan flanking movements. Kundt disregarded them, and this proved his undoing. By December he became the victim of his own dreaded double envelopment. He failed to fully protect his flanks, the first lesson taught in Prussian military kindergarten. Foiled by his own strategy, surrounded, his troops dropping from dehydration, Kundt's army folded and ran. Those who escaped survived solely because the Paraguayans were too exhausted to complete the rout. When the two sides settled down, the Bolivian army had been reduced to only 7,000 men in the field and one single Prussian muttering in German about double envelopments. The Bolivians were right back where they had started at the war's outset.

The defeat was too much even for the Bolivians. Das Ringer got jackbooted. Auf Wiedersehen to El Aleman. He lingered on in La Paz for a while, then submitted his resignation in February 1934. But the sacking of Kundt did not improve Salamanca's rocky relationship with the generals.

After such a defeat it would seem logical that Bolivia would listen to the peace talks that were once again floated about. But logic just wasn't their style. They pressed on. As the deaths mounted, the League of Nations scrambled to justify its existence by negotiating an end to the affair. Politicians made high-minded speeches about the senseless slaughter and how an arms embargo on both countries was necessary. Countries around the world all denied they were selling the combatants arms. "Not us," they declared. Yet somehow, fresh arms flowed to the front. Despite the casualties neither country was willing to give up the fight. They had yet to score the victory both countries sorely needed and had represented as their sole war aim. Neither could sign a peace treaty that did not recognize one as the clear victor. The fight had to continue.

Another big blow to Bolivia was the taking of the supposedly impregnable Fort Ballivian. It had withstood numerous Paraguayan assaults. As an election in Bolivia neared—yes, they actually held them, but since coups happened with shocking regularity they were more like nonbinding resolutions—President Salamanca wanted to notch victories to rally the country behind his pro-war party. In mid-1934 Sala-manca pulled his troops from Fort Ballivian and marched them north to take on Estigarribia, who was poking around up there. He had left the fort empty, believing it folly to have any more than a skeleton crew in his impregnable fort. The strategy worked as the Bolivians scored some battlefield vic-tories, which Salamanca's Genuine Republican party rode to electoral success that November.

But to the Bolivian's surprise, Estigarribia popped up in front of Fort Ballivian. His feint to the north had drawn the Bolivians out of the fort, and the Bolivian Verdun fell with-out a shot. The impregnable was suddenly pregnant with Paraguayans. Paraguay now had an open path to the Boliv-ian border. Victory was in sight, always a dangerous situa-tion with these two countries.

Outraged, Salamanca sped to the front to fire his com-mander in chief. When he arrived the officers instead de-manded Salamanca's resignation. He submitted it meekly while his vice president, Luis Tejada Sorzano, back in La Paz, declared that Salamanca had deserted. Tejada declared him-self the new president. Democracy Bolivian style!

Incredibly the Paraguayans kept advancing through the vi-cious Chaco heat. At the battle of El Carmen in November, they surrounded two Bolivian divisions and captured 4,000 prisoners while almost 3,000 Bolivians perished from thirst. By the end of 1934, the Bolivian retreat had succeeded in reaching the far western end of the Chaco. They were now getting beat on their own turf. President Tejada Sorzano now ditched fighting on the cheap and proclaimed a full mobiliza-tion. The ranks of troops swelled. Even as they suffered bat-tlefield defeats, the number of soldiers grew. By April 1935 the grim, leathery Paraguayans, whose thinning ranks had to be bolstered by teenage recruits, had pushed as far forward as their supply lines would allow but much farther than they

LEAGUE OF NATIONS

Formed by Woodrow Wilson during the peace talks that ended World War I, the League of Nations was designed to end war forever by having all its members gang up on any attacking country. Considering that World War II started while the League existed amply demonstrates the success of this little group. But the demise of the League was quickly hastened from its failures to resolve the Chaco war. Time after time, delegates from the League met with leaders from the two combatants . . . and they struck out each time. In addition, League members tried to impose strict arms embargoes on Bolivia and Paraguay, but to no avail. With the world in turmoil during the 1930s, it became clear to the powerful troublemakers of Japan, Italy, and Germany that if the League couldn't stop Bolivia and Paraguay, it couldn't stop them. The notion of collective security failed and was abandoned like a broken-down truck in the harsh lands of the Chaco.

ever dreamed. They stood at their closest point to victory and, unknown to them, their closest moment to defeat, just like the Germans during the summer of 1918.

Sorzano's draft swelled the Bolivian army to 45,000 troops. Finally, their numbers paid dividends. They rolled forward with stiffened sinews to defend their homeland. They slashed through the beleaguered Paraguayans, a big chunk of whom were teenagers far from home. The original Bolivian strategy proved correct after all.

By June 1935 both sides were willing to at least listen to the latest—the eighteenth—attempt to broker a peace. Paraguay realized it was at the breaking point and agreed to end the war. Diplomats from the five nearby countries—Brazil, Argentina, Chile, Uruguay, and Peru—along with the United States, pushed the sides to stop the senseless slaughter. When the meeting was about to break up without a deal, the U.S. representative, Alexander Wilbourne Weddell, ambassador to Argentina, demanded the sides work out their differences. They listened. A truce broke out while a commission from the mediating countries marked out a border across the Chaco to divide the non-spoils of war.

Bolivia and Paraguay agreed to stop the fighting at noon on June 14. All morning the two armies peered at each other from their trenches. With just half an hour before the deadline, for no apparent reason they started firing at each other. The fusillade grew, and soon both armies feverishly unleashed their weapons, blowing through stores of ammunition. The casualties mounted. At noon, whistles blew and the firing stopped. Half crazed from the slaughter and delusional from knowing it was actually over and they had survived, soldiers on both sides cheered and danced with enemies that only minutes earlier they'd tried to kill. It was a bloody, senseless end to a bloody, senseless war.

The war's only purpose was to prove to any doubters that a meaningless war, fought over a meaningless and barren land, is not enough to spring a country from the losers' bracket.

WHAT HAPPENED AFTER

Jubilation broke out throughout South America when the war ended. So relieved was the world that the organizer of the peace conference, Carlos Saavedra Lamas, the Argentine foreign minister, received the Nobel Peace Prize for his efforts. In fact, ending the war propelled him to the presidency of the assembly of the League of Nations. The peace conference met for three years before they settled on the treaty's final terms on how to divide the Chaco.

Bolivia and Paraguay endured enormous casualties from the fight. Bolivia suffered nearly 50,000 deaths; about 2 percent of its total population, while Paraguay had about

40,000 dead, nearly 3.5 percent of its population. This would translate percentage-wise to about 10 million dead for the United States today.

As for the leaders, Estigarribia was forced into exile after a coup in 1936 but returned from Argentina three years later. On August 15, 1939, he became Paraguay's president. Unhappy with the temporary nature of the country's presidents, he promoted himself to dictator, but in 1940 he renounced his position and declared he would hold elections. Since no good deed goes unpunished, a few months later his plane crashed, killing him along with his wife and the pilot.

In 1938 the six-member commission finally drew the border between the two warring countries. Paraguay received the bulk of the Chaco; Bolivia got a chunk of the western section near its oil fields and a slice providing it with a small port on the Paraguay River with access to the Atlantic Ocean. It was a deal both sides could have worked out years before the war.

The Chaco is still wildly depopulated, amazingly worthless, and filled with flies. Both countries are still landlocked nanopowers.

★ ★ ★

NINE

THE WINTER WAR BETWEEN RUSSIA AND FINLAND

1939

Hubris is the theme of many ancient Greek plays and also some foolish modern plays for power.

It's hard to think of Josef Stalin as a tragic figure from a Greek drama, unless plays have been unearthed featuring a paranoid, murderous thug with a shag mustache. Although the Soviet dictator caused tragedy wherever he and his army went, he himself was not tragic. Nevertheless, in failing to understand or even entertain the idea that the Finns might put up some resistance to being invaded, Stalin showed a Siberian-sized amount of hubris.

And that is exactly what Stalin did when he decided to invade Finland in late 1939, in a fit of logic, to extend the Soviet borders at the expense of the Finns and prepare his country's defenses for the inevitable German invasion. Expecting a short winter romp in the snow, the Russians made no preparations for a prolonged campaign featuring actual fighting by a breathing enemy. The Soviets poured wave after wave of undertrained and ill-equipped troops into the dark, cold Finnish winter. They suffered one of the most lopsided defeats in modern warfare. All the while, Stalin's real enemy, Adolf Hitler, watched in glee as little Finland pounded the fabled Red Army.

THE PLAYERS

Josef Stalin—Evil Rex Soviet leader who signed a nonaggression pact with the equally evil Adolf Hitler, all the while fearing that—could it be true?—Hitler would stab him in the back and actually invade.

Skinny—Adopted the motivational program for his generals that those who finished in first place got to keep their jobs, those in second place got an all-expense paid trip to a Siberian gulag, and the third place winners got taken out behind Ukraine and shot.

Props—Equal Opportunity Killer.

Pros—Bested the Nazis in the mother-of-all-evildoer death matches.

Cons—Just about everything else.

Field Marshal Carl Gustav Mannerheim—Known as "The Knight of Europe," the aristocratic general was the supreme commander of the Finnish armed forces. For years he beat the drum for a stronger military to protect against the inevitable rambling of the Soviet Bear, but his Finnish leaders ignored him. In frustration, he resigned in 1939 but before it took effect the Soviets attacked, and he was named to lead the defense.

Skinny—His first language was Swedish, but then he spent thirty-five years in the Russian army, admiring the tsars. When he returned to Finland in 1918, he needed a translator to talk to his Finnish troops.

Props—Was so famous in Finland that the country's main line of defense against the Soviets was named for him.

Pros—Fought the Communists when they were called Bolsheviks

and fought them when they were called Soviets. He even fought
them as Hitler's ally. But he still couldn't bring back the tsar.
Cons—Never really felt comfortable with the whole democracy
thing.

THE GENERAL SITUATION

In 1939 the world had dissolved into a very dangerous place.
Hitler had swallowed Austria and Czechoslovakia without
much opposition. Poland was next. He was concerned, however, with how the Soviets would react to this little foray.
Hitler's people and Stalin's people had a chat, then a talk,
and finally a meeting. The result was the Nazi-Soviet Nonaggression Pact. It was reported to the world in late August
without a hint of irony that a treaty between two of the most
aggressive countries in history contained the word *nonaggression.*

Publicly, the treaty was all about trade and other good
stuff. Privately, Hitler got Stalin to agree not to object to his
planned takeover of Poland. Even better, they divvied up
Poland and the small countries between them like they were
M&Ms. Hitler got the blues and greens while Stalin got to
turn the others into reds. In particular, the treaty gave Finland to Stalin.

With the treaty signed, Hitler green-lighted the invasion of
Poland on September 1, 1939, and when the British and
French raced to Poland's rescue with a firestorm of angry
words about Adolf, World War II was on. Adolf swore up
and down that he would never, ever consider invading
Russia, but Stalin, to his credit, still had doubts about Hitler's character. Stalin decided to beef up the defenses of Leningrad and the navy bases surrounding the eastern end of the
Baltic Sea, just in case Mr. Hitler turned out not to be who
he said he was. A quick check of the map, however, revealed

to Stalin that the Finns actually owned most of the land approaching Leningrad.

Finland has a complicated history. It was part of the powerful Swedish Kingdom from the end of the fourteenth century until 1809 when it was traded to the Russian Empire. By the late nineteenth century, the tsars treated the Finns harshly and dominated all Finnish institutions. But the Finns waited and when the tsar fell in 1917, the Finns declared their independence. On December 31, 1917, Lenin formally recognized the newly independent state of Finland.

But the wave of Communist agitation that erupted throughout Europe had also infiltrated Finland. A civil war erupted between the pro-Soviet Reds and the Finnish bourgeoisie led by Mannerheim. To defeat the pro-Soviet Communist forces, the Finns called in help from Germany. With their assistance and troops, the Finns defeated the Reds. But the country now had a decidedly pro-Germany tinge, and the Soviets gazed at their lost Finnish territory with longing and a bit of murderous revenge.

In the 1920s Josef Stalin inherited the not-yet-totally-failing Soviet state following Lenin's demise. He vowed to retake Finland. Perhaps most important, the vital Russian city of Leningrad stood a mere twenty miles from the Finnish border. Leningrad sits on the Karelian Isthmus, a chunk of land only about forty miles wide situated between the Gulf of Finland on the west and Lake Ladoga in the east. It was not paranoia to assume that a Soviet enemy might launch an attack from Finland down the Isthmus, and quickly overwhelm the city and its important military bases. To prevent such an attack, Stalin prudently wanted to grab a chunk of the Finnish border as a buffer zone.

Along with the other Scandinavian countries, Finland had a white-knuckle grasp on a tenuous neutrality among the flying bar stools of Europe. In 1938 Stalin asked the Finns to promise they would not ally with Germany and to kindly attach some of their territory to Russia. At least he asked. The Finns declined. Stalin, unable to believe any country could actually resist attacking and conquering their neighbors, and not willing to contemplate someone might tell the truth during negotiations, immediately distrusted the Finns and assumed they were up to something. For their part, the indeed-trusty Finns could not see how their answer did not sit well with the Russian Rex. Despite warnings by Mannerheim that little Finland would get quickly overrun, its leaders refused to bow to logic and stoop to Russian servitude.

The negotiations stalled and Stalin turned the screws, demanding more territory and bases. The Finns turned him down every time. At the end of a meeting on November 3, 1939, Soviet foreign minister Molotov told the Finns that it was now time for the military to speak. Loudly. This is Stalinist diplomatic code for "You are about to get crushed." When the Finns still refused, they shook hands all around, and Stalin bade his Finnish counterparts best wishes, more code for "I'm digging your graves, fellas." He then left to twirl his mustache and plan the destruction of their country.

WHAT HAPPENED: OPERATION "WINTER OLYMPICS"

To the Finns it seems natural. Ski through the woods, rifle slung over a shoulder. Slip off the skis, lie on the ground, and pop off a few quick, accurate rounds. Then ski away. A sport was even created around it—the biathlon—the combination of skiing and shooting that goes together like pickles and herring. In competitions, the biathletes fire at stationary targets. For a few months during the winter of 1939/40, the Finnish competitors fired at live targets, even though sometimes they were even more stationary than the Olympic kind.

The snowy woods of Finland were suddenly filled with the easiest targets a soldier often dreams of: Russian soldiers.

As with most of Stalin's plans, this one was brutally simple: line up as many soldiers and tanks he could muster on the border, pour into Finland, and overwhelm the Finns. If that wasn't enough, they had thousands of planes to bomb the Finns back to the Ice Age. The whole romp would take no longer than two weeks, the generals assured Stalin. In fact, Stalin was more concerned that his army would roll through Finland so fast they would stumble into Sweden on the other side, angering a country that Stalin did not yet want to conquer.

The attack concentrated on three main areas. First, the Soviets would pound the narrow Karelian Isthmus with division after division, long columns of modern tanks along with hundreds of fighters and bombers. Then five divisions would sweep north of Lake Ladoga to outflank the Finns pinned down on the Mannerheim Line, which was the Finns' stout defensive line across the Isthmus. And much farther north, into the thinly populated Arctic regions, the Soviets would launch numerous divisions in a pointless attempt to cut the country in half.

Stalin modeled his attack on the German blitz of Poland. His plan was brilliant except for two significant flaws: (1) he didn't have the German army, and (2) Finland is not Poland. Hitler's blitzkrieg was designed for fighting on the broad, flat plains of Europe. The invasion of Poland went so well in part because the Nazis had plenty of room to maneuver their huge tank columns, and the weather was warm and dry. Under those conditions, the immobile Poles were easily outflanked, cut off, and decimated.

But Finland is forbidding to invaders even in the summer. Winter invasion is an act of insanity. One third of the country is above the Arctic Circle, and all of it is virtually ice-bound during the winter when darkness lasts twenty-three hours a day and temperatures regularly drop to 20–30 degrees below zero. Roads are few and narrow, incapable of handling a tank convoy. Between the roads stand deep, dark forests with snowbanks large enough to swallow a man.

The Soviets soon found out that the toughest part of Finland was the Finns. The country had about 4.5 million people, hardy souls all, since that was the only way to survive in the harsh environment. Finns possess exceptional know-how of surviving outdoors in the winter. This tenacity, which the Finns called *sisu*, would prove their strongest weapon in their struggle with the vastly superior Soviet forces.

Finland's army, capable of fielding at most 150,000 soldiers, was terribly overmatched. They had no tanks, few anti-tank guns, artillery dating back forty years, and only a skeleton air force. Mannerheim knew his troops would be armed with *sisu* and little else. The army would fight to simply survive in the hopes that some foreign power—Britain or France—would rescue them. If not, Mannerheim said, his army would endure an "honorable annihilation."

On the other side, the Red Army looked pretty good on paper, like a team loaded with high-priced free agents. During 1939 they prepared for the invasion by building railroads close to the Finnish border, allowing them to not only put more troops in the field than Mannerheim expected but also to keep the supplies flowing. The Reds now possessed lots of everything. That was perhaps the last smart move they made. In the field, however, the Soviet army stank. It had never fought against a real army, so it was not battle tested. Stalin had purged the officer corps during the 1930s and replaced most of them with drones who lacked any initiative and simply followed orders. Any risk taking was rewarded by a firing squad.

Another minor problem was that the plan did not take into account the weather or terrain. Only in the Isthmus could large numbers of troops operate; the rest of the country was too heavily forested to move by truck. And although on the Soviet maps the forests didn't look like a barrier, in reality skiing was the only feasible way to get around. No Russian troops, however, received training in ski-fighting tactics. Some were supplied with skis but not instructions on how to use them. Others just got the instruction manual without any skis. Perhaps the plan was to strap the manuals to the soldiers' feet and turn them loose. But since the attack was only expected to last two weeks, they didn't bother schlepping along all that heavy winter clothing. Many of the troops simply marched along in cotton jackets with felt shoes.

Two items reveal the level of planning that would spell trouble for the Soviets. First, they trucked in large numbers of antitank guns even though the Finns had no tanks. Second, despite not having winter coats, they were well supplied with Communist propaganda and printing presses, just in case some Finns needed a refresher on the glories of life in the workers' paradise.

The war started on November 26 when the Soviets fired a few artillery shells into Finland. With well-honed insouciance Stalin claimed Finnish aggression and, appropriately outraged, declared he had to take steps to handle this "Finnish question." On the morning of November 30, the Soviets threw four armies across the border. Six hundred thousand troops flooded into Finland over their eight-hundred-mile border. Planes roared overhead, bombing and strafing the Finnish countryside and cities, killing hundreds of civilians. It was a glorious beginning. Watch out, Sweden.

The Finns staggered back, outnumbered by more than ten to one. In the north, soldiers quickly donned their white winter ski jackets and homemade skis and took to skiing circles around the Soviets, machine-gunning the invaders before slipping away into the frozen forest.

After the first day of the invasion, the Soviets trucked in a Finnish Communist, O. W. Kuusinen, who was living in Moscow since losing the Finnish civil war in 1918, and declared him the new leader of Finland. The puppet provided the Soviets with the refreshing change of attitude they were looking for as he rapidly agreed to the Soviet demands. Three cheers all around!

To further boost the puppet, the Soviets created an army just for Kuusinen. Made up mostly of other Finnish Communists living in Russia, the pathetic herd paraded around for the world's press. Unable to find any other clothing, the army dressed in ancient tsarist-era uniforms pillaged from a local military museum. Outraged by this aggression and charade, the rest of the entire world threw Russia out of the League of Nations and rooted for the brave little Finns.

As they slowly were pushed back up the Isthmus, the Finns booby-trapped everything. They planted mines, wired barns with bombs, and even turned frozen livestock into deadly traps. The Russian steamroller slowed to a crawl.

Mannerheim's plan was to deny the interior rail system to the invaders. By keeping the Soviets on the back roads, he knew they would bog down and become easy prey for his mobile guerrillas. It might not spell victory but would at least buy time.

The first problem the Finns encountered was fighting the Soviet tanks. Mannerheim's men had virtually no antitank guns and where they did exist, ammunition was in short supply. To throw off the tanks they relied on *sisu* and ingenuity. The most common weapon was the "Molotov cocktail," which they perfected and named. It consisted of jars filled with gasoline, kerosene, and other flammable liquids, thrown at the tanks from close range. The technique was simple;

someone jammed a log into the tracks of the tank to stop it, and then the tank was attacked with flaming bottles of gasoline. The Finns also used bags of explosives and hand grenades against the Soviet armor. That also took loads of *sisu*. About eighty tanks were knocked out in the first few days but with sharp losses for the brave tank-attackers.

Despite the stout resistance, by December 6 the Soviets reached the Mannerheim Line, which consisted of an eighty-mile-long series of concrete blockhouses, smaller pillboxes, and firing trenches. Manned by determined fighters, it was a formidable barrier. But it was short of antitank guns, artillery, and antiaircraft weapons. The Finns dug in. The Soviets pushed ahead, ready to stomp their enemy. "Tactics," they sneered, "we don't need no stinking tactics."

The Soviets launched their siege on the defenses but quickly fell into a predictable rhythm. They would move out just after first light, slowly approach the defenders, make furious assault after assault in tight formations, causing few Finnish casualties but resulting in piles of Soviet dead, sometimes numbering a thousand an hour. The Russians would retreat at dark and form defensive circles around huge campfires. Then the Finns would reoccupy any lost ground and snipe at the nervous Soviets all night. Some attacks broke up under well-aimed artillery; others evaporated from intense machine-gun fire. Throughout December the Soviets pushed against various sectors of the Finnish line only to suffer the same results everywhere. Finnish gunners mowed down row after row of attackers who slowly moved forward in virtual suicide attacks, unprotected by any trees or tanks. The Soviet dead were so numerous that some Finnish soldiers broke down emotionally from the stress of killing so many of the enemy. True to form, the Soviets never wavered in their tactics.

Finns live for winter—they know how to dress, ski through

the dense woods, quickly remove the skis for fighting, and keep warm. The Soviet army, despite living in an equally cold country, inexplicably knew none of this. Many didn't even know where they were. So while the Soviet troops suffered miserably from the cold in their dark uniforms that stood out against the white world in which they had plunged, the Finns donned camouflaging white sheets, slept in well-stocked and -heated dugouts, and even enjoyed the occasional sauna. The Soviets built huge campfires every night and the men huddled around, easy targets for snipers. For the invaders, simply surviving another day became an achievement. It was almost an unfair fight, except the Soviets had ten times the strength. Actually, it still was an unfair fight.

As the battles raged at the Mannerheim Line, the Soviets threw divisions against the overmatched Finns on the north side of Lake Ladoga. Here the Soviets pushed relentlessly forward as the Finns engaged in a fighting retreat. As the Soviets approached key crossroads that would allow them greater movement, Mannerheim committed his reserves in early December. Even with his forces boosted, the Finns were still greatly outnumbered. Mannerheim knew he needed a victory to revive the spirits of his men. On the moonless night of December 9, two companies of Finns crossed a frozen lake to attack the camped-out Soviets. One company got lost. The other, led by Lt. Col. Aaro Pajari, snuck up on an entire regiment of Soviets, took careful positions, and opened fire. In a few minutes it was all over and the entire regiment lay dead, over a thousand men wiped out. The raid unnerved the Soviets, who remained immobile for two days, while the Finns found a new bounce in their step knowing the Reds could be beaten.

The Finns kept pushing. One Soviet probe of about 350 men got ambushed by a Finnish task force, killing every Russian. Another Russian night attack into the Finnish rear was halted when the attackers stopped to eat sausage soup from an abandoned Finnish kitchen. As the Russians dined al fresco, the Finns regrouped and wiped out the sausage eaters. The Finns spotted another Russian night advance on a lake and opened fire, not stopping until all two hundred Soviet attackers lay dead on the ice.

On December 12 the Finnish commander Mannerheim moved his troops forward. They pressed the attack, despite fierce Soviet resistance. When the Soviet troops were too beaten up, they would just call up fresh ones. The Finns lacked this luxury, but they kept fighting with their dwindling numbers. By the time the attack petered out on December 23, the Finns had pushed the Russians far enough from the main roads to feel secure. The cost was about 630 Finnish deaths and over 5,000 Soviet dead and another 5,000 wounded. While a stunning victory for Mannerheim, it also showed that even with a 10:1 kill ratio, the Finns would run out of troops well before the Soviets.

By Christmas the Soviets paused to regroup, still not home. They had thrown more than seven divisions against the Line, and the Finns *sisu*ed them all back, destroying about 60 percent of their armored vehicles. The Mannerheim Line was undented. Now, when you have purged most of the officers in the army, staged mock trials to eliminate your political friends and rivals, and airbrushed out any historical inconveniences, you have not established a system for obtaining strong feedback from your underlings. But the chief of the Soviet armed forces, Kliment Voroshilov, foolishly lay the failure at Stalin's feet for his army purges and backed up his point by smashing a suckling pig on the table in front of the Russian Rex. Instead of killing Voroshilov, the evil genius in Stalin extracted revenge by making Voroshilov his whipping boy for years to come, always keeping the specter of the firing squad on hand.

Most attackers would have either changed strategy or simply given up. Stalin had a different system. He brought up fresh divisions from the virtually limitless supply of unhappy manpower and readied to repeat the whole affair. Soldiers who declined to volunteer for suicide attacks faced the firing squad. It was mass murder under the guise of determination.

Incredibly, farther north the Soviets suffered even worse defeats. Roads were fewer and not much bigger than paths. Soviets tank columns quickly bogged down, and a division might stretch out over more than twenty miles. A key battle took place for weeks at the Kollaa River, where the Finns dug in along its north bank. At first the Soviets threw a division of troops against a few thousand Finns. Then the Soviets added a second, then a third, and finally a fourth division. Still the Finns held firm. In late January the Soviets launched an all-out offensive, but they simply totted up about a thousand dead a day to the growing casualty list. In one instance, four thousand Russians attacked thirty-two Finns. There the Line cracked. Finally, the Soviets had found their winning ratio.

To fight the overwhelming odds, the Finns adopted the tactic called *motti*: cut the long Soviet column into tiny pieces and slowly destroy each fragment. Mannerheim knew the tactics would work as he anticipated the response by the petrified and doltish Russian officers. The Soviets would fight hard but would never venture into the dense woods, and if a column got cut in half, they would simply sit tight and wait. For what, no one is sure, but that was the closest thing to a plan in the Soviet playbook.

The first use of *motti* took place against a Soviet division on the shores of Lake Ladoga. Here the Finns minced a well-stocked Soviet division into little pieces and slowly strangled it. The Soviets formed defensive pockets but slowly suc-

cumbed to the cold and hunger, fighting with dwindling supplies of ammunition.

But the real Soviet disaster occurred in the far north
woods. There the Finns perfected *motti* against the 163rd
Division. About 10 percent of the division died from the cold
before the first shot was even fired. On December 12 the
Finns sliced through the Soviet division in short, sharp, and
well-planned operations, cutting the division in two. The
Finns launched two or three of these raids a day, slowly
chopping the division into smaller and smaller sections.

To rescue the division the Soviets sent in the Forty-fourth
Division. A series of quick raids on December 23 stalled its
advance. It simply stopped, its commander suffering from an
outsized case of brain freeze. After a month of warfare the
Soviets still had no idea how to gain the initiative or counterattack effectively. The Finns turned up the tempo on the
163rd, and it collapsed on December 28. A few breakout attempts by survivors failed, and in a typical Winter War
battle, about three hundred Soviets got machined-gunned in
the open with not one Finnish casualty. Meanwhile the relatively fresh Forty-fourth Division simply stood idle.

The Finns next turned on the hapless Forty-fourth. By
January 1, the *motti* had begun. The petrified Soviets began
to crumble. They would fire wildly into the woods, burning
up their ammunition. Slowly the Finns closed the ring. The
Soviets planned a breakout, then called it off. The commanders seemed to be paralyzed as their troops slowly died from
cold and hunger. Meanwhile, the Finnish troops rotated between the front lines and their warm bunkers with hot food
and a sauna every few days. The Finns picked their targets
carefully, focusing on the large Soviet field kitchens, assisting
the Soviets in their agony. On January 6 the Soviet commander declared every man for himself, and all organized
resistance collapsed. The second Soviet division perished.

Overall, the Finns killed more than 27,000 Soviet invaders, destroyed about 300 armored vehicles but lost 900 of their own, an outsized 30:1 ratio. The commander of the 163rd made his way back to the Soviet Union where he was court-martialed and executed. There has never been an explanation for his failure to move. He simply sat and waited for two divisions to die.

The Finnish victories stunned the world. Leaders hailed the Finns for fighting the dreaded Soviets, but that was essentially all they got. Sweden provided some aid, and Italy donated seventeen bombers, while its citizens provided a good stoning of the Russian embassy in Rome.

Manly, mustachioed hubris had started the war but finally it took two women to bring about its end. Hella Wuolijoki, a Finnish playwright, started talks with her friend Alexandra Kollontay, the Soviet ambassador to Sweden. Through these talks the Soviets on January 31 severed their relationship with Kuusinen's bogus government, paving the way for direct negotiations with the Finns. Stalin wanted out—if he could make the deal he liked. He had had enough of this sideshow. His mighty army was humbled before the world, and he feared becoming bogged down in Finland as the spring and summer marching season in the plains of Europe approached. He also feared the British and French would intervene and attack the Soviets either in Finland or in the Soviet Union itself.

Unknown to Stalin, the British and French had different ideas for Finland. They wanted to use the war as a pretext for sending thousands of troops into Sweden and Norway to fight the Germans. Northern Sweden's iron ore fields supplied almost half of Germany's growing need for steel. To deny them to the Germans would boost the Allied war efforts. Plus, the wily French thought if they could get the war against Germany started in Scandinavia, it would not take place in France. Basically, they wanted to export the battle-fields. So they cooked up lavish plans to help the Finns, not bothering to tell them that the bulk of the troops would stay in Sweden.

But the Swedes had no intention of helping the British and French. They wanted the war to quietly end with a surviving Finnish state acting as a buffer between it and Russia. The Swedes, however, sniffed out the French strategy of dumping the Germans onto them by remaining neutral, except for the face-saving trickle of aid. The Germans wanted the war to end to keep relations peaceful with the Russians so they could focus on destroying Britain and France, still higher up on Adolf's target list than Russia.

But the French were doing their damnedest to keep this war alive. As the Finns and Soviets neared final terms on a cease-fire, the French, in a fit of Gallic exaggeration, promised fifty thousand troops and one hundred bombers, as long as the Finns kept fighting. The offer stunned the Finns. They reconsidered the deal with Stalin. All their hopes and dreams might actually come true. Perhaps the French would really come to someone's rescue, they thought.

For a moment the lineup for the Big War stood suspended with the Finns holding the key. Had the Finns publicly asked for the Allied aid, the British and French would have come over. And that would have probably meant teaming up against the Russians. In turn, Germany would have invaded Finland to fight their British and French enemies. This would have pitted the Germans and Russians against the British and French. It was potentially a history-altering moment.

But the French military soufflé soon deflated under the weight of British reality when they said only twelve thousand French troops would actually arrive and then only in mid-April. The Finns fell back to earth. They never called for the aid.

In January, as both sides paused on the ground, the Soviets picked up the pace in the air war. Despite an overwhelming numerical advantage, the Soviets achieved little from their air forces and—this is getting monotonous—got mauled by the Finns. When the war started, the Finns had only forty-eight fighter planes, few of them modern. But they tore through the Soviets and attacked using their tactic of two pairs of two planes called "finger four," which outmaneuvered the Soviet planes flying in a single formation of three. By the war's end they had shot down 240 Soviet aircraft with a Finnish loss of only 26. Overall, including ground fire, the Soviets lost eight hundred planes in the war, about eight per day. For these losses, the Soviets actually succeeded in blowing up lots of snow and killing thousands of trees. They also managed on rare occasions to actually hit Finnish people and buildings.

Meanwhile, back on the ground, the Soviet divisions fattened up for the kill again, but the Finns were now running low on shells. While Stalin altered his tactics somewhat, he refused to give up one key negotiating point: if the truce talks failed, he would endure endless casualties to achieve victory. On February 1 the Soviets opened with massive artillery and aerial bombardments, the largest yet in military history. The bombing stunned even the stoic Finns. As usual, the Soviets surged forward in tight waves. Then they died in tight waves. The Finns continued to fight furiously, despite being bombed out of their bunkers. The Soviets simply ground down the Finns and forced them to expend their ammunition into the chests of the hapless Russians. Thousands fell in each assault with second and third waves climbing over their frozen comrades. At one point twenty-five hundred Russians died in less than four hours.

Then on February 11, the Soviets moved up eighteen fresh divisions. But the Finns held firm. Back and forth the fighting

MOLOTOV COCKTAIL

The Molotov cocktail has been the weapon of choice for revolutionaries and angry youth throughout the world. While the gasoline-filled bottle with the flaming rag has held a key place in many a soldier's arsenal, few armies got better use from it as the Finns against the Soviets. Although it was invented by troops under Spanish dictator Francisco Franco during the Spanish Civil War in the 1930s, the Finns perfected it and honored Soviet foreign minister Vyacheslav Molotov by naming it after him. During the Winter War, the Finns found the homemade weapons so effective they created a factory to mass-produce them. More than half a million were eventually turned out with an improved design that no longer required a flaming rag. Instead, a capsule of sulfuric acid was used to ignite the flammable liquid in the bottle as it shattered against another Soviet tank.

swirled, the exhausted Finns never breaking. Finally, on February 15, after the Soviets punched a hole in the resistance, Mannerheim ordered part of his line to retreat to their second layer of defenses. The Soviets pushed on. On February 28, Mannerheim withdrew to the final line of defense. As the diplomats dickered and the French made their empty promises, the Russians hammered the rear line with a total of thirty divisions. By March 10 the Finnish army was down to half its prewar strength. The rear line consisted of sporadic pockets of Finns taking on huge numbers of Russian tanks and troops. They were fighting on fumes, but still fighting.

On March 8 the Finns met the Soviets in Moscow, ready to sign away their battlefield victories. It was a typical brutal Soviet negotiation: sign or keep fighting. The Finns pushed their points. But the Soviets sat in stony silence: sign or keep fighting. The Finns got Stalined. Soviet foreign minister Molotov presented the Finns with the agreement, which had harsher terms than they had previously discussed. Stalined again. Facing a total breakdown of their army, the Finns had no choice but to sign the agreement, handing Stalin his territory. Just before the Finns signed the surrender, the French and British both announced they would help Finland *if* they kept fighting. The Finns could only shake their heads at the pathetic little men in London and Paris.

In an act of revenge, fifteen minutes before the cease-fire was to begin on March 13, the Soviets opened up with a massive artillery bombardment. Stalined a third time.

The Soviets got their land, so in a limited sense they won the war. But enough victories like this can destroy a country. The Russians suffered about 250,000 dead and a similar number of wounded. The Finns had about 25,000 dead, a ratio of ten Russians per Finn. The Finnish wounded amounted to about 43,000. In a one-hundred-day war, that was solely a sideshow as 2,500 Russians died each day. They suffered so many casualties that after the war a Russian general grimly joked that they had won "just enough land to bury our dead."

The biathlon became an Olympic sport in 1960. A Finn grabbed the silver medal, just beating out an opponent from—guess where—the Soviet Union. And he didn't even have to shoot him.

WHAT HAPPENED AFTER

The spectacle of the little Finns bravely fighting the Russian bear fascinated the world. World leaders delivered outraged tongue-lashings at the evildoing Russians with the level of indignity rising in direct relation to their distance from the action.

In a bizarre twist, Stalin's paranoid delusion about Finnish aggression turned true as the Finns joined hands with the Nazis in 1941 and invaded the Soviet Union, with Mannerheim once again leading the army. Mannerheim refused to advance beyond the 1939 border, and the fighting quickly stalled. Teaming with the Nazis destroyed the good will that Finland built with the West—and it was from then on treated like a friend of Hitler's. By 1944 Stalin's troops were once again pushing back the Finns, and Mannerheim became president of Finland. He negotiated a peace with the Russians and fought to rid the country of Germans. He resigned in ill health in 1946 and retired to write his memoirs in Switzerland. For decades thereafter Finland lived under the heavy hand of the Soviets, who kept a keen eye on their neighbor.

While the massive casualties suffered in the war did impress upon Stalin the need to reform his army, the biggest impact was to let Hitler know that the once-feared Red Army was beatable. Hitler mocked Stalin by privately offering to subdue the Finns. Hitler no longer feared the Russians.

Stalin led the Soviets through the war that killed some 20 million Russians and, to everyone's relief, died in 1953.

★ ★ ★

TEN

ROMANIA FIGHTS BOTH SIDES IN WORLD WAR II

1941

Choosing the wrong friends can lead to unpaid loans, unpleasant dinner parties, and possible jail time. In a war, choosing the wrong friends can be much, much worse.

On the eve of World War II Romania faced a decision of who to befriend. In a spasm of nationalist doltishness, Romania joined hands with the Nazis in the hope that Hitler would hand them the gift of Transylvania, their ancestral homeland.

To achieve this goal and make Adolf happy, Romania's Hitler-wannabe dictator Ion Antonescu decided to attack Russia, the largest and only undefeated country on earth. As Ion would painfully learn, any war plan based on the idea of making Hitler full of smiles and puppy love needs a thorough reevaluation.

But taking a moment to reflect on this decision apparently never occurred to the Romanian strongman. His decision led little Romania to eventually duke it out with the United States, Great Britain, the Soviet Union, and Germany, all in the same war. Romania fought so hard and inflicted so much damage to its allies and/or enemies that when the war ended, no one knew how to treat it. The West abandoned Romania and left it to rot under Soviet control for decades.

Romania's role in the war was so fickle and so bizarre that during World War II it had the dubious distinction of being the third most powerful Axis country and the fourth most powerful Allied army. Romania allied itself with everybody at the party but still went home with no friends.

THE PLAYERS

Ion Antonescu—This brutal dictator of Romania, known as the "Conducător," led Romania into the attack on the Soviet Union to regain Transylvania, stolen the year before by the wily Hungarians.
Skinny—Personal slogan was "Death before Dishonor." He managed to obtain both.
Props—Hitler loved him. He got the big picture about who really should be controlling the world, the Germans and the Romanians.
Pros—Had blue eyes so Hitler assumed he came from good Aryan stock.
Cons—Eager participant in the Holocaust.

Lt. General Carl A. "Tooey" Spaatz—One of the most decorated air commanders in U.S. history, he held the title of Commander of the United States Strategic Air Forces in Europe and was the architect of the strategic bombing raids on the Axis countries.
Skinny—Prepped Europe for its postwar revitalization by bombing its cities flat.
Props—Was present at the surrender of all three Axis powers.
Pros—Never promised to bomb an enemy back to the Stone Age despite directing the dropping of two atomic bombs on Japan.
Cons—Became a writer after the war.

King Mihai of Romania—He became the Romanian king at age nineteen in 1940 when Ion booted his anti-German father King Carol from the country.
Skinny—Did nothing as king for four years as his country fought a devastating war.

Props—Last surviving head of state from World War II. Great-great-great grandson of Queen Victoria of England.
Pros—Before his country got crushed by the Russians he surrendered to them.
Cons—He assumed the Soviets would forgive Romania for invading, looting, pillaging, and killing. Wrong! Also assumed the Americans and British would give him credit for taking on the Germans at the end of the war. Wrong Wrong!!

THE GENERAL SITUATION

It was not easy being Romania in 1939. On one side the German menace, aggressively looking to stomp on anything that moved. On the other side the growling bear of the Soviet Union. In this tough neighborhood it was important to make the right friends.

Romania, in its first attempt at making friends and influencing people, had shrewdly waited until World War I was three years old before joining the Allies, hoping to cherry-pick from the victors' spoils. The vastly more powerful Germans and Austrians smashed the Romanians. But like the little engine that could, Romania did not give up. Instead, the tiny country manned it out and lost more territory to the Germans before finally calling it quits in early 1918. When Germany collapsed later that year, Romania regained its fighting mojo and again joined the fray, hoping it would be easier to defeat an already conquered enemy. This short second fling so impressed the hard-pressed Allies that Romania won itself a seat at the peace talks in Paris where the spoils were carved up, and it walked away with an outsized share of the local swag. In this case, the minuscule country got enough territory, including Transylvania, to create Great Romania. All was well. Romania had chosen right.

During the 1930s, as German power grew and sovereign neighbors disappeared with little resistance, Romania's leader, King Carol II, a former playboy, became increasingly nervous. When World War II broke out in Poland in 1939, Romanians feared their little corner of Europe would be the next entrée for Hitler. Romania's only safeguard was to ally with the British and the always-eager-to-make-agreements-it-can-never-honor French. But in 1940 when Germany defeated France and threw Britain off the continent, Romania was on its own.

Romania faced its own volatile political mixture. King Carol had ruled since 1930 with a strong hand. But the driving force in the country's politics was the Iron Guard: religious fanatics, right-wing nuts, and violent anti-Semites. Unsurprisingly, they were much loved by the always-on-the-lookout-for-thugs-who-like-to-kill-the-helpless, Heinrich Himmler of the German SS. The Iron Guard was like a posse of Bible-toting SS thugs. They were not happy with Carol and probably wouldn't have been happy with Hitler, either.

Fearing an Iron Guard takeover and unhindered by such notions as fair play, King Carol suddenly showed some impressive fascistic chops by orchestrating the assassination of the Iron Guard leader Cornelius Codreanu in 1938 and outlawing the group. Carol also excluded General Ion Antonescu, the head of the army and former defense minister, from his government. In May 1940, with Poland already conquered by Hitler and the collapse of the west imminent, King Carol wrapped up a treaty with Germany giving the Nazi war machine access to Romania's plentiful oil. The king, believing his hard work was done, was now able to relax and get back to his real interests, living the high life amid the gathering storms of total war.

Teaming up with the Nazis somehow angered the Soviets, so in June of 1940 the Reds grabbed two northern Romanian provinces, Bessarabia and Northern Bukovina, primarily because the Russians didn't already control them. Hungary, with Hitler's approval, then jumped into the land grab and took most of Transylvania in August. And in September, Bulgaria took a cheap shot at its northern neighbor and reclaimed the area of Dobrogea. In all, Romania lost about one-third of its territory and population. The country had now become Less Romania.

Ion denounced the king over the humiliating loss of territory and prestige, so Carol dismissed him from the army and tossed him into prison. But this could not prevent the population from realizing their country was shrinking and party boy King Carol started to catch the blame. Demonstrating that even louche kings read polls, he desperately sprung Antonescu from prison directly into the prime ministership in September 1940. As a show of gratitude, Antonescu squeezed Carol to abdicate and flee the country. Carol reputedly loaded up a train with royal swag and decamped to Portugal. With the backing of the army, Ion grabbed dictatorial powers and appointed as his deputy the head of the Iron Guard. Touché! The circle of lunacy was complete again, for the moment.

With the instincts of a true dictator, Ion burned to see the day when he could extend his irrational rule over the ancient homeland of Romanians, Transylvania, as well as the other stolen territories. The problem, however, was that the lost lands were held by two opposite sides of the war. But Ion, starting to warm up to his job as dictator, began to limber up with some Houdini-like reversals and escapes of his own. He soon came up with a plan to fix Romania's territorial problems by throwing his lot in with Hitler.

In November 1940, Ion met with Adolf in Germany. In dictator-to-dictator talks, Antonescu ranted about the Jews, Slavs, and Hungarians. The two got along great. Hitler found the Conducător to be an eager ally. He bonded with the German generals. They in turn had little difficulty recognizing the rampant greed of a true sucker. Ion gleefully accepted an invitation to join the Axis.

In January 1941, Horia Sima, the head of the Iron Guard, was unable to repress his deep-rooted, coup-making urges and tried to overthrow Antonescu. Hitler preferred the order of Antonescu to the anarchy of the Iron Guard and supported Antonescu in crushing the coup. Sima and the other Iron Guard leaders were whisked away by Himmler and stashed in Germany in preparation to take over Romania if Antonescu turned woolly-headed on them. Ion now ruled alone.

Adding to the volatile mix of greed and hate swirling around Romania was the country's huge oil reserve. Romania was the largest European oil producer, the West Texas of the Balkans. At the start of the war, the British and French tried to buy as much of the oil as possible and even tried to sabotage the oil transport system, just to keep it away from the tank-happy Germans. Their plots failed, and in August 1940 Germany and Romania cut a deal whereby Germany got virtually all the oil it wanted. Romania got to charge Germany whatever it wanted. You could call it the Hermann Goering Plan.

The only cloud marring the clear blue sky of the perfect Romanian future, Transylvania included, was an invasion rendezvous with the German army in Red Square.

WHAT HAPPENED:
OPERATION "TRANSYLVANIA DREAMIN'"

Throughout 1940 and 1941, the Germans primped the Romanian army for the coming dustup with the Soviets. They were the first foreign power informed by the Germans of the invasion date of June 22, 1941.

Initially the plans for Romanian forces, called Army Group Antonescu, were to simply block the Soviets from taking over the oil fields and then later join in any needed offensive operations. All told, Romania's order of battle numbered about 325,000 troops.

With the Soviets reeling in the face of the German blitzkrieg, Romania easily recaptured the two provinces of Bessarabia and Northern Bukovina lying between Romania and Russia. The army then halted while Antonescu pondered whether to invade the Soviet Union. Or not. For most people this is a simple decision—NO. But Antonescu was one of the few people on earth who awoke one day and said, "Yes, I think invading Russia will be a good thing." (For anyone unfamiliar with basic geography, Russia is just about the largest land mass on the face of the earth, and its citizens live in such desperation that the state of total war is often indistinguishable from normal daily life.)

As a reward to the country for his work so far, Ion promoted himself to Marshal. With Russia seemingly on the ropes, Antonescu pushed all his chips into the middle of the table: invasion of Russia, full partnership with Adolf. It would all be worth it once Count Dracula's homeland, Transylvania, was returned to Romanian hands.

With the decision made, on August 3 the Romanians invaded Russia with the goal of capturing the city of Odessa. They eventually succeeded, with the Soviets withdrawing on October 16, but only after Romania suffered heavy casualties. Getting beat up by the retreating Russians should have been a big hint to Ion that his army wasn't what it was cracked up to be. Despite high-quality German arms and a dose of Prussian training to stiffen them, it was clear that the Romanians were ill equipped and ill prepared for a major war with their more powerful and, most important, more numerous enemy. The brutality of the fighting guaranteed that the Soviets would never forget that Romania had entered the long hall of sworn Russian enemies to be humiliated eternally after the inevitable defeat. In fact, the Romanians fought with such gusto against the Russians that they suffered a higher proportion of casualties than did the German forces in the east.

Not satisfied with going toe-to-toe with the behemoth Russia, the cocky Romanians joined Japan, Italy, and Germany in declaring war on the United States, the richest country on earth, in the days following the December 1941 attack on Pearl Harbor. Romania was now taking on half of the developed world to acquire a few provinces smaller than Pennsylvania.

Despite its small size and distance from Britain, the Allies had Romania squarely in their sights. The only patch of Romanian soil of strategic importance was the relatively puny few square miles of the Ploesti oil fields and refineries. From the very beginning of the war, it was well known that Germany's war machine ran on Romania's oil. The Allies were now cranking out thousands of long-range bombers like so many murderous Fords and Chevys. Carl Spaatz, the head of the U.S. air forces in Europe, had a particular jones for the Ploesti fields and couldn't wait to unleash his air armada on them.

After the Allies secured their position in North Africa in 1942, they prepared to hit the Romanians. The first attack was a slight affair, a jab and a slap but with symbolic importance. In all, twelve B-24 bombers made the run from Egypt to the oil fields, the first strategic bombing attack by the United States in Europe. They caused minimal damage and no planes were lost. It simply proved that the bombers could reach their target. Unfortunately, for future bomber crews, it also alerted the Germans that the Allies were eyeing Ploesti. They instantly beefed up their antiaircraft strength and deployed fighters to the area.

It took over a year before Spaatz could orchestrate another raid. This was one for the ages, perhaps the most spectacular bombing attack of the entire war. On August 1, 1943, from a base in Benghazi, Libya, 177 planes, mostly B-24s, flew at rooftop level for a point-blank attack on Hitler's oil. The mission was the largest U.S. air attack of the war, to date. So important was the destruction of the fields that the Allies green-lighted the mission even though some of the planners expected half the planes never to return. The planes faced German and Romanian fighters, mechanical troubles, getting lost, intense flak, and at such low altitude, even rifle fire. Handling the massive bombers like fighters, the planes braved the strong defenses to strafe the oil fields with tons of bombs. Fires raged as gas tanks exploded, bombers weaved through plumes of oily smoke, and stricken planes plunged to the ground. Despite the spectacular pyrotechnics, the raid caused only temporary damage to the huge oil complex, which soon began producing more oil than ever. The raid cost the Americans heavily as fifty-four bombers were shot down, a 30 percent kill rate. Spaatz knew more attacks would have to be mounted, but never again from such a low altitude.

On the ground things were faring even better for Romania. During the spring and summer of 1942 they blitzed along, riding the coattails of the Germans to the gates of the city of Stalingrad. While the Germans penetrated the city, the under-equipped and under-supplied Romanians guarded the flanks. With the Germans poised for victory the Russians counterattacked in November 1942, slicing through the crumbling Romanians whose collapse allowed the German Sixth Army to become surrounded. After two more months of brutal fighting, the Germans and Romanians surrendered. It was perhaps the bloodiest battle in history and marked a major turning point in the war. From that point on, the Germans and the Romanians fought on the defensive.

As 1944 started, the war had turned decidedly against Romania. The Allies were preparing for the European invasion;

their bombing force had grown considerably and was raining death on the Axis countries, and the Russians were on the march west. But loyal Ion still saw Adolf through rose-colored glasses.

Spaatz, from his headquarters in Great Britain, upped the ante and pushed for the "Big Oil" plan that would unleash the full strength of his bomber force onto Romania. After the Allies landed in Normandy on June 6, Spaatz was freed to pursue his plan. Just two days after the invasion, on June 8, 1944, Spaatz giddily declared that the strategic air forces' primary mission was destroying Hitler's oil supply. The largest bomber force ever created was now focused on Romania.

Spaatz led off with a dive-bombing attack featuring his long-range P-38 fighters, equipped with extra fuel tanks. Then he turned to the heavy bombers. For two months his Fifteenth Air Force flew bomber run after bomber run at the facility from its base in Italy. Defenses started to crumble, destruction began to surpass the ability to repair it, and oil production declined. Soon the German and Romanian fighters, now badly outnumbered by the hundreds of Allied bombers and their fighter escorts, hid in the skies far away from their enemy.

Even the British got into the action. They attacked Ploesti four times in 1944, lighting up the dark sky and adding to the slow devastation of the oil fields. Spaatz's plan was working. Oil production was cut in half from March to April 1944, and halved again by June.

The attacks culminated with the nearly seven-hundred-plane raid on July 15. By this time Ploesti was getting plastered once or twice a week. The German army was frequently abandoning their beloved Panzers and trucks for lack of fuel. Big Oil was having big impact.

Finally, the last bomber dropped its load on August 19 to rattle the dust a little more. Ploesti was dead. When the Russians captured the area on August 30, they told the Americans the place had been totally destroyed. In all, the Allies ran twenty-four missions against Ploesti involving almost 6,000 bombers. While it cost the Americans 230 bombers and their crews, the results were spectacular. The Germans completely ran out of oil in late 1944. The dividend paid off during the Battle of the Bulge that December, when the Germans abandoned their Panzers with empty gas tanks and walked away.

Too slowly it had dawned on Antonescu that he was losing. While spending the majority of his time conducating the retreat on the Russian front and pretending to be an effective general, the Germans were running his country while fighting off the growing storm of bombers over Ploesti. Ion had installed the baby-faced son of King Carol, Mihai, as a symbolic ruler in 1940 when he had thrown King Carol out. From his palace in Bucharest, Mihai knew the end was near and teamed up with officers loyal to him and political leaders who opposed Ion to overthrow the Conducător.

Mihai's plan was to quit the war and ask the British and Americans to occupy key parts of the country to prevent Russian occupation. Mihai realized that the Russians might be somewhat miffed at Romania's role in the devastating invasion, but he believed the Allies would want to help keep the Russians at bay. The small problem with the plan was that the Allies had no intention of occupying Romania and had already slotted Hitler's Stalingrad buddy into the Soviet sphere of control.

Mihai's plan was further complicated by the fact that the German troops in Bucharest were actually running the country and could easily eliminate the few Romanian soldiers stationed in the capital.

On August 23, Antonescu came to Bucharest and agreed to swing by for a visit to the young Mihai, who was now determined to act. Ion, undoubtedly surprised that the useless young king was suddenly stepping forward to vent his completely irrelevant feelings, walked into the meeting blindly confident and without a weapon or guards. King Mihai demanded he quit. Ion laughed him off. Then King Mihai simply arrested Ion and proceeded to take command of the country, appointing his fellow conspirators to lead the government.

Once word got out, the Germans never flinched but simply added Romania to their growing target list. The ever-practical Germans used the same air bases they shared with the Romanians in attacking the Russians to now attack the Romanians. The Romanians and Germans suddenly found themselves fighting each other from the same air base. It was like a time-share for air forces. The Germans pounded Bucharest without the slightest hint of nostalgia for their former ally. Meanwhile, the Russians watched all of this with glee. In a horrifically clumsy diplomatic sleight of hand, Romania had turned a friend into an enemy but neglected to turn an enemy into a friend. The Germans conducted a fighting retreat to the west while the Russians swept in from the east. Romania had managed to briefly turn World War II into a three-way affair: the Allies and the Axis versus Romania.

Happy to be able to start working out the kinks of their postwar plans, after weeks of confused fighting the Soviets occupied Romania, retook the disputed territories, and placed their Communist thugs into the government. In September 1944 Mihai's delegation traveled to Moscow to naïvely negotiate terms of a peace treaty. Negotiations quickly turned Soviet-style as Foreign Minister Molotov handed the Romanians his terms: namely, take it or leave it. When they protested, he responded by sarcastically asking what the Romanians had been looking for in Stalingrad. Ouch! The pain was just starting. To wrap things up the Russians grabbed all

B-24 BOMBER

Ploesti met its doom primarily from the bomb bay of the B-24 bomber, the Liberator, the most produced of any bomber in the war. The U.S. Army in 1939, realizing that long-range bombing would play a key role in any future war, looked to upgrade from its B-17 bomber force. The Liberator was a flawed machine—difficult to fly with fuel and hydraulic systems that often malfunctioned. It smelled of jet fuel, was bitterly cold at even medium altitude, unpressurized, possessed not a shred of comfort, and required its crew to pee down a tube. But it carried lots of bombs, flew long distances, and destroyed pretty much all of Europe. In warfare, this qualifies as a raging success.

the gold the Romanians had earned selling their oil to the Nazis.

The war was still not over for the Romanians, however. The Soviets forced their new "friend" to reform its punch-drunk army and form up alongside their new allies to fight the Germans in Hungary. In all, about 210,000 Romanian soldiers fought in Hungary, suffering 47,000 casualties. The high casualty rate stemmed from the Russian tactic of "allowing" their new "friends" the "honor" of leading risky attacks.

After dispatching Hungary, the fun continued in Czechoslovakia when, in early 1945, the Russians prodded the Romanians into invading their third country of the war. They fought hard and suffered harder, again taking more than their share of casualties from the retreating but still formidable German ex-friends.

Romania's sorry postwar fate was sealed at the Yalta Conference on February 4, 1945. Roosevelt and Churchill traded away nothing in exchange for allowing Russia to control the country after the war. They didn't even ask for a province to be named later. It's safe to say that this was the last time the Western leaders thought about Romania for more than forty years.

In the years 1943 and 1944 Romania ranked second to Germany as an Axis power. In 1944 and 1945 Romania suffered the third highest Allied casualty rate. In less than a year, the Romanians contributed 540,000 troops to the Allied cause, behind only that of the United States, the USSR, and Britain. They suffered 167,000 casualties, more than the British in Northern Europe in that same period. For this effort, the Soviets bestowed a medal on King Mihai, and Romania got blackholed by the West.

WHAT HAPPENED AFTER

As might be expected of anyone who leads an army into Russia, the Soviet-backed Romanian government took Ion out behind a prison and shot him on June 1, 1946. It didn't go smoothly. The first volley merely wounded the Marshal, who was smartly dressed in a double-breasted suit and his hat raised high in his right hand, just before being pumped with bullets. Still believing he was in charge he ordered one more death; his own. The soldiers quickly finished their work. An officer then shot him in the head a few more times because he could. The Conducător's Aryan blue eyes would lovingly gaze into Adolf's no more.

As for the young king Mihai, surrounded by Soviet-directed Romanian puppet troops, he abdicated in 1947 and fled the country. Mihai spent the next forty years or so in Switzerland, working in the airline industry. He finally was able to return to Romania in the mid-1990s. He is the last World War II head of state still alive.

General Spaatz went from triumph to triumph; after having helped turn Europe into rubble, he went on to drop two atomic bombs on Japan. He retired in 1948 with a chest full of ribbons. Upon his death in 1974 he was buried on the grounds of the U.S. Air Force Academy.

The Romanians, after feeding oil to Hitler's war machine, eagerly participating in the Holocaust, fighting the Soviets for three years, absorbing the pounding of the vast American air force, seeing their only national asset of any great value destroyed, getting robbed and overrun by the Reds, taking on the Germans, invading Hungary and Czechoslovakia, and getting treated like a crazy uncle by everyone involved, were completely ignored by the entire world for two generations. All with a little help from their friends.

It turns out Antonescu did find a way to get Transylvania back. It simply required fighting every major combatant in World War II on both sides of the war and enduring a Soviet occupation.

His beloved Transylvania has been a happy part of Romania since 1947.

★ ★ ★

ELEVEN

THE GENERALS' COUP AGAINST HITLER

1944

Apparently, Adolf Hitler made many enemies. It might strike some as hard to believe that the madman who killed millions and started the most devastating war in history did not make friends as easily as Jimmy Stewart or Elmo. But people seemed genuinely angry at the Der Führer.

This select group was not limited to Russians, French, Czechs, Jews, Poles . . . you know the list. Most Germans who dared publicly express their dislike for Hitler—and even some who expressed these feelings only in private—were locked away and executed. But a few with actual power and the ability to strike back at Hitler did exist. Surprisingly, many were leaders of the German army. These officers were the descendants of the master warfare technicians of the vaunted Prussian General Staff, which had reordered Europe for nearly two hundred years. These plotters gathered, talked, and planned ways to kill Hitler, the despised former lance corporal and HQ messenger.

After numerous close calls that required evading Hitler's body armor of SS and Gestapo, the plotting climaxed in one last great thrust at Adolf. On July 20, 1944, as the German military desperately fought off the growing weight of Allied forces, this small group took their boldest step. They planted a bomb practically under Hitler's feet at his headquarters in the East Prussian forest. With Adolf blown up, the plotters planned to seize control of Germany in a swift coup d'état. The generals would then immediately appeal to the Allies for peace terms and bring the horrible war to a close.

But this effort, like their numerous prior attempts, failed. The plotters' abject failures over many years stemmed from fighting a twentieth-century dictator with a nineteenth-century mind-set. The dwindling number of plotters, steeped in the ways of the Prussian military tradition of noble combat, clung to their outmoded beliefs in the sanctity of honor and following orders, despite Hitler's use of their revolutionary blitzkrieg tactics, which he used to brutally carve up Europe. Hitler and his gang were radicals who believed in total war and killing anyone who got in the way. This clash of principles, in many ways a clash of centuries, doomed the plotters to failure.

THE PLAYERS

General Ludwig Beck—The old wise man of the German army, Beck held the post of chief of the German General Staff, the top staff officer in the entire army, and achieved renown in Germany for deftly handling the humiliating retreat of ninety divisions from the western front at the end of World War I.

Skinny—Between the wars he authored the seminal work on military tactics.

Props—In a rage of Prussian honor, he resigned in 1938 to protest Hitler's aggressive maneuvering against Czechoslovakia. It was a parade of one.

Pros—Ringleader of the anti-Hitler cadre.

Cons—Looked like the mean old man down the street who always scared children.

Colonel Klaus Schenk Graf von Stauffenberg—He descended from a long line of military leaders, meaning his ancestors invaded virtually every country in Europe, while also holding the title of *Schenk* (meaning "Cup-bearer," and yes, this was an important title). The young colonel, who was the chief of staff of the Replacement Army, despised Hitler and was the one who actually set off the bomb on July 20.
Skinny—Tall and noble, he was one of the most famous soldiers in Germany.
Props—Heavily decorated war hero, Stauffenberg lost an eye, an arm, and two fingers in battle in North Africa under Rommel.
Pros—Motivated to kill Hitler on moral grounds.
Cons—Don't bet on three-fingered assassins.

General Friedrich Fromm—The rotund general held the sleepy post of commander of the Replacement Army, which put him in control of the troops in and around Berlin that would take over the city once Hitler was killed.
Skinny—Supported the coup, then didn't, ate more schnitzel, flip-flopped again, then couldn't decide. Backbone was not his middle name.
Props—The corpulent commander believed he was a big deal because he was defending Germany from unsightly, undernourished foreign workers.
Pros—At least he carried a weapon to the office.
Cons—Cowardly executed the conspirators to save his own skin.

THE GENERAL SITUATION

Hitler and his generals had a tense relationship. On one hand, the army did his bidding and conquered most of Europe, expanding Hitler's murderous empire. On the other, the army hated Hitler and tried to thwart his ambition at virtually every stage. Many of the generals saw Hitler as an upstart corporal, his rank during World War I. In turn, Hitler distrusted the army and was so afraid of an assassination attempt by them that he virtually refused to meet with any of its leaders.

To further cement dominance over the military establishment, Hitler built his own separate command structure, the OKW, with himself as the leader, which he erected over the army's command, the OKH. Hitler now directly controlled the military.

Hitler and his generals lived like a warring couple forced to share the same house. Since at least the time of Frederick the Great, the army had been the backbone of the modern German state. It's leaders came almost exclusively from nobility, Junker families with large estates where son followed father into the army.

After their humiliating defeat in World War I, the army, besides having to watch the French preen as victors, was reduced to the size of a police force. The old Prussians were determined to keep the army alive, and many supported Hitler's mesmerizing vision of using the army to rebuild Germany to its former glory. Survival of the army was paramount. The army *was* the state, and whatever it took to ensure its survival, including striking a deal with the odious Nazi ideology, was acceptable. In 1934 Hitler required every member of the armed forces to declare undying loyalty to him personally by swearing to the Fahneneid, the blood oath of the Teutonic knights. The deal was struck. The army could not resist sacrificing their honor for the chance to ride Hitler's coattails to world domination. Stymied by their oath, they were incapable of resisting Hitler's Nazification of the army.

A few key generals, however, spoke out bravely against Hitler. The leaders of this group were General Baron Werner Freiherr von Fritsch, the commander in chief of the army and his chief of staff, Gen. Ludwig Beck. Hitler knew of their opposition and quickly moved to isolate them. But Hitler, being Hitler, overreached and succeeded. The moment took place in early 1938 when Hitler accused Fritsch of homosexuality. Fritsch resigned in a pique of honor, hewing to the old rules of his caste. Unfortunately for history, the other army leaders failed to take up arms in Fritsch's defense at this critical time. Hitler gambled that if the army remained silent when he humiliated their leader, they would never have the balls to oppose him in anything else.

A few officers, however, joined forces in a secret society designed to overthrow Hitler, the *Schwarze Kapelle*—the "Black Orchestra." Over the next few years, the Schwarze Kapelle was led by General Beck, who plotted from his armchair while suffering from cancer in his suburban Berlin home. Rear Admiral Wilhelm Franz Canaris, the crafty head of the army's intelligence wing, the *Abwehr*, was his coplotter. Twice the conspirators came mighty close to achieving their coup against Hitler. First, in 1938, as Germany made plans to attack Czechoslovakia, the plotters stationed troops to pounce on the SS and Gestapo, and seize power from Hitler. All they waited for was some sign that Great Britain would oppose Hitler's takeover. As negotiations strung out, the plotters' hopes rose and fell. At one point they were sure the British would reject any agreement and fight for the Czechs. Then British prime minister Neville Chamberlain caved in to Hitler's demands at Munich and agreed to carve up Czechoslovakia, dashing their hopes as well as teeing up World War II very nicely for Adolf. The plans were burned.

In March 1943 the plotmates struck again. Two bombs, disguised as liquor, were placed on Hitler's private airplane by giving them to one of Hitler's unwitting aides, Col. Heinz Brandt. The fuses were set, and the plotters waited in Berlin for word of the führer's death. But the bomb failed to detonate: the explosives had frozen at the plane's high altitude. One of the plotters was then forced to retrieve the frozen bomb from Brandt's office the next day where Brandt joshingly tossed the package in the air at the plotmate who nervously hustled it away. Hitler's amazing luck had held again. The plotmates were stymied yet again and retreated to wait for their next chance.

But the Schwarze Kapelle did not give up. Plot after plot was either canceled or failed through some last-second change in plans by Hitler. In 1943 the group welcomed Col. Claus von Stauffenberg as a new leader. Despite his valiant efforts to kill Allied soldiers, he held deep personal opposition to the Nazis. He was disgusted at Nazi war crimes, which offended his dainty sense of Prussian honor and the deeply held belief that his country (and the world) should be ruled by Prussians like himself, not some poorly mustachioed watercolorist and ex-corporal from Austria.

WHAT HAPPENED: OPERATION "ARMY OF NONE"

Throughout the fall of 1943 and spring of 1944 the plotters met in their regular how-do-we-blow-up-Hitler-and-get-away-with-it meetings but failed to come up with any new juicy ideas. In the late spring of 1944, in a stroke of luck, Stauffenberg was given a job that provided him with rare direct access to Hitler.

The plotters had two problems, however. Like a rich man without any pocket change, it was oddly difficult for German army leaders to obtain explosives during the biggest war in history. But they quickly overcame this by fashioning the bomb from captured British explosives. The second issue was a lack of cheerful volunteers, other than Stauffenberg. No one else had the courage and the access to plant the actual bomb. That meant Stauffenberg would be absent from the plot's center in Berlin during the crucial coup-making hours. Leadership would fall to his colleagues, who lacked the passion and determination to complete the mission that Stauffenberg held. But with no other viable options, the plot was set in motion.

Twice that July, Stauffenberg showed up at a weekly group meeting with Hitler in his Russian front headquarters, packing a plastic explosive in his briefcase, right next to his charts of the phantom divisions that fed Hitler's fantasy of turning back the Russians. But both times Stauffenberg changed his mind at the last second. For a while the plotmates had agreed they would only detonate the bomb if it would kill both Hitler and SS leader Himmler. But their bad luck held, and Himmler stopped attending these meetings, so they agreed to settle for just Adolf. On July 13, Stauffenberg set out for his third meeting with Hitler at his Prussian HQ with the bomb jammed into his briefcase. This time he was determined to light the fuse.

Back in Berlin, confident that finally Hitler would be blown up, Gen. Friedrich Olbricht, deputy commander of the replacement army and a key plotmate of Beck and Stauffenberg, ordered the start of Operation Valkyrie, which was the army's standing plan to seize control of the country in cases an internal uprisings. The plotters would use the cover of Valkyrie to seize the government, take out the SS, and neutralize the vast Nazi apparatus. Then they would be in position to open peace talks with the Allies. Orders were sent out to army units throughout the country to be on the alert for further instructions. Soldiers maneuvered into position around Berlin to seize Gestapo and SS positions. But the overly cautious Stauffenberg got cold feet when Himmler failed to attend the meeting, even though the plotmates had agreed to go ahead with the plan anyway. He nervously called his colleagues Beck and Olbricht in Berlin, and they agreed to cancel the plans. Olbricht hastily withdrew the Valkyrie orders, but when Fromm found out that the orders had already been issued, he laid into Olbricht.

The following week, Stauffenberg was called to attend another meeting with Hitler. For the fourth time he packed his bomb.

The morning of July 20, Stauffenberg took a flight to Hitler's HQ retreat at Rastenburg, in the forest of East Prussia, the ancestral home of the German army. He traveled with his aide, Lt. Werner von Haeften. In a shocking turn of events, the plotters prepared a backup plan: Both men carried bombs in their briefcases; in case one briefcase was lost, the show could go on.

The plan was simple. Perhaps too simple. Stauffenberg would kill Hitler with the bomb. A coup member in charge of communication at Rastenburg would cut all communications with the outside world. Troops and police loyal to the coup would seize key government centers in Berlin and other German cities, and the army in France would round up SS and Gestapo members, execute them, and open talks with the Allies. What could go wrong? It wasn't quite the scale of a Russian invasion but the plotters—all colonels and generals— thought they could handle it.

To prepare for the meeting with Hitler, Stauffenberg and Haeften ducked into an empty office to light the fuse. A getaway car and speedy airplane waited to whisk them back to Berlin. But Stauffenberg, with only three fingers, had trouble setting the time-delay fuse. Outside the office, an impatient General Keitel, Hitler's pet general, sent in a soldier to rush the two along. While Stauffenberg did manage to set his bomb, he was unable to insert Haeften's backup bomb into his briefcase.

Stauffenberg entered the meeting and took his place next to Hitler at a large wooden table covered with maps. He placed his explosive luggage as close to Hitler as possible. But unlike prior meetings that took place in a concrete bunker, this one was in a lightly built wooden hut with open windows, which would reduce the impact of any blast. After a minute or two, just before 1:00 P.M., Stauffenberg excused himself from the meeting and dashed to his waiting car with Haeften, trying to not look like a guy about to kill Hitler and become outlaw number one in Europe.

But back in the hut, the same stoogy Colonel Brandt, who had unwittingly carried the liquor bombs onto Hitler's plane, became annoyed by Stauffenberg's briefcase blocking his way. He moved it to the other side of the solid wood table support, away from Hitler. For his trouble, Brandt was blown up when the bomb exploded moments later. In their getaway car, the three-fingered assassin and Haeften saw the explosion and concluded the overdue deed was finally done. Despite being stopped by SS guards manning the gate, they talked their way out and sped toward the airport. Along the way, Haeften ditched his briefcase with his bomb.

Back in Berlin, Beck and Olbricht, not known for their dashing drive, did nothing except sweat and wait. Because of the uproar caused by the premature launching of Operation Valkyrie the previous week, Olbricht hesitated in activating the plan until he confirmed that Hitler was dead. Better wait, he figured, than risk a dressing-down from Fromm and a negative job review. So he did nothing. He and Beck, who was decked out in his uniform for the first time since his 1938 resignation, were awaiting the call from Gen. Erich Fellgiebel, the coup member who headed the communications at Hitler's headquarters in Rastenburg. The plan was that Fellgiebel would phone Beck and Olbricht when the bomb went off so they knew that Hitler was dead. Everyone would skate through the coup without actually putting their lives on the line. Everything depended on Hitler dying from the bomb.

But the bomb didn't kill Hitler. The heavy oak table shielded Hitler enough so that he suffered only minor wounds. When he staggered out of the bombed-out building, Fellgiebel spotted him and froze. Rather than call his plotmates telling them Hitler was alive, he did nothing. He did try to shut down all communications in and out of Rastenburg but succeeded only in tipping himself off to the SS.

Fellgiebel's reaction proved to be a typical plotmate response. Now that the time to fish or cut bait had arrived, everyone involved either froze or waffled in their decisions, unwilling to sacrifice themselves and desperate to escape the inevitable backlash by Hitler. The SS quickly took control over Rastenburg's communications, and Fellgiebel never sent any signal to Berlin that Hitler was alive. In fact, they never heard from him again.

Beck and Olbricht nervously shuffled papers as the afternoon wound down; Stauffenberg winged to Berlin. The plot was frozen in place. Plotmate Wolf Heinrich, Count von Helldorf, head of the Berlin police, anxiously waited for orders to move out. So far it was the armchair coup.

Finally, just before 4:00 P.M., Stauffenberg landed outside Berlin and phoned Olbricht to announce that Hitler was certainly dead. At last, the plotters snapped out of their sweaty lethargy and issued orders. But they had already lost three precious hours while the Nazis didn't even know there was a coup afoot. The initiative slipped away.

At 4:00 P.M. sharp the coup lumbered to life: Olbricht sent out the Valkyrie orders; the troops in Berlin, commanded by plotmate von Haase, were dispatched to seize key government buildings; the Berlin police jumped at strategic locations; and Nazi and military leaders throughout the country were ordered to secure themselves and their locations against a revolt by the SS.

At first, things were going well, but troubles soon began

to pile up. First, Olbricht went to Fromm in the Bendlerblock army HQ, to enlist him into the plot. Fromm,
shocked, absolutely shocked that the coup he was nominally
part of had actually started but, not wanting to be caught
on the losing side, promised to join only if he received assurance that Hitler was dead. At Olbricht's suggestion, he
called Rastenburg. Olbricht was under the illusion that all
communication was cut. But Fromm got through immediately and was told by Keitel that Hitler had survived the
bombing. Fromm was furious when he found that Valkyrie
had been started in his name. The plotters demanded he join
them, and he simply drew his pistol and placed them all
under arrest. The dim-witted plotters had forgotten to bring
their guns. They didn't even post guards to protect the headquarters or surround themselves with loyal troops. They
had armed themselves only with attitude, their dubious
honor, and wishful thinking.

Facing the collapse of the coup and in many ways deter-
mining the future course of World War II, cancer-ridden
Beck, Olbricht, and the three-fingered assassin Stauffenberg
wrestled Fromm to the ground and took away his pistol.
They locked him in his office without a snack. Fromm received the first time-out of the revolution.

Had the plotters drawn up a pre-coup checklist, it probably would have looked something like this:

Stiff Prussian attitude—check
Note pad for dictating orders—check
Indignant look for questioning underlings—check
Loyal soldiers or weapons—Not needed!

At about 6:00 P.M., rebel army troops led by Maj. Adolf
Remer, not a party to the plot, surrounded the Propaganda
Ministry, with its Radio Berlin transmitter. Inside, the par-

THE OATH

I swear by God this holy oath, that I will render to Adolf Hitler, Führer of the German Reich and people, Supreme Commander of the Armed Forces, unconditional obedience, and that I am ready, as a brave soldier, to risk my life at any time for this oath.

Few things hindered the army's resistance more than the oath. Once taken, most officers couldn't see how they could violate it and remain in the army. To these men the oath was like some pixie dust sprinkled in their eyes. In a way it served as their security blanket. If they ever doubted what to do, they could always fall back on following the oath and sleep well, knowing they did their duty.

boiled Josef Goebbels, Hitler's propaganda chief, saw them coming and sprang to action. The plotters, trapped in their Prussian traditions of duty and honor, expected Remer to capure the transmitter, as ordered. Goebbels, wise to Hitler being alive, took advantage of the same instinct to follow orders and invited Remer into his office for a little chat. The slick Goebbels convinced Remer that he was unknowingly taking part in a coup. To back up his claim, Goebbels got Hitler on the phone—the plotmates never thought to cut his phone lines—and he told Remer to obey him and not the army. Remer, his common sense overwhelmed once again by the potent mix of German order-taking abilities and Nazi craftiness, now clicked his heels and ordered his troops to protect Goebbels. Fortified by clear orders, Remer turned on the plotmates.

With one slick move Goebbels, a shriveled PR hack in a poorly fitting suit, had flipped the troops actually carrying the guns over to Hitler's side. A single phone call had outwitted the career army men, some of the cream of the crop of the General Staff. As usual, the plotmates had no idea the ground had shifted under their feet. Their belief was that all orders would be followed; even if the order meant sending an unknown army major to inexplicably arrest a key member of the Nazi high command. This, however, was not their father's Germany—it was a whole new world, and the fast-talking, initiative-taking Goebbels ran circles around them. The plotters had stupidly trusted that the officer would explicitly follow their orders. They lost the one great chance to overwhelm the Nazis.

By 7:00 that evening, the troops under Remer marched back to the Bendlerblock and surrounded the plotmates. Inside they were still obliviously issuing orders to their phantom revolutionary army. Somehow they never noticed that no one was replying. Had they bothered to investigate, they would have found their communications had been cut an hour earlier. Now, they were isolated.

But they were not alone. True to form, the plotmates had failed to clear the Bendlerblock of pro-Hitler soldiers, and many still roamed the halls. Later that night some of these officers burst into the offices of the plotters and opened fire. It was a one-sided affair, as the plotmates were still unarmed. They were quickly overpowered, and Fromm, now freed from his time-out, confronted them. Remer's troops flooded into the building.

Fromm now found himself in a tough spot. He was marginally part of this whole affair. If Hitler had been blown up, Fromm would have taken on a key role. But fate had turned him against his former allies. He latched on to the opportunity to save himself and issued an immediate death sentence on all four conspirators: Beck, Olbricht, Stauffenberg, and another ally, colonel of the General Staff Mertz von Quirnheim. All but Beck were taken away.

Fromm gave Beck a chance for the honorable way out by using a pistol on himself. Beck fired a shot that merely grazed the top of his head. An annoyed Fromm grabbed the gun away, but Beck pleaded for another chance to take his own life. Fromm gave the pistol back to the cancerous general. Still the old soldier, who had spent his entire adult life in the army, failed again to accurately shoot a bullet a few inches. A disgusted Fromm brutally ordered a solider to finish off his old, former boss.

Fromm then turned to his old plotmates and ordered them shot in the courtyard of the Bendlerblock. And there, in the dark of night, highlighted by the headlights of a truck, a squad of German soldiers ended the last gasp of German resistance to Hitler. They had been bred in the generations-old traditions of the Prussian officer corps, had conquered most of Europe, and were now holding their ground against enemies whose size and strength dwarfed their own. Yet they still could not conquer a few square miles of their own city, and the enemy didn't even know a fight was on.

Outside of Berlin, the coup stumbled blindly forward, not knowing their leaders had fallen. Upon being told that Hitler was dead, Gen. Karl-Heinrich von Stülpnagel, the military governor of France and an avid member of the coup, leapt into action and ordered the arrest of senior officers of the SS in the Paris area. Then he headed over to see Field Marshal Günther von Kluge, the commander of the German army on the western front.

Kluge was yet another one of those halfhearted fence-sitting generals; earlier that afternoon he had received two interesting phone calls. First, Beck had found some downtime to phone Kluge and urge him to join the coup. A short time later, Keitel at Rastenburg rang to let him know that Hitler was alive and Kluge should obey orders from him and not the plotters. Kluge was stunned. Before hearing from

PRUSSIA

It has been said that Prussia is not a country with an army, but an army with a country. Settled by Teutonic knights way back in the thirteenth century, the country occupied most of today's eastern part of Germany, Poland, and sections of the Baltic countries. Following the unification of Germany in 1871, Prussia had a big country of its own: Germany. The Prussian king became the German king, the Prussian army became the heart of the German army. But after World War II, the Germans who weren't dead fled Prussia; it was officially dissolved, and the Soviets took a blowtorch to the homeland of the German nobility. The core of Prussia, the estate-rich east, was split up with a section absorbed into Poland and another chunk still an isolated outpost of Russia.

Rastenburg, he had been planning to join the coup. But now, that meant violating his oath to Hitler and worse yet, facing his wrath if the coup failed. He was torn—the fate of the war and the lives of millions waited for his decision. Finally he made his choice: he would wait and see what happened to Hitler. Then he would throw his support behind the winning side. When he sat down for dinner with Stülpnagel, Kluge made up his mind and betrayed his caste. He denied any knowledge of the assassination plots, even though he had held discussions about them for years. A stunned Stülpnagel did nothing other than stutter a few syllables. He knew he was a dead man if the coup failed because he had a jail full of angry SS officers being prepped for the firing squad. But once again, the plotmates did nothing when confronted with disaster. Stülpnagel took the bad news in stride, finished dinner, and returned to Paris to release his SS prisoners.

Like the other plotmates, Stülpnagel lived in the old world of honor and oaths. Unknown to the plotters, however, that world had long passed them by. It was a nineteenth-century

world, and they were fighting Adolf Hitler, the archetype of
the twentieth-century dictator. In their country's and the
world's darkest hour, these men of outmoded ideals could
not muster the courage and will to abandon them. It was a
loss the whole world suffered.

WHAT HAPPENED AFTER

Hitler scoured the continent to wipe out any distant relative
of Stauffenberg. Thousands were killed, even those connected by the slimmest of threads. The resistance to Hitler
from inside the German high command died.

The street outside the Bendlerblock where he was executed
in Berlin now bears Stauffenberg's name.

The noble-born generals of the Prussian cabal, who had
elevated their survival above all other concerns, while ac-
commodating Hitler's evil, were now paying the ultimate
price. For years after the failed putsch of 1923, they could
have had their way with Hitler. But they realized only he
could give them what they wanted: control of Europe. They
put the awesome might of their resuscitated armies under his
control and on a cataclysmic collision with the rest of the
world. It was too late when many realized they could not
control him. Even with the terrible end in sight, and with the
knowledge of the horrible crimes committed in their name,
the generals couldn't summon the courage to sacrifice themselves to kill Hitler. Ultimately both were destroyed by their
enemies who learned Hitler's lessons better than the generals,
that they were in a fight until death or bitter victory.

★ ★ ★

TWELVE

THE BAY OF PIGS INVASION

1961

Invading a country is a big deal. It usually makes the news.
John F. Kennedy, the youngest president ever elected, seemed to be very mature for his age. Perhaps it was his World War II experience combined with his movie-star aura and privileged upbringing that led him to imagine he could cloak an invasion in total secrecy. But when the invaded country is well known as the rabid enemy of a world superpower like the United States, it's hard to hide the looming colossus shooting from behind the sand dunes. Even a platoon of CIA flacks disguised as press aides proclaiming full deniability can't spin away an invasion. But Kennedy tried.

To many Americans, Cuba seemed a natural extension of Florida. Only a mistake of geography prevented the United States from exercising its natural domination over the island. Ever since Teddy Roosevelt charged up San Juan Hill during the Spanish American War, Americans treated Cuba like their little brother. Of course, that's if you don't like, treat well, or respect your kid brother. But then one day the little kid got pissed off and dressed up in army fatigues, lit a cigar, and fought back. In 1959 Fidel Castro took over Cuba, kicked out the American business interests, and declared himself in charge.

Immediately the United States began looking to take out Castro. In 1960, under President Eisenhower, it turned to its master spies, the CIA. While not strictly in the job description, the CIA was willing to overthrow foreign governments if requested by the government. The upstanding Yale men, Skull and Bones types, who had controlled the agency since its founding as the OSS in World War II, were still dining out in their Brooks Brothers suits on the stories of overthrowing the leader of Guatemala in 1954 with a slingshot and two broken walkie-talkies. They figured if it worked there, it could work in Cuba. Both countries are filled with Spanish-speaking people and have nice beaches, so what could go wrong?

When Vice President Richard Nixon grabbed the reins from a disinterested Eisenhower, the CIA rounded up the old Guatemala gang and set them loose on the problem of "saving" the little *hermano* to the south from their new leader. With Richard Bissell, the patently brilliant head of covert operations running the show against Castro, the CIA just knew his days were numbered. They tweaked and jimmied up various plans, each one more foolproof than the last, finally settling on the perfect plan of a tidy little invasion of just a few hundred lightly armed, disgruntled former citizens.

Kennedy, who inherited the plan along with Bissell and his gang of bureaucratic revolutionaries, agreed to do it if they could pull it off without anyone guessing that the giant, superpower, archenemy ninety miles to the north was involved.

THE PLAYERS

John F. Kennedy—Young, exceedingly lucky and charismatic, the new president was ready to push the United States into a New Frontier of, well, everything. But beyond the hype he was an inexperienced, untested president who won a very close election and needed to prove he had the mettle to stand up to the Russkies and more important, the Russki-haters.

Skinny—Probably won the election because he had a closer shave than Nixon.

Props—Marilyn Monroe was a key member of the bedroom cabinet.

Pros—After the invasion tanked he sheepishly admitted his mistake by saying "How could I have been so stupid to let them go ahead?"

Cons—This epiphany came a week too late.

Fidel Castro—Young, exceedingly lucky and charismatic, the new dictator was ready to join forces with the Soviet Union in the worldwide struggle against the shopping mall. Before taking command with his merry band of a dozen comrades, he convinced the world he was a major threat to Cuban dictator Batista. When Batista suddenly fled the country, Castro found himself in charge.

Skinny—Mass executions not as fun since Ché bought it in Bolivia.

Props—Knew an invasion was coming. He read about it in the U.S. newspapers.

Pros—Big baseball fan. Found it easy to motivate players with jail time and random killings.

Cons—Tested the revolutionary zeal of his underfed and TV-deprived citizens by requiring them to sit through four-hour harangues.

Richard Bissell—The reputedly brilliant chief of covert operations for the CIA, he was managing his first major coup without a net, notes, or a plan. He conceived the entire operation and was the one person who knew all the ways it could fail, and he was determined to keep them secret.

Skinny—Yale man. Studied there, taught there. Never featured on the cover of the course catalog.
Props—Overthrew countries from a desk in Washington, D.C.
Pros—Created the U-2 spy plane.
Cons—Needed a spy plane to find his career after the invasion flopped.

THE GENERAL SITUATION

When Castro first took over Cuba in January 1959, following the New Year's Day flight of dictator Fulgencio Batista, he had everyone confused. No one knew quite what he stood for. He told the world that he led a people's revolution that aimed to install all the trappings of the good society; free press, elections, good schools, and health care for all. Crowds cheered him during his first visit to the United States in April 1959. Many in the CIA wanted to support him. Even after a three-hour meeting with the famed Red-hunter Richard Nixon, the true picture of Fidel remained fuzzy. He was a tantalizing blend of Lenin and Elvis.

It didn't take long, however, for the real Castro to emerge. Starting in mid-1959 Castro took over the large hotels and then, outrage of outrages, outlawed gambling. Even more ominously, he rounded up political opponents and summarily shot them. He slowly closed his grip on Cuban society. Many people fled; airline pilots often hijacked their own planes and flew them to the United States. After Castro's takeover, the Cuban community in Miami swelled with exiles. They demanded immediate coup action. Some shipped arms to anti-Castro guerrillas in Cuba; others brawled with Castro's supporters in Miami. The tipping point occurred once Castro linked Kalashnikovs with the Soviet Union in 1960. Now he represented a real threat, and soon thereafter Washington joined the Cuban exile chorus demanding immediate coup action.

It was 1960, the height of the Cold War. Kennedy was campaigning by denouncing the Republicans for allowing the United States to fall behind the Russians in strategic missiles. The Communists kept pushing forward around the world while the country shouldered the effort to roll back the Red Menace. Americans fervently believed that when one country came under Soviet domination, other countries were sure to topple. The inescapable logic of the domino theory, which led to numerous international experiments, such as the war in Vietnam, dictated immediate coup action: if the U.S. government stood idly by and let Cuba go Red, the next domino to fall would surely be the United States.

Starting in January 1960, CIA honcho Richard Bissell took the lead in cooking up a strategy. Plans were discussed, meetings held, calls placed. Many of these activities received hearty backing by Nixon, who was particularly eager for the invasion to happen that year to boost his presidential plans. Eisenhower had no qualms about coup action. But in his last year in office, he focused more on his putting game than on pushing for the invasion. He let Nixon run with the ball.

Invading Cuba was actually the backup plan. The first choice was simply to kill Castro. In a striking example of real life imitating a bad movie, in August 1960 the CIA hired the mob to rub out Castro. In a chain of command, bedazzling in its complexity, Bissell instructed his CIA compatriot Sheff Edwards to head the project, and Edwards ordered James O'Connell, also of the CIA, to handle the job. O'Connell then outsourced the work to Robert Maheu, a private investigator who handled odd jobs for the agency, and Maheu brought in mobster Johnny Roselli. Roselli recruited Momo Salvatore Giancana, Chicago mob chief, and Santos Trafficante, former mob ruler of Havana. And those two paragons of national security were tasked to hire the actual killer.

Shockingly, it almost worked. Giancana and Trafficante had numerous plans to kill Castro: (1) assassinating him via a facial defoliant to his famous beard, (2) killing him with a poisonous cigar, (3) drugging him into a rambling mess during a live radio talk, (4) poisoning his favorite meal, and (5) staging the "accidental death" of his trusted brother Raul. But due to the combination of absurd plans, Castro's charmed fate, and bad luck, all failed. Methods left untried include a laser aimed at his crotch, and dipping him in a huge pot of boiling oil.

Bissell and the CIA had tasted success and knew where to get the recipe. In 1954 the agency had launched a mission to oust Guatemalan president Jacobo Arbenz Guzmán, guilty of flirting with Communists. Arbenz fled to Europe, Moscow, and landed eventually, of all places, in Cuba itself. Flushed with victory from one successful coup, the agency felt confident it could take its show on the road. And Cuba was the next logical stop.

WHAT HAPPENED: OPERATION "DAY AT THE BEACH"

In 1960 Bissell's original vision for the conquest of Communist Cuba required only a tidy group of a few dozen infiltrators, dropped in under cover of darkness, who would foment a guerrilla insurgency. A key added benefit to this plan was that the operation would be small enough to appear organically Cuban. Richard Bissell, however, was not in the habit of thinking small. Mission creep crept in as Bissell tinkered with his plan. When he finally unveiled it, the plan called for "a shock action," CIA-speak for a full-scale military invasion. Bissell's enthusiasm got the best of him. Then he forgot to tell anyone.

Bissell went dark for strategic reasons. His own CIA reports in November 1960 stated that a Cuban military invasion, even with upward of 3,000 troops, would fail. The CIA concluded that the only way to oust Castro would be to land the Marines. Bissell never breathed a word of this report to anyone; instead, he beefed up the invasion all by himself.

Bissell's plan now ran as follows: 1,500 American-trained Cuban rebels, shipped in from Guatemala, would land on a remote beach on the southern coast of Cuba, hold on for a few days while makeshift air support fended off the Cuban army of 200,000 men. The country would erupt in anti-Castro hysteria, and the rebels, now joined by their Cuban leaders (who would be holing up in a Manhattan hotel until the invasion worked) would simply walk into Havana and take over, just like Castro had done, with the occasional stop for a refreshing Mojito. A fun and easy covert op with full deniability for the United States.

The problem for the CIA, as with all of their home-brewed revolutions, was creating an invading force powerful enough to win . . . but not so strong that it would reveal the American backing. The invasion, in essence, had to be Cubanized—made to look unprofessional. As events later proved, unprofessional military operations came quite easily to the CIA.

Like a Broadway show working out the kinks on the road, the CIA held a preview invasion. In May 1960 the agency conquered Swan Island—"Bird Drop Island"—a lonely outpost in the western Caribbean, which was coated in the stuff. The CIA set up its own radio transmitter to broadcast anti-Castro messages into Cuba. To capture Swan (Codename: Operation Dirty Boots) required a secret deployment of a destroyer to evacuate some drunken Honduran students found partying on the island. The pre-invasion reviews: two thumbs up.

To train the rebel army, in July 1960 Bissell established a base in a remote area of Guatemala, with the help of the country's superfriendly president Miguel Ydigoras Fuentes.

The camp grew as the CIA flew in more Cuban fighters, mostly recruited from the pool of cranky exiles around Miami, who trained under the eyes of sunburned CIA trainers and army drill masters disguised in civilian clothes and sporting aliases, to keep up the fiction that America was in no way involved. The growing force was named Brigade 2506 after an early volunteer, secret ID number 2506, died in training. In a shockingly clever twist, the CIA gave volunteers ID numbers starting with 2500 to fake out Castro on the size of the force, should he happen to discover its existence. This turned out, unfortunately, to be one of their craftier moves.

One complication with Brigade 2506 was the high rate of rebel soldiers going AWOL. When the CIA found the rebels were taking off to frolic in a distant brothel, the agency didn't hesitate to make the logical move; they opened a whorehouse on the base. For security reasons the whores were recruited from El Salvador and Costa Rica.

A larger issue was that security of the plans was a top priority. If word of the CIA's project leaked, it would destroy the myth that the American invasion of Cuba was organically Cuban. But in mid-1960, the *Miami Herald* discovered Cubans being trained for war and planned to run a story on the whole affair. Pressure from the U.S. government, however, killed the story. On October 30, 1960, a Guatemalan paper ran an article about the training camp, which was largely ignored in the United States, as often happened to events in Guatemala. Then on January 10, 1961, the *New York Times* ran a front-page story disclosing the CIA training of Cuban guerrillas. Now the cat was out of the bag, it seemed. But Bissell and company remained unperturbed, convinced that few people actually paid attention to the front page of the *Times*.

After Kennedy's election in November 1960, Bissell had

briefed him on the plan. The young president had been as uninterested as everyone else. Bissell tried to get Kennedy to focus on the plan but failed in maneuvering the young president into green-lighting the project.

As the invasion planning went forward under Kennedy's new administration, it occurred to only one key person during the planning, Antonio de Varona, one of the Cuban exile political leaders, that the plan's math hardly spelled success: the invasion brigade of a few hundred men would face about 200,000 Cuban soldiers. Bissell had a one-word response that calmed everyone: "umbrella." The invasion would be protected by an umbrella of air power, one of the inviolable laws of modern warfare. American planes would lay waste to any ground forces the invaders would meet. The umbrella was not only the key to victory; it was a sedative for restive and questioning minds. The umbrella would solve all problems.

A bigger problem that nobody seemed to notice was the lack of any clear chain of command for the operation, a gross violation of basic military strategy. While Bissell created the plan, and the CIA controlled every aspect of the operation, Kennedy retained final authority on all decisions. He lacked, however, a firm grasp of the details. The lack of clear U.S. operational lines of control was matched by the paralysis of the rebel Cuban leadership. For example, the main ground force, Brigade 2506, reported to no one in particular. Various groups vied for control: some were former Batista cronies, some were disgruntled hangers-on from Castro's entourage, others were former government leaders. They hated and distrusted one another. Each had his own idea of how a post-Castro government should look, with each one seeing himself as the next top dog. If the invasion succeeded, it was not clear who would take over for Castro. It was a revolution without a revolutionary.

Despite the mushrooming cloud of problems, Bissell remained convinced that none of them were unsolvable and that the correctness of getting rid of Castro would swing Kennedy to his side. Bissell's interactions with Kennedy throughout the early months of 1961 confirmed this, as the new president rarely asked probing questions whenever Bissell swung by the White House to update Kennedy on his invasion plans.

As a result Bissell's little invasion plan began to suffer from scope creep, which he conveniently forgot to mention. The series of small infiltrations designed to inflame an internal Cuban uprising had morphed into a mini D-Day, complete with a beach assault from amphibious boats and the motley crew of Cuban exile rebels standing in for a division of Marines. He consulted no one but simply tried to bamboozle the new president into agreeing to what was quickly becoming a full-scale invasion.

On March 11, an alarmed Kennedy rejected Bissell's mini D-Day as overblown. And he wanted the plan reworked to ensure a 100-percent organically Cuban provenance. But it still wasn't canceled. Bissell stomped off to massage his plan.

Kennedy was holding true to his lifelong predilection of getting exactly what he wanted, in this case a double victory to start off his presidency. There was no reason Castro couldn't be crushed and the whole operation hidden behind a well-tailored cloak of invisibility. Like the "help" his father provided to secure his election or the beautiful "secretaries" he kept stashed in the basement of the White House, he didn't see any reason whatsoever to suffer any blemishes on the sheen of perfection on his shiny, new administration. He seemed to have full confidence that the CIA could pull this off without him having to even miss his weekend sail off the Cape.

In late March 1961, a month before the invasion, Bissell came back to Kennedy with a new softer version of the inva-

sion, one that included a change that Kennedy never bothered to understand. It was still a military invasion, just
slightly smaller. But now its location had moved from the
foot of the guerrilla-friendly Escambray Mountains to about
sixty miles away in the swampy, isolated Bay of Pigs. Unreal-
ized by Kennedy, this change meant that if the invasion
failed, the rebels could not simply melt into the mountains as
guerrillas to continue the fight and continue the fiction that
the invasion was a "100 percent Cuban affair." Kennedy obviously had not thought the whole thing through, and consulting a new map was not part of Kennedy's approval
process. The young president was a man of action without
the fail-safe backup his father's money and planning had
provided. The confident Bissell assured him the plan would
succeed, even better than in Guatemala. Kennedy was caught
in a trap: if he canceled the operation he would look weak—
both to the Republicans and to the Russians.

One thing remained the same, though. The deciding factor
of the entire invasion was control of the air—the key to
modern warfare. If the rebels controlled the skies, they could
land reinforcements at will. But if Castro had air superiority,
he would pick off the rebel ships, and the invading force
would wither on the beaches. It was obvious, given Kennedy's insistence on maintaining the total veil of secrecy, that
the United States could not simply flood the skies with jets
emblazoned with USAF. The rebels needed their own air
force, and Bissell gave it to them.

To create this winged behemoth, Bissell turned to mothballed vintage World War II B-26 bombers owned by the air
force, but they, wary of becoming entangled in this mess, refused to just hand them over. They had to be purchased. The
two sides haggled over the price, like rug traders in a Turkish
bazaar.

Bissell also realized his invading army needed a navy, as he

quite reasonably deduced—they could not walk from Guatemala to Cuba. Now the *navy* refused to cooperate and provide any ships. In order to get his hands on some ships,
Bissell first had to get permission from the Joint Chiefs on
February 10, 1961. The bulk of the rebel navy consisted of
rickety merchant ships chartered from a Cuban businessman
hell-bent on taking out Castro.

The ruling junta at the Pentagon had qualms about the
plan that ran deeper than holding up ships and planes. After
JFK took office, the CIA briefed a committee established by
the Joint Chiefs on their plan. Some plans occupy thick brief-
ing books; others take up just a few pages. This one existed
solely in the minds of its planners—nothing was written on
paper. The Joint Chiefs were stunned. They took notes and
ran it through their own patented invasion process. They
concluded in February 1961 that their plan had about a 30
percent chance of success. Not wanting to look like wussies,
however, they told Kennedy that the plan had a fair chance
of success, without ever mentioning the 30 percent figure.
Even this slight chance required total air superiority and a
popular uprising in Cuba against Castro.

While Bissell hadn't seen the necessity of committing the
invasion plan to writing, the CIA did have its own PR department. Two in fact. At the very beginning the CIA hired
the same guy who had headed the propaganda for the Guatemala operation to reprise his role. His first step was to set up
a propaganda radio station on Swan Island. As backup, a PR
man and his assistant in New York spewed out press releases
dictated from the CIA in the name of a phony CIA "leadership council."

Finally, in early April 1961 the switch was flipped. The
troops were shipped to a port in Nicaragua for transport to
Cuba aboard the chartered Cuban navy. Along the way they
picked up U.S. naval escorts as protection. The force of

1,500 invaders received a joyous, dockside send-off from Nicaraguan dictator Luis Somoza. Viva democracy!

Then Kennedy developed a bad case of cold feet. He sensed problems with the cover story, and at the last second he tweaked the initial air assault, reducing the number of bombers from sixteen to eight. The first assault on April 15, a Saturday, knocked out a large chunk of Castro's air force but still left behind a number of decrepit, British-made fighters.

To create a convincing air of provenance to accompany the first air attack, a rebel pilot flew a CIA-supplied B-26 directly from the invaders' air base in Nicaragua to Miami and, before the assembled press, pretended to be a defector from Castro's air force. The charade dissolved under questioning from the meddlesome free press as it quickly became apparent that the plane had never fired its guns. Also, it had a metal nose; Castro's B-26 bombers were equipped with plastic noses. Bissell was able to fake out the State Department and the United Nations quite a bit easier. While news of the attack swept through the halls of power around the world, the U.N. ambassador Adlai Stevenson, a convenient egghead stooge, was assured by his superiors at the State Department that the "Cuban defectors" were, in fact, pure Cuban, which he unwittingly proclaimed to the world during a U.N. debate.

But the connection between the United States and the plausibly deniable air strike was beginning to reveal itself. Castro declared the United States was behind the strike, and the Russians seconded it. The veil of secrecy was in tatters. Kennedy, always more concerned about upholding the secrecy of the invasion than its success, panicked. So when the time came to approve the next air strike for dawn the following Monday, which of course he theoretically knew nothing about, he canceled it. This air strike would be the one to wipe out the remainder of Castro's air force, and the most critical piece of the operation, if Kennedy wished it to succeed. He still wasn't sure.

With the cover blown for the first strike, a second one would make it plain that the invasion had U.S. backing, once and for all revealing that it was not Bermuda or Morocco behind the invasion, but Uncle Sam. Bissell and other CIA leaders pressed Kennedy and Secretary of State Dean Rusk to allow the attack. But the president didn't budge. And with that one executive decision, JFK sealed the fate of the invasion. It was doomed before the first rebel hit the beaches. In an effort to prevent the world from finding out what it already knew, JFK had flushed the entire operation down the drain. Bissell had failed to fully impress upon the president that the air attack was the crucial element in the whole affair. Kennedy failed to grasp this fact or knew it but didn't care. JFK closed the umbrella.

As the rebel bombers stood down, the doomed invaders churned toward the beach during the early morning of Monday, April 17, blissfully unaware the air strike had fallen victim to JFK's whims. Led by Cuban frogmen whose job was to scout out the beaches shortly before the arrival of the main force, the invaders waited a few miles offshore ready to land during the night. At the last moment, the frogmen were joined by their trainer, Grayston Lynch, a former army special forces officer who had signed on with the CIA in 1960. Lynch was a veteran of the actual D-Day landings and winner of two Silver Stars.

Lynch planned to establish a command post a few plausibly deniable yards offshore. As they neared their landing spot, the frogmen found a well-lit beach and a bodega full of people. Seeing the confidence of the Cubans slipping, Lynch, who was more gung-ho to liberate Cuba than many of his Cuban comrades, steered his dinghy toward a dark stretch of beach. Just before they landed, a Cuban army jeep stopped nearby and swept the area with a spotlight. Lynch opened up with his machine gun, knocking out the jeep and killing two Cuban soldiers. His rattling machine gun had given up the element of surprise, but the frogmen still secured the beach and radioed the rebels to land. Lynch, realizing that nobody was actually in charge of the landing despite months of preparation, took command. The Cubanization of the invasion didn't survive the campaign's first shot.

Shortly after Lynch took out the jeep on the beach, Castro was told of the invasion. He sprang into action and made two phone calls. That call, coupled with Kennedy's refusal to send the second wave of bombers, sealed the doom of the invasion. Castro notified the head of the Cuban military academy and ordered him to take his cadets and repel the invasion. He also phoned Enrique Carreras, his ace pilot, with instructions to attack the invading transport ships with his Sea Fury, a World War II–era propeller fighter. That was all Castro needed to do. He could have gone back to bed.

By the end of that first day, the invaders were pinned down on the beach, their ammunition nearly exhausted, their spirits declining, two of their key ships sunk by the creaky sharpshooter Carreras. Castro kept up the pressure by rushing more troops to the scene.

As a comparison in leadership between the heads of two ideologically opposed systems, the differences were stark. Back in the dynamic States, Kennedy issued orders from his retreat in Virginia; down in the totalitarian state, the dynamic Castro personally joined the attacking columns and took active command of his defenders. He positioned his troops, directed which routes they should take, and kept in constant contact with his military leaders. Kennedy meanwhile was kept apprised of the situation from wire reports that were hours behind the pace of the actual fighting. This distance did not deter Kennedy from issuing orders directing troops on the ground, trying to micromanage the war from the White House. The president made snap decisions without fully understanding their implications, thus putting politics over victory. Castro made snap decisions with a total mastery of the situation focused solely on a quick and decisive military victory. The landing zone happened to be one of the dictator's favorite fishing areas. He was intimately familiar with all its back roads and villages. And he knew that its isolation behind impenetrable swamps made it an ideal location to establish a beachhead. Success depended on speed.

As the situation on the beach deteriorated, just after midnight on April 18 Kennedy broke away from a White House reception to hold a quick meeting in tails. Bissell told him the situation was dire, but one way out existed: send in American jets from the carrier *Essex* stationed off Cuba to clean up Castro's forces. Bissell always expected that when this moment of truth arrived, JFK, a dedicated Commie hater, would openly commit U.S. forces rather than see the operation die. In fact, since Bissell had read the CIA's analysis the year before, he knew this was the only way it would work.

But JFK insisted the United States would not become mixed up in the affair. Admiral Burke, chief of naval operations, snapped at the president that the country was already involved. The president stood fast. Apparently, American involvement to Kennedy meant nothing less than having the White House staff actually machine-gunning enemy tanks. But at this point he was not thinking about victory for the invaders. His focus was trying to save himself politically from what he now realized was a huge mistake. Kennedy told Bissell it was time for the invaders to melt into the mountains and continue the fight as guerrillas. Bissell pointed out that since the invaders were sixty miles from the moun-

E. HOWARD HUNT

Whether he was especially unlucky or just idiotic is not clear, but either way E. Howard Hunt is a two-time loser. First, he played a key role in the Bay of Pigs debacle, as a spy in Cuba trying to organize the rebel political leaders, using the code name Eduardo, a sly attempt to blend in with the Cubans. A decade later, now working out of the basement of the Nixon White House, presumably under his real name, he led the botched Watergate break-in that turned a second-rate crime into the greatest presidential scandal of all time. A good hint that his failures were of his own making comes from the company he kept. His key sidekick during the Cuban debacle was Bernard Barker, the very man who was caught red-handed in the Watergate hotel on that fateful night. With him was the Cuban Eugenio Rolando Martinez. Both men had address books with Hunt's name and phone number alongside the note "W. House." How anyone was able to then link the robbery to the White House with those paltry clues is unknown. As one CIA colleague said, Double Trouble Eduardo had consistent judgment. "It was always wrong."

tains, it was not an option. At this point, on the fifth day of military operations, one can assume Kennedy should have understood the importance of moving the invasion site. A kingdom for Google maps!

Kennedy agreed to one concession, allowing jets from the *Essex* stationed off Cuba to escort the B-26s as they attacked the Cuban airport in hopes of knocking out the few Cuban planes that had been terrorizing the invaders. The jets were not to engage the enemy, but just fly alongside the bombers so as to discourage Castro's planes from shooting the B-26s. The Cubans, however, refused to fly the planes because it was viewed as a suicide mission, so American volunteers— mostly Alabama Air National Guard pilots who had been training the Cubans for the CIA—took the controls. In an invasion that was not supposed to have any U.S. forces,

American navy planes were escorting American planes with American pilots to attack Castro's air force.

In another crowning moment of deskbound operational brilliance, CIA planners failed to realize that Cuba and Nicaragua, where the B-26s were based, were in different time zones. As a result of this oversight, the bombers arrived an hour before their navy escorts, and four were shot down by the same handful of Cuban fighters flying on duct tape and hope. Even the time zones were working for Castro. The rebels held on throughout all of Tuesday, but the situation remained hopeless. By dawn on Wednesday, April 19, the fight was lost. Castro's troops tightened the noose on the rebels. That afternoon, Lynch, who had stationed himself offshore shortly after the landings and assumed the role of de facto rebel field commander, took command of a small landing craft packed with ammuniton and guided it toward shore.

But it was too late. Before he could land, the rebels gave up. Their leader, Pepe San Roman, radioed Lynch that he was destroying his communications equipment and heading for the swamps. Brigade 2506 was no more. The survivors stumbled around the swamps until rounded up by Castro's men a few days later. The spin continued. The exiled Cuban leaders, having learned the PR lessons from their CIA trainers all too well, declared that the invasion was really a small supply operation that had failed to achieve all its objectives. And they swore up and down the United States was not involved.

In all, 114 rebels died and 1,189 were captured. Castro returned most of the captors to the States in late 1962 in exchange for $53 million in drugs and food.

In a ceremony held on December 29, 1962, at the Orange Bowl in Miami to honor the returning fighters, Kennedy prasied their courage and vowed that the rebels' flag would one day fly over a Castro-free Havana.

Eight presidents later, the wait continues.

WHAT HAPPENED AFTER

From the ashes of Kennedy's biggest disaster sprang his greatest triumph. To protect Cuba, the Soviets parked some nuclear hardware in Fidel's backyard. When discovered in 1962 by the United States, Kennedy confronted the Soviets and forced the Russkies to back down and remove the missiles. The Cuban Missile Crisis stands as the world's closest known moment yet to a nuclear exchange.

The failure of the invasion provided Castro with a good cover story to imprison tens of thousands of dissenters, further strengthening his hold on power. Even after the Soviet missiles were removed, Castro has kept a vigilant, paranoid guard against external enemies. Since 1962 he's been waiting for the next invasion to overthrow him.

And for Richard Bissell, the genius behind the whole mess? Bissell left the CIA, with a national security medal pinned on him from Kennedy, and moved back to Hartford, Connecticut, where one can be quite certain no day is ever as exciting as running black ops for the agency. Bissell died in 1994.

THIRTEEN

THE SOVIET INVASION OF AFGHANISTAN

1979

Cars have cruise control. Planes have autopilot. And empires have auto empire control.

Without thinking, empires will respond to the same situation the same way time and time again, disregarding other options that might be better suited. It worked once before, their thinking goes, so let's not mess with the plan. When two superpowers run on reflex and fight a pilotless war against each other, however, the situation is ripe for disaster.

In December 1979, the Soviets invaded Afghanistan in order to prop up its failing Communist regime. Just like in the old days when the Red Army crushed opposition in Hungary in 1956 and Czechoslovakia in 1968, the Russians felt that the philosophy of Marx and Lenin was best taught by tanks machine-gunning the populace, repeating as necessary.

In knee-jerk response, the Americans stepped in and supported anyone, absolutely anyone, who was willing to fight the hated Soviets. The result was a long, bloody, and destructive war that left Afghanistan in ruins, rapidly put the Soviet

Union on the fast track to disappearance, and created a whole new brand of enemy for the United States, just in time for the demise of the USSR.

Two superpowers fought it out, in the last great battle of the Cold War. Both lost more than they could have possibly imagined.

THE PLAYERS

William Casey—Head of the CIA under Ronald Reagan, the devout Catholic took command of the U.S. effort to supply the Afghan rebels and pumped billions into killing Russians.
Skinny—During World War II, he ran the U.S. spy program inside Germany.
Props—Mumbled so badly that few understood what he was saying. Turns out this is a great way to get what you want.
Pros—Killing godless Communists brought him to a state of grace.
Cons—Thought it was a good game plan to team up with the devout *mujahideen*.

Mohammed Zia-ul Haq—Dictator of Pakistan and the gatekeeper for the anti-Soviet operations. After spotting the opportunity, he enriched himself like a good ole American vulture capitalist.
Skinny—Started his life as an officer in the British colonial army.
Props—Murdered his predecessor, Zulfikar Ali Bhutto, made himself dictator, and created an Islamic state. This earned him status as a moderate in the region.
Pros—Spoke with British accent.
Cons—Looked the other way as a mob of students ransacked and burned the U.S. embassy in Islamabad in early 1979. Miraculously only a handful of the 139 employees died.

Ahmed Shah Massoud—The "Lion of the Panjshir," he was perhaps the most successful and famous Afghan to fight the Soviet invasion.
Skinny—Fought the Soviets, the Taliban, and al Qaeda and yet there is no statue of him in Washington, D.C.

> *Props*—Started his jihad against the Soviets with thirty supporters and seventeen rifles.
>
> *Pros*—Took the Russians' best shots and withstood six direct Soviet campaigns to wipe them out.
>
> *Cons*—Declared a truce with the Soviets in 1983.

THE GENERAL SITUATION

The Soviet Union's best export was always puppets. At every opportunity, the tireless revolutionaries in the Kremlin grabbed territory and installed puppet regimes to run the show. And when things went bad, as they usually did, such as the local people realizing they didn't like being an abused and overlorded nook of the Soviet empire, the Russians knee-jerked in their second most successful export, the army.

The knee-jerk strategy became so ingrained in Soviet thinking that it even had a name, "the Brezhnev Doctrine," bathing it in a gloss of scholarship as if produced by professors at Invasion State University. And of course once you create a doctrine, it needs to hit the road every few years so the battery won't die. It morphed into a doctrine looking for a target.

This one popped onto the Soviet radar in the 1970s along its southern border. For the first decades after the end of World War II, Afghanistan, isolated and poor, occupied a minor place in the Cold War. Both the Americans and the Soviets, however, shipped in small amounts of money and advisors to curry favor with Afghan ruler King Zahir.

Earlier, during the 1960s, two competing philosophies swept through Afghan schools and universities—Communism and Islamic fundamentalism. At the same time, the economy started to crumble. As the 1970s dawned, the United States had almost totally withdrawn to focus its nation-building energy on Vietnam.

In 1973, while on a trip to Italy, King Zahir was over-thrown by his cousin Mohammed Daoud, who leaned toward the Communists. The Soviets had, by this time, spent years training and equipping the Afghan army and held considerable influence in the country. And Daoud, seeing that his real opposition came from the Islamists, cracked down on them, and thousands fled to Pakistan. But much to the displeasure of the Soviets, who were expecting to control Daoud, he continued to exert an independent streak, insisting on such radical ideas as Afghans ruling themselves. This was too much for the Soviets. In April 1978, Soviet toadies in the army killed him.

Now the Afghan Communists, led by Nur Mohammed Taraki, took formal command of the country. He began immediately to create a cult of personality and insisted that the people call him the "Great Teacher." To the shock of the Soviet leaders, Taraki took Russian propaganda seriously. He was not content to create a "Brezhnev-style" dictatorship of leaders brooding over a stagnant economy. Instead, he took Lenin's most radical writings literally and began imprisoning and killing his political opponents. Caught by surprise that someone actually believed their own drivel, the Soviet leaders, especially KGB chief Yuri Andropov, cast about for a replacement.

What really alarmed the Soviets was the rise in power of the Islamists. The precocious mountain rebels announced themselves in February 1979 by kidnapping Adolph Dubs, the U.S. ambassador to Afghanistan. Taraki's troops, aided by the always-helpful KGB, succeeded in rescuing him but then managed to get him killed in the same raid. The United States responded by vigorously doing nothing. Taraki still didn't get it. He was too focused on choosing which glorious pose should adorn posters extolling his greatness to realize the Islamic fundamentalists represented his true threat.

By early 1979 the Islamic leaders had started to revolt, and the Afghan army, more loyal to their tribal leaders than Taraki, slowly dissolved to join the rebels. Taraki responded by waging a fight against his fellow Communist goon Hafizullah Amin, the country's prime minister, who contested Taraki for supremacy in the party. In September 1979 Taraki flew to Moscow for meetings with Soviet leaders. Upon his return Amin and his "elite guards" ambushed Taraki, took him prisoner, and had him executed.

Amin, the third to violently take over the country in six years, became its shortest lived. Everyone hated him. The Soviets, perhaps believing their own rumors, thought he was a CIA agent who had successfully infiltrated the Afghan Communist Party. The Afghans saw him as another tool of the Soviets. Amin hated the United States because he failed his PhD exams while a graduate student at Columbia University. The Americans hated him because he hated the United States. Another prime example of knee jerk.

Alarmed by the deteriorating condition of its Communist ally, the Soviets thought of ways to bail Amin out. A jolt of urgency hit their talks when radical students in Iran seized the U.S. embassy, taking fifty Americans as hostages. The Soviets saw the United States had now lost its most strategic ally on the southern rim of the USSR. The Soviets' knee-jerk reaction was to believe the United States would take over Afghanistan as a replacement.

With their usual dearth of planning, Andropov pulled out the KGB invasion template. It would be along the lines of Hungary and Czechoslovakia: some lightning strikes at key installations in the capital—key media posts, government ministries, military bases—a quick change of leadership and long tank columns to enforce the new law and order. After a short time the Soviets would leave and their puppet would rule unopposed. Pull out the old playbook and change the names.

The Soviets, however, were not the first country to invade Afghanistan. Geographically, the country lies between the Middle East, Central Asia, and India, and throughout history it has served as an entry point for invading armies to pass through, looking for someplace better to conquer. First the Persians, and later the Greeks and Mongols swept through the country's steep mountain passes while the hardy tribesmen remained unbowed.

In 1838 the British invaded Afghanistan with an enormous army from India. The goal was to grab Afghanistan before the Russians could, and thereby create a buffer between the sprawling Russian empire and India, the crown jewel of the British Empire. The British quickly captured the major cities of Afghanistan and installed their man as the country's new king. But the Afghans despised their new rulers; they buried their tribal feuds and hatched plans to oust the British in an eerie foreshadow of the Soviet invasion to come.

The Afghans broke into open rebellion in 1841. They cut the British link to India and turned on the British in Kabul. Thousands of troops and civilians were pinned down in their fort and slowly slaughtered. At a conference with the Afghan leader, a deal was arranged allowing the British to leave during the first week of 1842. Immediately, the slow-moving caravan suffered grievously from the harsh cold and attacks by bands of Afghans. The dead mounted over the ensuing days as the Afghan attackers swooped down at them as they staggered through snow-covered mountain passes. The death march lasted a week. One solitary survivor reached the British garrison at Jalalabad. Although the British army returned later that year to exact revenge on the Afghans, the British adventure in Afghanistan had arrived at a ruinous end.

The Soviets did not find this blazing example of defeat germane to their situation. Empire cruise control was turned on, the tanks were gassed up, and they were ready to roll.

WHAT HAPPENED: OPERATION "MASSIVE REFLUX"

The first week went perfectly. The next ten years were all downhill. In early December 1979, the Soviets infiltrated soldiers into Afghanistan to scout out key locations in and around Kabul. They also snuck in their latest puppet, Babrak Karmal, as Amin's successor and stashed him at an air base. Finally, on Christmas Eve the Soviets rolled. The Soviet Fortieth Army—yes, the Russians had lots of armies—crossed the Amu Darya River into Afghanistan as troops deplaned at the Kabul airport. By Christmas morning the army was racing forward. Two days later they entered Kabul, seized the radio and TV stations and key government ministries, and surrounded Amin in his palace. A siege raged over a few hours, but it ended as expected with Amin riddled with Soviet bullets. Another election Afghan-style, this one with Soviet monitors.

As the Soviets clucked over their brilliant stroke, the Afghan warlords and tribal leaders watched in anger. The descendants of warriors who fought Alexander the Great and slaughtered thousands of British troops, sharpened their knives. Once again it became time for them to repel foreign invaders. They put aside their many differences and focused on one goal: kill Soviets. They called themselves *mujahideen*—soldiers of God.

To the Americans, they were soldiers from heaven. Long before Amin was killed, U.S. national security advisor Zbigniew Brzezinski urged President Jimmy Carter to support the Afghan rebels and finally fight the Soviets. The final struggle of the Cold War was on.

This secret war screamed out for one group, the CIA, to take command. Starting with the debacle of the Bay of Pigs in 1961, the CIA had slowly lost credibility and power in the States, and by the late 1970s had fallen to its lowest level of prestige. Things got so bad even Congress was looking over their shoulder. Now opportunity knocked. Afghanistan would become their raison d'être. The CIA was stocked with bitter Vietnam vets who smiled at the thought of arming soldiers to kill the Soviets, a main supplier to the North Vietnamese. And the war would give a flagging CIA a leg up in Washington. As long as day-in-and-day-out Soviets were dying, the CIA was back on its game. Guns for all became their rallying cry.

The U.S. leaders had no illusion the rebels could actually defeat the Soviets. They were happy to just force the Soviets to fight—and die—in the barren mountains of Afghanistan. But the United States had a practical problem. To reach Afghanistan, supplies had to cross Pakistan. Fortunately, the Pakistan dictator, Mohammed Zia-ul Haq shared the American devotion to killing Soviets, as long as he could get a fat cut of the booty.

Zia was a devout Muslim who declared Pakistan an Islamic state when he took command in 1977, but he tempered his religious zeal with heavy doses of political realism. During the struggles within Afghanistan between the Communists and Islamists, he sheltered Islamic leaders, such as Massoud. Once the Soviets invaded, Zia saw both the need and the opportunity to risk a fight. First, he feared getting squeezed between a powerful Soviet puppet on his western border and Pakistan's traditional enemy India on his eastern flank. And by supporting the Islamic fighters he would gain serious street cred in the Muslim world. Once the Americans started tossing money around like drunken investment bankers at a strip club, Zia seized his golden opportunity. He would help the United States fight the Soviets and help himself to unlimited, unmarked CIA cash and military toys. It became a textbook case of doing well while doing good.

As the Afghan resistance geared up with American hardware, the CIA station in Pakistan took control of the U.S.
supply operation. It was a humble, mom-and-pop shop, confined to a handful of people who funneled about $30 million
in cash and arms to the rebels. But to satisfy Zia, the United
States had no direct contacts with the Afghan rebels. Instead,
the money went directly to the Pakistan intelligence service,
ISI, who doled it out as they wished to their favorites. The
CIA didn't know who got what, nor did they care. They were
big-picture Russian killers, not micromanagers.

Zia, seeing the value in his position, turned down a $400
million aid package from the Carter administration. Peanuts!
When Reagan took office in 1981, the money became serious, and Zia got a tidy $3.2 billion package to bolster his
own military and fledgling nuclear weapons program.

On the ground in Afghanistan, the situation quickly
turned bad for the Soviets. Babrak Karmal's army dissolved
further when deserters brought their weapons over to the
rebels. Most of the soldiers had more loyalty to the various
tribes and warlords they were fighting than to Karmal or his
foreign supporters. Uprisings that sprang up in the streets of
Kabul were quieted down by Soviet machine-gun fire. But
like the British 150 years earlier, the Soviets never succeeded
in controlling the harsh mountainous countryside —and
that, as it has throughout Afghan history, is where the resistance thrived.

By the spring of 1980, rebel fighters were ambushing
Soviet army units and honing their hit-and-run tactics. The
Soviets responded by destroying villages and killing civilians,
the knee-jerk superpower plan to win over the local hearts
and minds, as perfected by the United States in Vietnam.

To help the rebels, the CIA scoured the world for weapons
that would not reveal their source. CIA buyers fanned out to
purchase thousands of Soviet-made rifles from Egypt and

Poland, chuckling to themselves over the irony of Soviet weapons killing Soviets. Even better, China proved a major ally in the cause, and the CIA secretly bought thousands of guns from them too, providing the Chinese with a handsome profit. In a war against Communists, a Communist country was engaging in aggressive capitalism to kill other Communists, natch. Oh, the biting irony of clandestine war.

To help the mujahideen, Zia set up training camps along the Afghan border. As the war grew, the entire region became dedicated to the fight with packed camps, warehouses, hospitals, and a road network. The CIA money flowed, and the Pakistan army and ISI partook handsomely from the American swag.

The U.S. involvement increased when President Reagan appointed William Casey to head the CIA in 1981. Casey first joined the spy business during World War II when he commanded the operation by the OSS—the predecessor of the CIA—to run spies into Nazi Germany. Casey deployed a secret weapon to achieve success within the Washington bureaucracy: mumbling. Few could understand him. Tired of asking Casey to repeat himself, people would simply politely nod and agree with him. Reagan himself would give up and just tell Casey to go ahead with whatever mumbled plot he had just hatched. Casey always maintained total deniability that he mumbled. The problem was with the listeners, he thought, all thousands of them.

Casey repeatedly flew to Pakistan to meet with Zia and the head of ISI to take the fight to the enemy. He not only supported the Islamic fighters but, as a devout Catholic, believed a combined squad of Christian/Islamic militants were a sure bet to take down the godless Soviets.

By 1984 Casey ratcheted up U.S. contributions to $200 million, with a matching contribution pledged from the Saudis. Zia funneled the money—after taking his cut—to the

Islamic fighters, virtually excluding the moderates and non-religious elements. One of those excluded was Ahmed Shah Massoud, perhaps the most successful and famous of the Afghan fighters. He came from the Panjshir Valley, a narrow strip north of Kabul along the Panjshir River. A religious Muslim, he fled to Pakistan when the pro-Communist Afghan government cracked down on the fundamentalists in the early 1970s. But unlike other Afghan fundamentalists, he held a more moderate line.

Shortly after the Soviet invasion, the twenty-seven-year-old Massoud took thirty supporters, a handful of rifles, and pocket change into the valley to fight the Reds. The Panjshir Valley occupies an important strategic position in Afghanistan. Along either side stand steep, high mountains where rebels can hide with impunity. From their mountain hideouts they can sweep down and attack Soviet convoys along the Salang Highway, the only route from Kabul to the Soviet Union in the north. This lifeline of the Soviet occupation was laid bare to the crafty Massoud. He captured weapons for his growing army and raided Soviet columns without retribution.

To rid themselves of this pesky rebel, starting in 1980 the Soviets threw attack after attack against Massoud. Each time they had him seriously outgunned; he not only survived but also became stronger. Rebels flocked to him as his reputation as a fighter grew. With his battlefield successes he acquired the very cool nickname of "Lion of the Panjshir."

Frustrated, in 1982 the Soviets launched a massive push and threw 10,000 Soviet troops, 4,000 Afghan troops, tanks, helicopters, and fighter jets at the Lion. But Massoud, tipped off by informants in the Afghan army, hid his fighters in the mountains and swept down on the Soviet column in the narrow valley, slicing them to pieces and capturing tons of equipment. Once again, the defeated Soviets slouched back to the safety of Kabul where they resumed their scorched-earth policy in an already scorched country.

A huge Soviet offensive in 1984 punished Massoud, after he broke off a short-lived truce. The Russians introduced two new weapons: thousands of special forces troops with the skill and dedication to take on Massoud's men in the mountains, and attack helicopters that could withstand anti-aircraft fire. Now it looked as if the Soviets might actually win the war. Massoud barely hung on. By this time the Soviet price for propping up their puppet was more than steep. A CIA report stated the Soviets had suffered 17,000 soldiers killed or wounded, and lost up to 400 aircraft, 2,750 tanks, and 8,000 other vehicles.

The new Soviet weapons forced Casey to push more chips to the middle of the table. More money than ever flowed, with Texas Democrat Charlie Wilson as chief war booster from his perch on the committee that controlled the budget. Casey also sent in sophisticated communications equipment along with experts on explosives and commando warfare. What had started as a mom-and-pop operation had mushroomed into a full-fledged U.S. government agency. It also became impossible to pretend to the Soviets that the United States was not involved. Congressmen inspected training camps in Pakistan, journalists spent weeks with the rebels, and President Reagan, in his best "win one for the Gipper" voice even pronounced the mujahideen "Freedom Fighters." Casey and Zia glowed.

As the war ground on, life for the Soviet soldiers became intolerable. Their enemy were ghost soldiers who appeared from nowhere and just as quickly vanished. Armed with U.S.-supplied sniper rifles, rebels picked off Soviet officers by the dozens in Kabul. Death hung around every corner for the Soviets. Clever bomb makers fashioned plastic explosives into ordinary objects—pens, cigarette lighters, thermoses—

and sold them to the Soviets. Many died while writing letters
home; others were poisoned in restaurants. Soviet morale
plummeted as despair and drug abuse swept the ranks. Word
of the failure seeped into the Soviet press, and the citizens
back home began to notice that their country was fighting a
disastrous foreign war. To stop the slide, the Soviets pushed
Babrak Karmal into retirement and replaced him with head
of the Afghan secret police, Najibullah, the one-named tor-
turer.

As the war expanded, it grew from a Soviet/Afghan fight
into one embraced by the entire Islamic world. Afghan leaders flew to Saudi Arabia for fund-raising tours at mosques
and returned flush with cash. But more important, the Arab
countries sent their young men. Spirited with dreams of fighting the godless invaders, these young men flooded to U.S.-
financed terror camps along the Pakistan/Afghan border
ready to take up arms against the hated Soviets. These rebels
studied the tricks of guerrilla and terrorist warfare from
Pakistani trainers, and absorbed the credo that Islamic fighters should fight all nonbelievers. One of the newcomers was
a tall, very rich Saudi named Osama bin Laden.

As the seventh year of the war sped along, what had been
a secret CIA operation to fund a small group of Afghan fighters had blossomed into a U.S.-financed effort to equip, house,
and train Islamic fundamentalist warriors without any concern where these thousands of soldiers would end up and
who they would fight. Blowback hung in the air.

But the Soviet dream of empire died hard. Seeing that the
rebels needed a more potent weapon capable of destroying
Soviet helicopters and aircraft, the United States began supplying Stinger missiles to the Afghans in the fall of 1986. Few
weapons altered the war as much as the Stinger. Once the
cheap, lightweight, shoulder-fired weapon entered the fray,
they immediately turned the tide against the Russians as the

RECOVERING THE STINGER MISSILES

After the Soviets took off, the CIA realized that it might not be prudent to leave thousands of these deadly missiles in the hands of Islamic terrorists. Congress secretly authorized millions of dollars to buy back Stingers. The CIA, falling back on its old ways, outsourced the process to Pakistan's ISI, who scoured the back roads of Afghanistan looking for anyone with a missile stashed under his bed. The CIA paid between $80,000 to $150,000 per missile, with ISI taking a commission that would make a loan shark blush. In some years the United States spent as much buying missiles as it spent on humanitarian aid in the country. And where did all the money go? To the mujahideen and their new legions who used it to buy more weapons. Despite the recall, the CIA failed to round up all the Stingers. A few made their way to a foreign country where they were dissected, copied, and eventually produced locally. That country: Iran.

rebels knocked down hundreds of Russian helicopters and aircraft. Missile-fear forced the Soviets to keep their aircraft above the missile's 12,500-foot ceiling, meaning they had minimal impact on ground operations. The Soviets never developed a way to counter the Stingers.

Back at the Kremlin, the new Soviet leader Mikhail Gorbachev was doing his best to destroy the empire from within. He knew the country had to undertake dramatic economic reform in order to stay alive and compete with the West. At the same time, Gorby allowed more openness in the country, including more liberalization of the press. As a result, everyone knew the catastrophe that was taking place to the Russian army, but the hard-liners refused to surrender to reality. For Gorby it was not a question of *if* they would withdraw but *when* and *how*, without sparking a coup against himself.

By the end of 1986 the war had blossomed into a grotesque Disneyesque spectacle of U.S.-sponsored terrorist training. The border along Pakistan was swimming in money from the American sugardaddy as volunteers from around the Arab world all tried to muscle in on the Russian slaughter. And Osama bin Laden had taken up permanent residence in Peshawar, the center of the Afghan war effort in Pakistan. Alarm bells failed to ring at the CIA. In fact, they welcomed the new additions to the mujahideen. Guns for everyone.

Looking to get closer to the action, bin Laden moved his operation into Afghanistan. In April 1987 the Soviets attacked his hideout in the mountains just inside the border. His soldiers held on bravely, and bin Laden sustained a slight foot injury. After a few days he and the survivors withdrew to Pakistan. Several journalists chronicled the fight, and bin Laden succeeded in turning this small battle into a public relations bonanza. He toured the Arab world with exploits of his fighters' bravery and quickly became the face of the Islamic jihad against invaders, Soviet or otherwise. Young men willing to die for him flocked to his banner. Massoud fought on in anonymity.

Later in 1987, Soviet foreign minister Eduard Shevardnadze secretly told U.S. secretary of state George Shultz they wanted to withdraw from Afghanistan. Shevardnadze asked for U.S. help, however, as they believed the Islamists were becoming too strong and posed a threat to the Soviet control of their Islamic republics. In exchange for a quick exit, they asked the United States to stop supporting the rebels. Here was a golden moment: the Americans had a chance for a double victory. They would get more than they ever dreamed out of Afghanistan, not just a Soviet bloody nose but also an outright defeat. And, they would get the cooperation of the Soviets in controlling the rise of the Islamic fundamentalists. The kind of help that would possibly cut the threat off before it became serious. The Americans, however, doubted the sincerity of the Soviets. They were blind to any other threats and rejected the Soviet offer, holding on to their knee-jerk view of the world. So entrenched was this knee-jerk thinking that Robert Gates, who took over the CIA after Casey's 1986 death, bet $25 that the Soviets would not withdraw from Afghanistan within a year.

In 1988 Gorby proved Gates wrong. Rather than agree to cut support for the rebels once the Soviets left, the United States sped up arms deliveries. In Moscow the new policy of *glasnost*, or openness, allowed longtime dissident Andrei Sakharov to publicly denounce the Afghan war as a criminal adventure. Gorby's cool draft of honesty had turned into a cyclone of white heat. Other parts of the Soviet Empire took note.

Once the Russians started pulling out, the issue became who would run postwar Afghanistan. The CIA predicted the Soviet-backed leader Najibullah would quickly collapse. To prepare for this they did nothing. Even after Zia died in August 1988, the CIA continued to support his pro-Islamic policies while the Islamic radicals stood poised to snatch power in Afghanistan.

October 1988 saw a leading CIA officer from Afghanistan, Ed McWilliams, deliver his critique to Washington. The report stated that all the money the United States had spent had been hijacked by the Pakistani ISI and used to create a powerful Islamic fundamentalist movement ready to seize Afghanistan and turn it into an anti-American Islamic state. The CIA leaders, angered at his conclusions, recalled McWilliams and tried to sabotage his career.

Soviet troops continued to roll north out of Afghanistan throughout that year. By February 1989 only a handful remained. On February 15, the final vehicles stopped on the Termez Bridge, and Gen. Boris Gromov, commander of the Fortieth Army, left his tank and walked to the Soviet Union into the arms of his son while the international media

watched. What began secretly in the dark rooms of the
Kremlin died in the open, a stunning display of the changes
Gorby's cyclone had wrought. The trusted playbook had
been torn up, the Brezhnev Doctrine shredded, and those
living under the thumb of the Soviet army everywhere no
longer feared the tanks.

Once the Soviets left, the Americans followed, quickly
losing interest in the venture without the fun of killing Russians. They abandoned Massoud and the other rebels, and
mentally blackholed the entire area. After dominating the
CIA's thinking for years, once the Soviets pulled out the
United States left the whole situation for Pakistan to deal
with. Najibullah hung on for three years without his Soviet
backers.

By the end of 1989, the Russians soon realized they had
lost more than Afghanistan. Throughout Eastern Europe,
people who had lived in fear of Soviet tanks stood astride the
Berlin Wall, whacking it with sledgehammers. The invincible
Red Army and the Soviet empire died in the snowy mountains of Afghanistan, and the Soviet Union slipped under the
waves two years later. Meanwhile, champagne flowed at CIA
headquarters, its leaders too drunk on success to understand
the danger of the mujahideen factory they had built. Massoud planned his attacks on Kabul. Bin Laden trained his
troops at American-built bases and honed his recruitment
videotapes. The final struggle of the Cold War was over.

Two superpowers fought. The Russians knew they had
lost. The Americans thought they had won.

WHAT HAPPENED AFTER

In 1986 William Casey suffered a brain seizure and died.
Robert Gates claimed Casey's final words were argh . . .
argh . . . argh. Two years later Zia, still firmly in control of

Pakistan and now one of the most important allies of the United States, died when his private plane crashed, also killing the head of Pakistan intelligence and the U.S. ambassador to Pakistan. While initially foul play was suspected, it was later shown to be an accident.

The Lion survived the war and became a major figure in postwar Afghanistan. Massoud held on as one of the most powerful leaders, and when the Taliban began their sweep through the country in 1994, he retreated to the north where he became the military commander of the Northern Alliance and the sole effective fighter against the Taliban and their al Qaeda allies. Then, during an early weekend in September 2001 he entertained some journalists who turned out to be assassins sent by Osama bin Laden. Their bomb ripped through Massoud. He survived long enough to die on a helicopter taking him to a hospital in nearby Tajikistan. Two days later bin Laden's minions turned their wrath on the World Trade Center and the Pentagon.

★ ★ ★

FOURTEEN

THE FALKLAND ISLANDS WAR

1982

War at its most basic.

No grand principles at play, the great driving force behind twentieth-century wars. Instead, this war was about nationalistic macho: who had more of it and who was going to get pushed around. In an age of aircraft carriers, supersonic jets, and high-tech missiles, it was as meaningless as a schoolyard fight.

Sometimes when one country's nationalism rubs up against another country's, conflict breaks out. Historically, few countries have been as vigorous defending their nationalism as Great Britain. Sneeze wrong on one of its outposts and you can expect a nasty letter from the Queen. When the Argentines grabbed the useless islands in 1982, the British didn't hesitate to sail a big chunk of their navy to the other end of the world to take back the Falklands. The world was shocked, none more than the leaders of the invading Argentine junta, because their citizens were among the few people who knew where the Falklands were and among the even fewer number who cared. At the height of the Cold War, the world was treated to the sad spectacle of a shooting contest between two countries that really had nothing to fight about. And oddly, there was not a Communist anywhere in sight.

THE PLAYERS

Margaret Thatcher—*¿Quién es mas macho?* Nobody beats Maggie. The first woman to head Britain's formerly world-dominating government, the "Iron Lady" was appalled over the spectacularly mistimed Argentine aggression and pushed for the massive military operation to retake the Falklands, despite often being able to communicate with the islands only by relayed ham-radio messages.
Skinny—Spoiled for a fight with the Russians but had to settle for the Argentines.
Props—Pushed the rusty British fleet to its breaking point and beyond.
Pros—Revived British economy and its standing in the world.
Cons—Never confused with Minister Congeniality. Not even third runner-up.

Gen. Leopoldo Galtieri—The ruling head of the Argentine military junta in 1982. He took over in December 1981 when a reshuffling put him in the corner office where he shared the reins on decision making for the country's economic and social policies, as well as who was to be tortured, killed, and made to disappear.
Skinny—While never subjecting the junta to the rude dictates of the electorate, he was nevertheless sensitive to pressure from the public to shore up his poll numbers.
Props—Well liked in Washington where the Reagan administration admired him for his willingness to kill thousands of people on the off chance that some of them may turn out to be Communists.
Pros—Head of the catchily named "National Reorganization Process" as a front for the dirty-war crackdown on the ungrateful populace. Also looked impressive in his uniform while being cheered in front of the palace by huge crowds who imagined they were going to defeat the British.
Cons—Failed to inspire a Broadway show about his life.

THE GENERAL SITUATION

The Falkland Islands lie just outside the Antarctic Circle. The islands are barren, and their most numerous inhabitants are birds and seals. A small number of people, amounting to no more than a village or two, have inhabited the islands for hundreds of years since people first put down roots into its thin soil.

The primary aspect of the Falkland Islands has been their complete insignificance in every way. The islands have no practical use except as a whaling station, weather observatory (although dreary is what people usually observe), or naval coaling station, useful in the rare case your ships still use coal. When English sea captain James Cook discovered the islands, he declared them "not worth the discovery." On the other hand, he did feel it was worthy to note that it was not worth discovering.

Despite this persistent insignificance to humans, the Falkland Islands have been the subject of power grabs throughout modern history. In the 1760s the French, British, and Spanish, all eagerly gobbling up colonies around the world, eyed the worthless islands as an easy addition to an empty quadrant of their colonial empire map. In 1764 the French set up a colony on the islands—followed a year later by the British—with both colonies ignorant of the other's existence. When the French and British discovered each other's heinous presence, the British demanded the French declare their allegiance to King George III. The French spurned their offer and, sensing perhaps their only value existed as an object of desire to the British Empire, quickly sold their interest to Spain.

As the Spanish colony grew, the British colony withered, and in 1770 the British retired, but not before the British foreign office issued its standard diplomatic threat to start a war of honor with Spain. The Spanish agreed to a secret peace treaty that supposedly maintained Spanish sovereignty over the islands while allowing the British to keep their main colony at Port Egmont. This treaty, whose exact terms have never been made public, forms the main dispute over who exactly holds the deed on the insignificant islands.

Despite having their colony restored, the British pulled up stakes in 1774 and continued with their empire building for the next sixty years. During this time the Spanish Empire continued to melt while the British Empire grew to ever-greater glory. Tellingly, the fortunes of both empires were apparently completely unrelated to their respective colonial position in the Falklands.

The dissolution of the Spanish Empire left in its wake a host of new countries in South America, including Argentina, the closest country to the Falklands. The Argentines, a new nation eager to grab its own worthless possessions, declared the Falklands theirs and in 1820 landed a ship to plant their new flag. Soon, colonists established a fishing port, a logical use for the barren islands, but one that proved to be a festering affront for unknown reasons to the maritime-minded English, who were inclined to claim any gathering of dirt protruding above the waves as their own.

In 1833 a British warship swooped down to the Falklands, (known to the Argentines as the Malvinas), claimed them for Britain, and escorted the fisherman-provocateurs back to Argentina. The ousting of the fishermen caused an uproar in Argentina. National honor had been insulted and they vowed revenge.

One hundred fifty years later, the Argentines made their move.

WHAT HAPPENED:
OPERATION "DEFEND THE CRUMBS OF THE EMPIRE"

In 1982 General Galtieri and his fellow juntos were successfully waging the "dirty war" that killed something like
30,000 of their own citizens. Despite the seeming success of
the dirty war, the junta felt that things were not going well
for the country and that happiness was not widespread
throughout the land.

The reason was that although the country had undergone
the junta's "National Reorganization Process," the economy
was still a mess. This fact, combined with the gnawing suspi-
cion that the junta had been responsible for the disappearance
of thousands of citizens, had resulted in many unhappy Argentines. In order to cheer them up, Galtieri and the juntos
came up with the idea of reflagging the Falkland Islands,
humbling the British overlords, and taking revenge for the
ousted fishermen from 150 years ago. Maps of Argentina
always showed the Malvinas as part of their country; many
depicted them as supersized islands lying close to the Argentine shore. Since very few people had actually been there, no
one was the wiser. To Galtieri, taking the Falklands would
restore national pride and make the citizens forget about the
staggering economy and the hordes of disappeared citizens.

After a short period of careful study, the junta came up
with a plan to make a quick invasion, declare victory, and
reap the benefit of the public relations bonanza. Their little
fantasy world failed to take into account the willingness of
England's leader—"Iron Lady" Thatcher—to fight to the
death over insignificant crumbs of the former British Empire.
Her autobiography contains a matchless bit of British understatement, admitting that the Falklands were "an improbable
cause for a twentieth-century war."

The junta gave the nod to a crack team of scrap-metal merchants to spark the invasion by landing on South Georgia Island on March 19, 1982. South Georgia Island is administered by the Falklands governor and lies a thousand miles east of the main Falkland Islands. Its only other claim to fame is that it had been the location of an abandoned whaling station inhabited by a British Antarctic survey team. The determined metal gleaners landed unopposed and brazenly planted the Argentine flag—without informing the British authorities—and then started to aggressively collect metal whaling scrap. The British governor of the Falklands, Rex Hunt, had the scientists confront the scrap harvesters and ask them to have their passports stamped with a British landing permit.

Outraged over the proposed soiling of their passports, they refused, as it would acknowledge the despised British sovereignty. The British governor insisted that the flag be lowered. The Argentines agreed and lowered the flag but still refused to get their landing permits.

In response to the South Georgia invasion, a Royal Navy ice patrol boat, the HMS *Endurance*, was sent with twenty-two heavily armed Royal Marines on board to remove the incursive scrap seekers. The juntos then told the gullible British that the scrap-metal men had left, so the *Endurance* turned around. But the next day the British scientists on South Georgia radioed Hunt saying the Argentines were still there. The *Endurance* made a quick U-turn and stood ready off South Georgia as Thatcher's government told Galtieri to remove his men from the island. Both sides girded for a big confrontation over the tiny island off the small islands.

Galtieri refused to dial down the macho. No self-respecting member of the junta, having successfully dominated millions of unarmed Argentines, would take orders from the British.

The scrap-metal men stayed. The Royal Marines landed and confronted the Argentines. To the juntos this scene was a repeat of the humiliation they suffered in 1833, almost nine short generations ago.

Galtieri countered with an ice-breaker loaded with one hundred marines. They landed the first blows of the war by defeating the British force and occupying the barren island. Casualties during the short, cold fight were minimal, with one Argentine killed and no British deaths. Apparently the soldiers themselves were unaware of the necessity of risking their lives for the worthless islands.

Thatcher, feeling the phantom pangs of empire, assembled an armada to counter the Argentine navy steaming to the Falklands to invade. Meanwhile, the Americans, led by over-reaching power-grabber Al Haig, the secretary of state, opened negotiations with the Argentines to forestall potentially embarrassing hostilities between one of its favorite democracies and one of its favorite military dictatorships. The United States also found itself in somewhat of a corner diplomatically: the Monroe Doctrine calls for resisting European aggression in the Western Hemisphere; America's greatest ally and NATO treaty partner is the U.K., and the United States is bound to defend it if attacked, even if only on the toenail of its former empire.

But the Argentines were not to be deterred. On the eve of the invasion of the main islands, Galtieri refused to take Thatcher crony Ronald Reagan's phone call until after the invasion had already begun. Take that!

On April 2, 1982, the Argentines moved boldly against the main city, Stanley, really just a small town that was home to about half of the island's 2,000 people. To capture the island, which was defended by a few dozen troops, the Argentines sailed virtually its entire navy, including its lone aircraft carrier. The British defended with a garrison of seventy lightly armed marines. The British troops, apparently still not convinced that the Falklands were worth losing their lives over, managed to surrender while suffering only one casualty. The war was on, if just barely.

Al Haig was now dispatched to serve as a "shuttle diplomacist" to mediate the dispute. After two weeks of jetting between London and Buenos Aires, he failed to convince Thatcher to accept a deal that resulted in anything less than restored British sovereignty to the islands, despite the embarrassing fact that the Falkland Islanders did not in fact enjoy full British citizenship.

The idea of giving Argentina sovereignty and leasing the islands back from them was floated again. Since the 1970s the British had considered the idea a neat way to resolve the sovereignty situation without reminding the populace that the empire was evaporating. But the lease-back proposals had been rejected flatly by the Falkland Islanders, so the British government was forced to continue supporting yet another worthless overseas territory. In consequence the Falklanders returned to their forgotten existence. But now that the long-expected but completely surprising and unprepared-for invasion had taken place, the Falklands quickly moved from last to first on the importance scale, like a tiny English soccer team rampaging into first place. Thatcher's view, that "the reputation of the Western world was at stake," now virtually guaranteed that the conflict would hurtle toward a bloody conclusion unless the gang of Argentine dictators backed off. Fat bloody chance.

About to be outmatched by Galtieri, Thatcher raised her own giant naval armada, including an aircraft carrier battle group, to prove Britain was also capable of a grotesquely overwrought military response. The armada also included Prince Andrew, Duke of York, who was not only the third in line for the Crown but also a crack chopper pilot. The task force of more than one hundred naval vessels set sail for the bottom of the planet with the honor of the Western world— the glory of its World War II role notwithstanding—apparently hanging in the balance.

The severity of the overreaction by the British caught the juntos completely off guard. They had fooled themselves into believing that the British would simply ignore the invasion and let the whole situation fade away. They had no idea that the British were unaware that the limits of their empire were now the English Channel—not the shores of Antarctica.

Apparently, the juntos felt that intimidating their own people into submission would turn Thatcher into a weak-kneed girl. They had underestimated the victors of Agincourt, Waterloo, and the Blitz. Throw in Thatcher's concern that being pushed around by Argentina was akin to empire hara-kiri, and it becomes clear why she couldn't resist bellying up to the bar with Wellington, Nelson, and Churchill and telling the world the Big Show was on the road again. The British, still mired near the bottom of their postwar malaise, loved it.

At the same time, the Argentines found a new love for General Galtieri. A hundred thousand cheered him, shining amid the glory of defeating a few dozen British marines. Galtieri, the son of poor Italian immigrants, bettered himself by joining the Argentine army as an engineer. He worked his way up the ladder by joining a coup against the government in 1976, stood on the balcony of the palace, and basked in their love. But perhaps underneath their cheering was the relief that the government was now trying to kill people from someplace else.

Following the capture of the islands, Argentina sent thousands of young, poorly armed and barely trained conscripts to defend their new land. They had little understanding of their role and without proper housing or food, they were highly motivated to simply survive. One would expect a military dictatorship to at least get the military part right, but apparently the bar had been set so low that military expertise was optional. The major qualifications were thick mustaches and high self-esteem.

The Argentines set about folding the islands into Argentina. They forced the 2,000 Islanders, who had staunchly held on to their British traditions, into horrifying acts such as driving on the right-hand side of the road and renaming everything in Spanish. The Islanders rebelled against this outrage by continuing to drive on the left side of the roads and speaking English. One must also assume they continued to drink a lot of tea.

The British task force assembled at the mid-Atlantic island of Ascension (a British territory containing a military base run by the Americans) to begin its execution of its boringly named "Operation Corporate." Haig, still jetting over the Atlantic to tease some personal glory out of the growing mess, failed to secure an agreement.

On April 21 the British, now amped up to full empire mode, began the unnecessary mission of recapturing tiny, remote South Georgia Island and its abandoned whaling station with a force of seventy commandos.

In a preview of the difficulties to come in the last gasp-of-empire, this operation took four days. The first British assault had to be withdrawn when several helicopters crashed in heavy fog into the glacier that dominated the center of the island. The action was halted again when the support ship withdrew in the face of an Argentine submarine found lurking in the area. Finally, on April 25 the British commandos captured the Argentine garrison led by Captain Alfredo Astiz, known locally as the "blond angel of death." He resisted savagely but managed to surrender without firing a shot. The Argentines were forced to abandon their precious scrap metal.

The British then started the main attack by sending over their long-range Vulcan bombers in something oddly called the "Black Buck Raids." These bombers, due to Britian's arthritic post–World War II status, were scheduled to be mothballed without ever dropping a bomb in anger. They required five in-flight refuelings on the way over, an aircraft ballet so complex that the refuelers needed to be refueled themselves, resulting in a total of eleven tankers flying to support two Vulcan bomb-ers. This orgy of in-flight refueling resulted in a single hit on the tarmac of Stanley's only paved airport.

This one-bomb barrage, however, proved powerful enough to spook the shaky Argentines into pulling all of their air-planes from the Falklands and winging them back to the mainland. Since the distance from the mainland to the is-lands would prevent the Argentine planes from lingering over the battlefields for more than a few minutes, the cold and hungry Argentine conscripts hunkered down around Stanley could expect an unchallenged British blitz.

Building on this faint momentum, the HMS *Conqueror*, a British submarine, sank the Argentine light cruiser *General Belgrano*, killing 323 crewmen, just outside the exclusion zone Thatcher had created around the islands. The *Belgrano* was a World War II–vintage survivor (American) of Pearl Harbor and, perhaps fittingly, was sunk by World War II–vintage (British) torpedoes. Half of the Argentine casualties in the war were due to the sinking of the *Belgrano*. The Ar-gentine navy quickly followed its air force back to the main-land, never to reappear. Their ground forces, denied air support, were suddenly without assistance of any kind except for nighttime supply flights into Port Stanley's airfield by

C-130 Hercules planes, the American-made mainstay of junta air forces around the world.

The Argentines, now on the defensive, cannily rejiggered their air strategy: they would use their French Mirage fighter planes to distract the efficient British Sea Harrier fighters and press their attacks with fighters carrying dangerous French-made Exocet antiship missiles.

The French, normally unembarrassable, were actually ashamed of the fact that they had recently sold planes and missiles to the Argentines and promised Britain—to whom they owed much of their existence as a non-German-speaking sovereign state—they would provide intelligence about the Exocet missiles.

Pressing with their new tactics on May 4, a single Exocet missile fired from an Argentine fighter (refueled in midair by an American-made Hercules tanker) sunk the British destroyer *Sheffield*, which was part of the "picket line" protecting the aircraft carriers. The armada's flagship, the aircraft carrier *Hermes*, narrowly escaped a similar fate. As a result, five nuclear submarines were posted just off Argentina's shore to serves as a last-ditch effort at deflecting Argentina's air attacks.

On May 21, 4,000 British commandos finally arrived in force on the northern shore of East Falkland Island in an amphibious landing.

The Argentine air force responded by sinking three British capital ships: the *Ardent*, *Antelope*, and *Atlantic Conveyor*. The sinking of the *Atlantic Conveyor* was the worst blow: it was carrying all but one of the American-made Chinook helicopters that were to be used to ferry supplies to their counterinvasion troops. The counterinvasion was on, but just barely.

Meanwhile, back in England, the BBC, apparently badly

out of practice since the Normandy operation of 1944, off-handedly announced to the world a day before the landing the first target of the British commandos: a position known as Goose Green. Goose Green contained an unpaved airfield on Eastern Falkland Island. The leader of the paratroopers making the assault, Col. "H" Jones, was reportedly incensed over this leak but was killed in the attack before he could file an official protest.

After the tough fight at Goose Green, the British commandos began to advance haphazardly across the fifty-mile-wide island toward the capital, Port Stanley, on the eastern shore. The British found themselves in trouble again due to the difficulty of supplying the troops with the single Chinook helicopter that was left. When some of the commandos commandeered the Chinook (like a stray puppy on a ship, it was referred to affectionately in the British press as "Bravo November") to leapfrog ahead to occupy some vacant villages without orders, they found themselves strung out halfway to their destination without their equipment. Since the equipment was too heavy to be carried, the soldiers loaded it onto ships for ferrying around the island to their advance position within striking distance of Port Stanley—an inlet named Bluff Cove. A disagreement between British officers during unloading as to the exact debarkation point resulted in such a long delay that the troop carriers were caught unguarded by the highly opportunistic Argentine air force. Fifty British troops died in the bombing and strafing.

The Argentine fighters continually surprised the Royal Navy ships out of nowhere as the British, despite having invented radar, proved incapable of creating an effective air defense. The Argentines sank a landing ship, another destroyer (the sister ship to the *Sheffield*), and badly damaged two frigates using plain old-fashioned bombs. The carnage could easily have been much worse except for the fact that

COMMANDER ALFREDO ASTIZ

Widely admired within the junta as one of Argentina's best tortur- ers and known as the "blond angel of death," Astiz was given command of the dozens of Argentine troops on South Georgia Island. When the British assaulted the island, Astiz turned into the angel of surrender. He fought savagely until the moment he surrendered to the British without having fired a shot. After his capture, Captain Astiz was separated from his troops and sent to the U.K. for questioning for his role in the Argentine crimes. He was sent back to Argentina a few weeks later after they decided not to prosecute him. In 1990, Astiz was convicted by a French court in absentia for killing potentially dangerous French nuns in Argentina during the 1970s. In 2001 he was placed on the world- wide Human Rights Watch, because Argentina refuses to extra- dite him to Italy. He remains at large and a threat to a free and British Falklands.

the Argentine pilots had been dropping the bombs from too low an altitude, with the result that many failed to explode (bombs arm themselves in the air after release). This helpful tidbit of information was subsequently tucked into a British Ministry of Defense press release, and the Argentines, who despite other weaknesses were always good readers of their enemy's press releases, adjusted the arming of the bombs with effective results.

At this point, the British had lost six capital ships and still had yet to attack the main body of mostly green enemy troops protecting Port Stanley. Some leaders may have had second thoughts about the invasion. Not the Iron Lady. She remained undeterred in the face of the ongoing diplomacy to resolve the war. Galtieri still felt the love of his people as the juntos were still able to keep bad news out of the press.

The British finally gathered their forces to press their attack on Port Stanley, supported by naval gunfire and artillery. The Argentine forces, lacking a major air force or navy to evacuate them, were surrounded but continued to perform wonders of dexterity with their Exocets, killing thirteen British on the HMS *Glamorgan* by launching one of the fifteen-foot missiles from the back of a truck. They also bombed the British troops at night with their British-made Canberra light bombers.

The British, undaunted by these setbacks and confident of their legendary ability to turn disasters into rousing victories, pressed home their attacks on the hilly outlying areas of Port Stanley on the nights of June 11 and 12.

The battles for Mount Harriet and Two Sisters were tough little fights that took naval gunfire and direct assaults to dislodge the Argentines from well-defended positions behind minefields. The Battle of Mount Longdon was the bloodiest with twenty-three British killed and forty-three wounded. The Argentines lost thirty-one and more than one hundred wounded in this fight.

The next night, the final two battles were fought for the hills directly overlooking Stanley. The Argentine defenders finally took flight but only after facing a British bayonet charge. The bulk of the Argentine conscripts, still cold and hungry from exposure, nearly 10,000 in number, defied Galtieri's order to fight and surrendered en masse on June 14 without engaging the British at all. The Falklands were British once more.

WHAT HAPPENED AFTER

Back in Britain, everyone loved Maggie. The victory propelled the Iron Lady to new heights of power and popularity. British troops paraded through the streets of London as victors for the first time since the end of World War II. The military in Britain received the respect from the population that it had not seen in decades. The victory provided a much-needed shot of optimism into the entire country, and Thatcher rode the victory to a huge Conservative Party majority in Parliament and nearly a decade as prime minister.

The defeat hit the Argentines hard. Little news of the impending defeat reached the public, and the surrender came as a blow to the country's inflamed psyche. The same crowds that had cheered Galtieri now turned on him.

The military failure proved the undoing of the junta and Galtieri. The Argentines suffered 700 dead and 1,300 wounded in their bid to fight a major leaguer. The senseless waste of life and the ignominious surrender signaled the total failure of the junta in a way that the dirty war had failed to do and energized the cowed Argentine citizens into finally standing up to the junta.

Strikes and demonstrations ousted Galtieri as president on June 17 when his fellow generals voted him out. This led to the end of the junta and the country's descent into democracy. Elections were held in 1983. Eventually Galtieri was tried for his role in the junta's crimes and sent to prison in 1986. He died in 2003.

As for the people of the Falklands, their rocky islands finally became a tourist attraction for Britons willing to travel to the ends of the earth for a faint taste of fading glory. In 1983 Falkland Islanders were restored to full British citizenship, and there have been no serious discussions between Argentina and Britain over sovereignty of the islands. A large garrison protects the islands from any further outbreak of Argentine macho.

★ ★ ★

FIFTEEN

THE U.S. INVASION OF GRENADA

1983

In 1980, the American people elected Ronald Reagan president.

He was elected partly based on his promise of making America proud again after the long nightmare of the Vietnam War and the humiliation of the 444-day hostage drama in Iran. A former actor fondly remembered as playing a straight man to a chimp, Reagan felt empowered to accomplish his mission by attacking the Communists wherever they popped up using whatever means he could muster. He was busy.

Reagan's dream required a vastly expanded military. He spent billions to add ships, bombers, tanks, and missiles to the U.S. arsenal. Armed with these new toys, the military leaders could hardly wait to try them out for real on a "deserving" country.

Meanwhile in Grenada, a tiny island at the bottom of the Caribbean near South America, its prime minister Maurice Bishop, under the banner of his "New Jewel Movement," was running the palm-tree-lined country with a Communist government so small and secretive that very few Grenadan citizens realized it was actually Communist. Interestingly, Bishop grabbed power in a coup against the kooky president Eric Gairy while Gairy was in New York trying to convince the UN to hold a conference on aliens. Bishop's main pledge project for the worldwide Communist fraternity became shoehorning a large airport into a corner of the hilly little island with the help of Cuban engineers. It could be used for tourist jets or—more ominously—military planes.

To the rabid anti-Communists in Reagan's administration and the Pentagon, it seemed obvious that the ten-thousand-foot runway was the first step by a brazen cadre of revolutionaries intent on turning the small island into a hub of revolution in the Caribbean. Nothing was done, however, until Bernard Coard, the number-two man in the island's micro-Marxist Party, felt that Bishop was somehow betraying the revolution by not letting him be number one. An American-educated economist who in reality was a crypto-Stalinist, Coard strongly agreed with himself that to further the revolution in textbook KGB style, Bishop should be lined up against a wall and machine-gunned.

The rabidly anti-Communist American government, eager to crush the tiny Grenadan threat and win a clear-cut victory with their new, shiny weapons, realized that hundreds of American medical students lived at Grenada's St. George's medical school, only a few hundred yards from the dreaded runway's edge. In the revitalized military, the United States had the diamond-hard might to get these possibly threatened young men and women, along with their hematology textbooks, safely home. Once Coard shot Bishop and took over, Reagan's anti-Commie crusaders fueled up the jets for a quick weekend invasion in the Caribbean.

No one wanted to miss the fun.

THE PLAYERS

Ronald Reagan—U.S. president, ex-movie star, anti-Communist who revived jingoistic military operation code names.
Skinny—Never let an invasion spoil a good golf game.
Props—Invaded one of Margaret Thatcher's commonwealth countries without her permission.
Pros—Once his aides advised him of a decision he should make, he stood behind it 100 percent.
Cons—Often didn't remember what his advisors had decided for him the day before.

Oliver "Ollie" North—Marine colonel on National Security Council staff and proto anti-Communist.
Skinny—Absolutely never tempted to skip an invasion to play golf.
Props—Hired leggy paper-shredder Fawn Hall as his right-hand man.
Pros—Pledged to defend the Constitution of the United States.
Cons—Believed the Constitution allowed him to do whatever he wanted.

Bernard Coard—U.S.-educated treasury secretary of Grenada's micro-Marxist party who promoted himself to island ruler by killing his predecessor, Maurice Bishop.
Skinny—Practiced a revolutionary theory of "lead the revolution by hiding" when the invasion began.
Props—Very organized, kept his folders stacked neatly on his desk.
Pros—Thought Communist revolution and industrialism would provide a better future for Grenada than tourism.
Cons—Had no idea that the United States could actually invade a country.

THE GENERAL SITUATION

In 1983, American soldiers were patrolling Beirut in a futile effort to establish democracy in Lebanon while desperately trying to fend off Syrian control of the Islamic militias. Nuclear missiles were being delivered to Western Europe to counter the thousands of Russian missiles already in place. The Contras were being funded to battle the Communist Sandinistas in Nicaragua, and the CIA was funding the mujahideen to fight the Soviets in Afghanistan. The Cold War was pretty damn hot.

Also that year the secret micro-Marxist party running Grenada was bubbling with dissent. Cuba had indeed supplied hundreds of engineers to build a giant runway, but island strongman Maurice Bishop's main partner in the government, Bernard Coard, wasn't happy.

Coard, the party's treasury secretary, had studied economics at Brandeis University in Massachusetts and at Sussex University in Britain and had somehow, inexplicably, managed to turn himself into an ardent Marxist hard-liner. Perhaps jealous of Bishop's power, Coard accused Bishop of betraying the revolution, despite the obvious evidence of the giant airstrip being slowly built by the Cuban engineers and the piles of weapons delivered by the Cubans and Russians.

As the money man, Coard knew that the revolution wasn't going well. The 100,000-person island nation was having trouble paying its bills, perhaps because turning it into a tiny version of such giant, failing states as Cuba and Russia was working all too well. Other than the production of nutmeg and some tourism, the one bright spot for the regime was St. George's Medical School, which paid the government a lot of rent. But for a government trying to foment Marxist revolution, relying on a couple of hundred B-level American medical students for funding was embarrassing. One thing everyone understood, however, including Bishop and Coard, was that you didn't mess with the American meal tickets.

The unhappy Coard finally confronted Bishop and bullied him into sharing power. But while he was on a trip, Bishop called Coard from Havana and reneged on the deal. When Bishop returned, Coard placed him under house arrest, which was easy enough because Bishop happened to live right down the street from Coard, on a sort of a Revolutionary Row of Grenada. When word of Bishop's arrest got out, most Grenadans, blissfully ignorant of the intraparty squabbling, were angry that the widely admired Bishop had been pushed out by Coard in the name of the "Communist revolution." Most Grenadans still didn't realize Bishop was a Communist or that any such revolution had taken place. Marches spontaneously began to happen; shops began to close; Fidel weighed in, and he wasn't happy. For five days the situation festered as Coard tried to force Bishop's ouster down his throat. He didn't accept. Realizing that he wasn't as popular as Bishop, Coard hid.

On October 19, a large crowd marched up the hill, past Coard's house, brushing past the armored personnel carriers (APCs) manned by soldiers who fired in the air to scare away the demonstrators. Undeterred, the crowd rescued Bishop. Coard watched from his living room window as the exultant swarm swept Bishop past his house again. The rescuing crowd carried Bishop into Fort Rupert, the army headquarters, on the other side of town.

At this point it was a standoff. Bishop, still getting his bearings after six days of house arrest, didn't move to arrest Coard. Concluding that since the soldiers hadn't fired on the crowd, he controlled the streets and the situation, he relaxed. But Coard grabbed the initiative and went after Bishop.

Under Coard's orders, three APCs drove over to Fort

Rupert, pushing through confused crowds that thought the vehicles supported Bishop. Coard's hastily conceived plan was to make it look like Bishop had thrown a coup and was killed while the government was retaking the headquarters. This would make it more palatable to the citizens who were solidly behind Bishop. It would, of course, just confuse those citizens who asked how the head of the government could coup himself. But no plan is perfect.

When the soldiers arrived at the fort, they machine-gunned the crowd in front, killing dozens, and stormed inside. Bishop was easily captured but refused to die fighting. After checking back with Coard, the army lined Bishop and seven others up against the wall and shot them. Coard had graduated to Stalinist first class.

Coard, who had declined to witness the executions, formed a new government called the Revolutionary Military Council (RMC). Their first official duties were to implement martial law and a curfew, creating great hardship in a country where the revolution had not included providing electricity or refrigerators for many people. Their second duty was to dispose of the bodies of the former government leaders, a two-day process involving a series of trucks and jeeps, and culminating in burning the decomposing bodies in a pit behind a latrine.

Coard, already proving that his style of leading-by-hiding was brutal but effective, now receded even farther into the background as General Hudson Austin, the army chief, was named the head of the RMC. The next day Austin went to the vice-chancellor of St. George's Medical School to assure him that the students would not be harmed. Until then the school administrator was totally unaware that any danger existed.

When news arrived in Washington of Bishop's execution, Reagan's cadre—always on a hair-trigger alert for any Communist provocation, even against other Communists—stood ready. Col. Oliver North, assisted by Fawn Hall, held the post of deputy on the National Security Council staff with the responsibilities of coordinating the various political and military departments. This role put him in a position to influence the legal decision-making process or to safely cut it out completely, as he later did during the Iran/Contra scandal.

On Grenada, however, North saw an opportunity to work within the system. Initially, the military chiefs were against an invasion of a sovereign country, no matter how small, without a really good reason. The students-who-could-easily-be-hostages concerned them, of course, but there hadn't been any reports of actual harm to them. The hard-liners, who were convinced that Grenada was poised to become the nexus of a Communist push into Caribbean tourist hot spots, felt that this was too good of an opportunity to pass up. They recommended an invasion.

The Joint Chiefs, despite being rabid anti-Communists to a man, were reluctant to invade a country even if it was Communist (albeit secretly) and could be conquered in about seventeen seconds. There was virtually no intelligence on the size or composition of the enemy they would face on the ground. The CIA intelligence reports roughly went as follows: the beaches were lovely, the drinks icy cold, the Cubans were building a runway, and yes, in fact, there were American students-who-could-possibly-be-hostages. The one bright spot was that the island had been discovered to be infested with easily beatable Communists who had wandered into their gun sights.

It was a stalemate at the NSC, but North kept pushing. A request was arranged from the Organization of Eastern Caribbean States (Antigua and Barbuda, Barbados, Dominica, St. Kitts-Nevis, St. Lucia, Montserrat, St. Vincent, and Grenada) asking for American armed forces to please invade one of their member states. The fact that Grenada was a fully sovereign nation and a member of the British Common-wealth didn't really matter much.

Over the weekend before the invasion, diplomats from the United States and Britain met in Grenada with RMC leaders and the vice chancellor of the medical school. American offi-cials wanted to get every student out. Evacuating all six hun-dred could not be done by air from the smaller airport in the north, and the larger airport in the south, the new nexus of Communism, was not actually finished, so a commercial jet could not be flown in. A warship was suggested, but the Gre-nadans didn't have any (they didn't have any airplanes either), and they rejected using an American warship as an embarrassment, since it would look like an invasion. Using a cruise liner for the evacuation was posed as an alternative but was never followed through. Essentially, the students had gotten onto the island but could not get off.

The RMC sent two telexes to try to ward off an invasion. The first one was sent to the American embassy in Barbados, not an obvious hub of U.S. foreign policy. It was ignored. The other telex was sent to London, where it arrived at a plastics company instead of the British government because the wrong number had been used. The plastics company called the British government who told them to drop the telex in the mail. There was no follow-up from the Grenadan Caribo-Stalinists, who despite the swirling rumors of an im-minent attack by the Americans, didn't really seem to be paying attention.

Back in Washington, North pushed on with the invasion planning without any formal warnings or notification to the Grenadans, the British, most of the Pentagon, and almost all elected U.S. government officials. The main feature of the plan was that it be secret and quick, a giant hostage rescue operation, to ensure the safety of the students.

The Pentagon had an invasion plan handy, as they do for many countries, but it was tossed aside as not germane. North's vision for the invasion did not include involving such hangers-on as the head of logistics for the Joint Chiefs of Staff, someone presumably critical to planning an invasion, who was not informed. North believed he could not be trusted to keep word from leaking out.

Reagan was presented with the plan on Friday, October 21, 1983, and was so staggered by the enormity of invading another country that he immediately left for a weekend of golf at the famous Masters Championship course in Augusta, Georgia. Rather than involving just the two obvious military branches in the invasion—the U.S. Navy and Marines— North had pumped up the plan to make sure all the branches would get a slice of glory. Nothing brings out the pro-invaders at the Pentagon more than an easy win in the Carib-bean followed by a lengthy beachside occupation.

As it turned out, however, a marine amphibious unit, about 1,600 strong on a flotilla of ships with everything needed for a nice small-scale invasion, happened to be on the way to Beirut, Lebanon. It was quickly redirected to Gre-nada. A navy armada led by the carrier *Independence* also sailed. Army Rangers and paratroopers from the Eighty-second Airborne would catch direct flights from the States and land right on Grenada's giant airfield.

On Sunday morning, October 24, terrorists blew up the marine barracks in Beirut, killing more than two hundred soldiers. Reagan couldn't get his last round in. He flew back to Washington to deal with the emergency. The whole ad-ministration became preoccupied with the enormous crisis in Lebanon, where large, pressing issues of national security were actually at stake. Grenada suddenly became an after-thought. The only thing that resonated with Reagan was that he did not want to repeat the Americans-as-hostages scenario. He did not want to get Jimmy Cartered so close to home. So, he gave the final go-ahead for the Grenada operation: Tuesday was D-Day.

When the commanders got the final orders, the first thing they did was look for their maps. They found that there were none.

WHAT HAPPENED: OPERATION "OVERKILL"

When the commanders of the RMC realized the rumors were true and their nearby superpower was going to invade, they hustled into tunnels under Fort Frederick. The fact that they would also not be able to communicate with their army by radio from inside the tunnels did not stunt their determination to stay safe from the inevitable bombing and strafing that happens when a superpower invades your tiny island.

In fact, they didn't have many troops to command. The main assault force of the RMC was a mobile company of about one hundred men with APC's, two antitank rifles, some mortars, and two antiaircraft guns. There were another dozen antiaircraft guns scattered throughout the island manned by the militia companies. The militias, which in peacetime counted over three thousand strong, had quickly dissolved back into the populace when Coard had taken over, and only about 250 showed up to tackle the superpower invasion. The regular Grenadan army numbered about 500. They had a half dozen or so of the handy APCs with machine guns, manned by brave, bloodthirsty troops, as had been proved emphatically when they wiped out Bishop without hesitation in the name of the revolution.

Castro refused to provide any reinforcements to the 600 or so Cubans at the airport, except to dispatch an officer at the last minute to make sure the Cubans stood firm before the inevitable collapse. Castro was determined to make sure that the rabid anti-Communist, running-dog imperialist generals of the superpower weren't tempted to go island hopping through the Caribbean, issued strict orders only to fire at invaders if fired upon. The RMC, sensing perhaps that fighting a superpower army without radio contact with their own troops could perhaps occupy all of their attention, left the Cubans to handle themselves.

Arrayed against them were thousands of heavily armed, technologically superior, highly trained superpower warriors in planes, helicopters, ships, and vehicles, tracked and untracked. The force was overwhelming. Resistance would be futile. Or so it seemed.

In 1983 the U.S. military was still recovering from the debacle of the Vietnam War. There were not yet precision, satellite-guided smart bombs that promised collateral-damage-free attacks, with streaming video footage to prove it. In order to blow things up with its vast arsenal of rockets, bombs, and artillery shells, Combat Control Teams (CCT)—actual soldiers with binoculars and radios—had to direct the attacks. These spotters were usually accompanied by some of the growing forest of special forces the American military now featured: Army Rangers, army Delta Force, Navy SEALS, and Marine Special Forces.

Special Forces had taken on a life of their own after the failed 1980 mission to rescue the hostages in Iran. With the entire U.S. military establishment desperate to chalk up a victory in the first real action since Vietnam, confidence ran very high. Ollie North's attitude was that coordination was for desk jockeys and ping-pong. But coordination of all these forces on such short notice proved to be complicated and as lethal as the enemy shooting back at them.

In addition to not knowing exactly where they were going, the commanders were not sure who they would be fighting, or how many of them existed. Old tourist maps were pulled out, and anyone who had actually visited the island was labeled an expert. While the maps provided little information on enemy strongholds, they did inform the U.S. commanders where they could rent mopeds.

After careful consideration, American commanders estimated that they would defeat the enemy, no matter how well armed or how many there turned out to be, in one day. They also assumed that all the medical students were at the True Blue Bay campus adjoining the runway. This information, which could have been confirmed by calling someone running the medical school or, perhaps, even a student there, was apparently beyond the operational scope of the mission.

The combination of an almost complete lack of intelligence, a dearth of accurate up-to-date maps of the island, and the scrum of interservice rivalry seemed destined to ensure communication gaps, miscues, and foul-ups. In a bureaucracy, this causes headaches. When that bureaucracy is the military, it causes deaths.

It was a rush to war, but an ambling sort of rush. Like a rusty car sitting on the lawn way too long, the engine of war had trouble turning over.

On the first night, October 23, Navy SEALs and air force CCTs planned a landing on the Point Salines runway to clear obstacles and set up navigation beacons for the incoming wave of troops. Because the invasion was so rushed, these vanguard soldiers were forced to rendezvous with the navy by (1) flying directly to Grenada from the States, (2) parachuting into the ocean, (3) in the dark, (4) somewhat close to the ships (5) from about six hundred feet up, in (6) high winds. The result was that four out of sixteen soldiers drowned, and their small boats, when they finally got aboard, were swamped on the way into the beach. The mission was canceled.

The second night, October 24, the Special Forces again

failed to get the small boats ashore in rough surf. This stung the American commanders. A flotilla of a dozen ships, including an aircraft carrier and an amphibious assault ship loaded with helicopters along with the thousands of soldiers and sailors, stood waiting in the dark off Grenada, held up by the failure to land sixteen (now down to twelve) soldiers on a beach. The Grenadans were winning . . . and they didn't even know they were fighting.

The result of this small failure was that the invasion would have to start during the day of the 25th, a Tuesday. And instead of landing on the massive airstrip at Point Salines, the first wave of invasion troops would have to parachute in. A daylight jump meant no cover, spoiling the element of surprise. Conversely, the only element of surprise for the Americans was how many enemies lurked below.

Fortunately for the Rangers, the Cubans defending the airstrip were more afraid of Castro than the Americans: they held their fire, just as ordered by the maximum leader. This saved the day for the Rangers, who floated down well within range of the Cuban gunners, most of whom were actually construction workers armed with AK-47s, which carried only about one hundred rounds each. Grenadan gunners manning the antiaircraft guns were held at bay by U.S. airpower. The Americans had landed.

The Rangers' goal was to capture the airfield and secure the True Blue campus. By 7:30 A.M. the Rangers rescued the students-who-would-be-hostages from the invisible people-who-could-be-hostage-takers. The Rangers' glee was cut short when they discovered more students living at the Grand Anse campus, between the airport and the capital. Darn! The empire for a campus directory.

The soldiers at the airstrip moved out and captured the Cuban positions around their work camp. At one point the Rangers' advance stalled under the fire of a single recoil-less rifle. Pausing to smash the enemy with an overwhelming display of technology, they called in an air strike but were bedeviled by the miscommunication that was quickly proving to be endemic. Four Marine Cobra gunships, and small two-man helicopters raced in but could not contact the army or air force planes to confirm their targets. Two of the Cobras were finally able to contact a ground air controller but then discovered they had different maps. They finally pinpointed the enemy rifle by a ground soldier using a broad-spectrum photon beacon deflector, known as a shaving mirror in non-military parlance. Unfortunately for the invaders, the parade of ineptitude was just getting started.

In the south, two battalions of the Eighty-second Airborne, the main invasion force of about one thousand troops, finally landed in the afternoon. Meanwhile, marine amphibious units landed in the north, capturing the small, undefended airfield there. But coordination between these groups and the Rangers at Point Salines never materialized. The Rangers found themselves cut off from the commanders on the USS *Guam* as well as the Marine units in the north. Why? Because in the rush to deploy, they had left behind their vehicles containing long-range radios. The radio-free Rangers lingered, reduced to waiting for orders to arrive by telepathy.

Later in the afternoon, the Grenadans boldly counterattacked at the eastern end of the runway in three APCs. Without any air or artillery support, the Rangers easily beat back the attack. American commanders, still lacking firm intelligence on the size of the enemy, worried that many more attacks awaited them.

By the end of the day, when the invasion was supposed to be wrapping up, the radio-free Rangers and Eighty-second still struggled to break out from their positions around the air strip, bogged down by their commander's lethargy. The

BLACK HAWK HELICOPTER

The war saw the emergence of the U.S. Army's newest weapon, the Black Hawk helicopter. Offering a significant upgrade over its predecessor, the Black Hawk allowed the army to transport an entire eleven-man squad right into the fighting, while also pulling out the wounded. And as it proved in Grenada, the chopper can take multiple hits from enemy fire and keep operating. It features an armor-plated cockpit and a cabin that can withstand crashes. Because it's so tough, pilots are not reluctant to fly it into places others would never consider. It even features twin engines in case one is knocked out. This ruggedness has turned the Black Hawk into an international star, and it is the standard helicopter for much of the world's military.

Grand Anse campus, only a couple of miles away, still contained students-who-could-easily-be-hostages. Assessing his troops deployment before his tiny enemy, the commander of the Eighty-second came to a worried conclusion: he needed more overkill. He sent his sweat-stained word up the chain of command: "Keep sending battalions until I tell you to stop."

The other attacks on the first day all shared disturbing signs of nonsuccess. The invaders had three crucial D-Day targets, excluding the newly discovered students not living at the True Blue campus. All these targets were handed to the Special Forces, the cream of the crop of the mighty technological superpower.

The first target was a radio station near the capital. A crack team of Navy SEALs successfully occupied it. But they were quickly counterattacked, by one solitary APC. The SEALs desperately needed an infusion of a massive technological advantage, but unfortunately no air support was assigned to them. The outgunned SEALs, products of some of the most arduous training in the military world, designed to hone them to the hardest edge of military steel, blew retreat and scampered back to the beach to hide. That night, under cover of darkness, the retreating SEALs redeployed farther afield by swimming out to a ship to snuggle under the safety of naval armor. The navy tossed its biggest five-inch shells at the transmitting tower but missed. It didn't matter anyway. The Grenadans were transmitting from their old radio station closer to town.

The second target was the rescue of Sir Paul Scoon, the island's governor general, a well-tanned and glorified ambassador who served as an official representative of the Queen of England. A different team of Navy SEALs was sent to rescue him at the Government House on the outskirts of St. George's. Facing intense ground fire, the brand-new Black Hawk helicopters withstood a baptism of fire but could not land. On the second try they lowered twenty-five soldiers down ropes onto the roof of Government House. The SEALs also found themselves quickly outgunned by more frisky Grenadan soldiers in an APC. Fortunately the SEALs had a Spectre gunship on call, a massively armed cargo plane, which held the APCs at bay. The soldiers, however, could not escape like their brethren. A rescue plan was cobbled together featuring troops still bogged down at the airstrip. What was supposed to be a lightning raid turned into a long siege. At noon the SEALs were still pinned down, the governor general huddled under a table without any relief in sight.

The third target was the Richmond Hill prison, perched atop one of the innumerable hilltops on the island. A tag team of army Delta Force and Rangers was sent to capture the prison and free the political prisoners—without adequate intelligence, planning, or preparation. Once they located the target, five Black Hawk helicopters zoomed into the small mountainous valley to drop the soldiers into the prison until

ERIC GAIRY

If people didn't take what was happening in Grenada seriously for a while, the fault probably lies in Bishop's predecessor, Eric Gairy. During his term as head of Grenada, Gairy turned quite weird and became exceptionally enamored with UFOs. He tried to declare 1978 the year of the UFO, even though *Close Encounters of the Third Kind* premiered in 1977. In fact, while Gairy visited the UN in 1979 to arrange for an international panel to investigate UFOs, Bishop launched his slightly bloody coup for his mini-Marxist party. After twelve years in charge, Gairy was out of work, becoming perhaps the only person actually harmed by UFOs. In 1984 he returned to Grenada and became a perennial election loser. He died on Grenada in 1997.

they realized, belatedly, that no landing areas existed. Worse, the ridge right next to the prison was actually higher, topped by Fort Frederick (where the RMC leadership was hiding in their communications-free tunnels) and dotted with anti-aircraft guns, which had clean, level shots at the helicopters.

The Black Hawks became sitting ducks for every gun at the fort and in the valley. The Grenadans blasted away. The fire brought down one of the choppers, while the others withstood numerous hits. One of the unfortunate pilots who crawled out of the wreckage waving his hat in surrender was gunned down by a Grenadan gunner. Later in the day the navy bombers finally plastered Fort Frederick but failed to dislodge the RMC leaders hiding in the basement tunnels. They did, however, manage to blast a mental hospital next door to the fort, killing seventeen patients and releasing many others to wander the streets.

Back at Government House, the SEALs remained trapped. As the radio communication problems reached a crescendo, a soldier reportedly made a call from the Government House to the Pentagon in order to reach the commanders on the USS *Guam*. In any event, a distinct sense of urgency that the invasion was not up to snuff was now starting to sweep through the U.S. commanders.

They slapped together a quick plan to rescue the rescuers at Government House. The plan featured one company of marines heading over from a north beach landing zone, while another company of marine choppers flew in, without any advance intelligence, of course. The amphibious landing was made at 7:00 that evening; the marines quickly headed out in the darkness with tanks and amphibious assault vehicles crunching down the single-lane roads toward the governor general. They left without their battalion commander, who in the haste wasn't informed his troops had been deployed. He spent most of the night helicoptering around in a desperate bid to find his men.

The first day was almost over. Nearly all the objectives still remained unachieved. Along with rescuing all the students, saving the British governor general had been a top priority—for no other reason than he was British. Neither happened. In addition, Camp Calivigny, the main Grenadan army camp to the east of the airport, hadn't been assaulted. The Grenadan and Cuban soldiers were still shooting back, and somewhere Coard and his Caribo-Stalinists remained unaccounted for. At the end of the day the score was Tiny Tourist Nation 1, Superpower 0.

The score was largely kept secret from the American public. For the first time in American history, journalists had been barred from an invasion. Unbeknownst to the commanders, however, seven journalists snuck into St. George's harbor by blithely sailing in on a boat, where locals greeted them casually. Seven scruffy reporters had succeeded where the entire U.S. military had failed.

The second day of the rescue mission, October 26, dawned

with the Grenadans having pretty much given up. It took a while for the Americans to realize it.

The marines finally rescued the governor general in the early morning after the noise of their vehicles frightened away the defenders. They walked into Government House and relieved the SEALs with no casualties. As originally planned by Oliver North, the governor general signed the backdated letter requesting the invasion. The Pentagon's lawyers rested easy.

Early that morning at Fort Frederick, the leaders of the RMC figured out that the gig was up and gave the order to the PRA soldiers to melt into the populace. The leaders also slipped away, hoping to escape the islands and justice. The marines who showed up to attack the fort walked in unopposed.

South of St. George's the Eighty-second Airborne finally started moving out from the airstrip. They attacked the remaining Cuban positions north of the airfield in the morning with some of the Cubans escaping by scurrying into the Russian embassy. Now they were in position to rescue the students at the Grand Anse campus. The soldiers, finally getting the hang of the screwy invasion, telephoned the students at the Grand Anse campus from the True Blue campus to gather intelligence on the enemy's strength. A medical student who was a ham radio operator at Grand Anse turned out to have one of the most reliable connections to the commanders on the *Guam*. This student turned into a nexus of communication for the invaders.

The first rescue plan was to have Rangers go in and return the students to the airstrip in trucks. But Gen. Norman Schwarzkopf, who had been hastily attached to the invasion as army liaison, came down on the side of overkill. He wanted the Eighty-second sent in on marine helicopters. Grenadan army positions were to be bombarded beforehand for ten minutes. The students were told over the phone to hit the deck while the dormitories were softened up for the assault. Even though unopposed, the United States still managed to sustain casualties as two choppers crashed into aggressively growing palm trees. It had taken approximately thirty-three hours, but almost all of the students were finally rescued.

Camp Calivigny, home of the Grenadan army, to the east of the airport, out past True Blue campus, still loomed as a threat. It was supposed to have been attacked on the first day, but yet it still stood, untouched. Intelligence estimates surmised that 600 Cuban soldiers and maybe some Russian advisors were in the camp. Russians! Probably with guns! It was an embarrassment to the generals in Washington. They would have to be taken out.

Situated at the tip of a narrow peninsula on the southern side of the island and perched atop a rocky plateau rising one hundred feet above the sea, Camp Calivigny was unapproachable from the water. Only one road ran into the fort from the town, making that approach unworkable. It would have to be assaulted by helicopter. The Special Forces girded themselves for a suicide mission.

The commander of the operation helicoptered over the camp before the jury-rigged attack to reconnoiter. He saw no activity but felt no reason to cancel the assault. The commander ordered up a one-hour bombardment from army and marine artillery, naval guns, air force bombers, and C-130 gunships. This crescendo of interagency cooperation, fueled by years of multibillion-dollar Pentagon budgets, would blast the obstinate Grenadans out of their little fort. Then the helicopter-borne Rangers could touch down and mop up. Only the Coast Guard was denied a role in this extravaganza.

The attack began when the 105-mm artillery shells from the army at Point Salines airport missed the mark and fell into the sea. The commander, watching from his helicopter, couldn't adjust the fire because the artillery spotter was not sitting beside him, and the artillery gunners had left their aiming circles back in the States. Then the fight was turned over to the navy. Its guns opened up but were soon silenced by the commander who realized they might hit aircraft flying in the area. So they turned to the air force gunships and navy bombers. Finally, the buildings were blown up and the rubble bounced. The Black Hawks cruised in. One landed in a ditch, shredding a rotor blade, killing three soldiers and badly wounding four others. The Rangers stormed in. Success. But they found an empty camp. The Grenadans had been out fighting the war for the last two days. The Rangers didn't even fire their weapons.

Day three, Operation Overkill rumbled on. A lone Grenadan sniper took a shot at some U.S. soldiers. They happened to be a CCT able to call in air strikes. Normal procedure required them to check with battalion HQ about new targets. They lacked the right radio codes to contact the HQ. But hey, they figured, why not call in the strike anyway. Navy planes screeched through the sky and smashed their target. Whoops. It was a U.S. Army command post, and three American soldiers were injured in the strike.

Even this gaffe didn't kill Operation Overkill. The generals in Washington realized that only half of the hoped-for 1,100 Cubans on the island had been captured. The other half must be hiding in the hills! Patrols were sent up the long, hot, winding roads into the island's jungle interior. The American troops, overloaded with equipment, suffered badly. Dozens dropped from heat stroke as they sweated in their polyester fatigues. The Cubans proved to be phantoms.

In Fort Frederick the Americans captured Coard along with his wife and family, all of whom had been in hiding since the day after shooting Bishop.

The invasion staggered to the finish line. The United States conquered Grenada. The toll was approximately sixty-seven Grenadan dead, twenty-four Cubans. American forces announced nineteen deaths, more than half from accidents, with over one hundred wounded. Special Forces casualties remain secret, except to their pride, which they suffered in public. The medical students returned to school the next semester. Some of the off-campus students had never left.

After it was all over, the Pentagon broke out the one weapon it hadn't fired. It handed out over 30,000 shiny new medals to the victorious American soldiers.

WHAT HAPPENED AFTER

When the last of the troops returned home just days before Christmas, Reagan declared the U.S. military as once again "standing tall." Imagine his pride if the United States had defeated someone really tough, like Barbados. But the invasion did boost the public's mood as people felt good the country had asserted itself and almost killed some Russians. This upbeat mood continued, helping to propel Reagan to a landslide victory in 1984.

Oliver North parlayed his supporting role in Grenada into a starring role in the Iran/Contra scandal three years later, where he became famous for having the snappiest salute in the military. He later ran an unsuccessful Senate campaign, then became a writer and media commentator. He still hates Communists wherever he can find them.

Fawn Hall became the most famous secretary in the United States by loyally shredding documents for Ollie North and telling the world about it. After getting fired she married music manager Danny Sugerman, and the couple shared a heroin addiction. The two eventually kicked their problem and stayed married until Sugarman's 2005 death.

Bernard Coard, who got the entire party started, was tried for the coup and killing Bishop, and was sentenced to death in 1986. That sentence was later reduced to life in prison, where he is to this day, still on the little island he ruled for a week. Even that has not gone smoothly: the prison was destroyed by Hurricane Ivan in 2004, forcing Coard to live in a small prison annex.

★ ★ ★

SIXTEEN

THE SOVIET COUP AGAINST GORBACHEV

1991

Few people ever face the question of how to respond when the life you have created is dying right before your eyes. Do you strike out ruthlessly at the cause of the demise? Do you accept fate and make the necessary adjustments for the impending death of the only world you have ever known? Or do you just sit back and have a couple drinks while it all falls apart, trapped because you know it is useless to resist, like struggling to escape quicksand, but with the full knowledge that no man knowingly becomes the agent of his own destruction.

The men who led the coup against Mikhail Gorbachev in 1991 were faced with this decision. They were the cream of the mediocrities running the Soviet otherworld: leaders of the army, the internal security forces, the government, and the biggest industries in the Soviet Union. Gorbachev's reforms, perestroika and glasnost, were tearing apart their world. How would they respond? What about a coup? It failed spectacularly, despite the fact that these men controlled much of the empire; their entire careers had been dedicated to pulling the switches on the greatest command-and-control system ever devised. The system died on their watch, and their collective failure became a symbol of the fate of the Soviet Union.

THE PLATERS

Mikhail Gorbachev—General secretary of the Communist Party, he tried to reform the USSR's floundering political and economic life but accidentally reformed it out of existence.
Skinny—Appearing in public with his wife established him as new breed of open-minded Soviet leader.
Props—Received the Nobel Peace Prize in 1990 for not invading his own empire as it tore itself apart.
Pros—Believed fervently in Communism.
Cons—Believed fervently in Communism.

Boris Yeltsin—Member of Congress of People's Deputies, president of Russia, inveterate drunk, and expert complainer. Started his rise to power in the Communist Party when Gorbachev noticed how successfully he had demolished the house where the tsars were executed.
Skinny—Believed Russia could fail spectacularly on its own without being yoked to the Soviet Union.
Props—Stood alone atop a tank to defend the nonexistent Russian democracy.
Pros—Ended the Soviet Union.
Cons—Forgot to replace the Soviet Union with something else.

The Coupsters—The cream of the mediocrities manning the repressive organs of the Soviet Empire.
Gennadi Yaneyev—Drunken vice president of the USSR and fat tick living off the Soviet society, he took the lead as figurehead of the coup.
Vladimir Kryuchkov—Head of KBG, many believed he was the prime mover behind the coup.
Boris Pugo—Minister of the interior, he headed the dreaded black-bereted OMON troops.
Valeri Boldin—Gorby's chief of staff and his chief turncoat.
Valentin Pavlov—Heavy-drinking prime minister.
Marshal Dmitri Yazov—Defense minister, who while nominally in charge of the most powerful force in the country, saw his troops flout his direct orders.

THE GENERAL SITUATION

When Mikhail Gorbachev assumed the post of Communist Party general secretary in March 1985, no one had any inkling of the revolution brewing inside him. For all anyone knew he was just another faceless bureaucrat, with a wine-colored stain on his forehead, who had clawed his way to the top of the Soviet political food chain. No one expected anything different from Gorbachev than what had been dished out by the previous Soviet leaders all the way back to Lenin: brutal housecleaning of the previous tenants, bullying of neighboring states, obtuse and indecipherable pronouncements on ways to "reform" or "improve" the massive seventy-year-long train-wreck of the Soviet "command economy," reshuffling of the blizzard of acronyms in the horrifyingly obscure bureaucracy, and, as always, the same bad suits and uninspired neckties. No one expected a genuine attempt at revolution from within, in a state that had supposedly institutionalized revolution and yet seemed to be collapsing in on itself from inertia and vodka.

But that is what Gorbachev, known sweetly as "Gorby" to the Western press, did upon gaining the reins of leadership. "Glasnost" and "perestroika"—openness and restructuring—were his keywords. Gorby's idea was to reinvigorate the gigantic barter-based economy by allowing Soviet citizens to learn some of the brutal truth about the criminal history of their country and to actually think, write, and speak about it. Despite the huge distraction of allowing the public to discuss the Gulags and the endless series of crimes committed by the Soviet regimes, Gorby still childishly believed that the gigantic felonious enterprise that was Soviet society was capable of fixing itself.

After gaining control, Gorby quickly proved that even though he was a skilled political climber, he had a tin ear for running a huge, totalitarian government. His first proposal targeted alcohol reform. Needless to say, in a country where the daily consumption of vodka is vast and as common an experience for the average citizen as standing in line with muddy boots, this was perhaps his most truly radical step. And clearly doomed. The program included new laws for prosecution of people drunk at work, raising vodka prices, and cutting movie scenes of alcoholic consumption. His program succeeded in gashing a hole in the federal budget (as production switched to the black market) and in retrospect was Gorby's first inadvertent step toward the complete dissolution of the Soviet Union. Drinking less did not apparently appeal greatly to Soviet citizens, as the regular overconsumption of alcohol seems to have played a key part to staying inured to a bleak daily life.

Gorby also had big ideas for the economy. His career had started when he helped his father harvest a record crop after World War II on a collective farm near his home in Stavropol, a sleepy farming region on the Caspian Sea. This accomplishment, for which he was awarded the Order of the Red Banner of Labor—a meaningless trinket highly valued by the chaff in the great command economy—apparently imbued him with a lifelong conviction that Soviet socialism could actually work. He held on to this view despite the persecution of his grandparents, who were labeled bourgeois farmers during Stalin's forced collectivization of farms.

Gorby's economic plans were novel in Soviet history because they didn't involve blaming, killing, or relocating large segments of the population for no apparent reason. Harkening back to that successful harvest in 1947, Gorby felt that the time was ripe to allow some measure of freedom for small business operations, know as "collectives." These encompassed such basic things as restaurants, which for the past seventy years the party had considered impossible to

serve someone food outside the home without it being subjected to party control.

In April 1986 the #4 Chernobyl nuclear reactor exploded,
and Gorby was faced with his first major crisis. At first, the
Soviet system responded in reflexive fashion by refusing to
respond. After three days, however, workers at a Swedish
nuclear plant found their work clothes covered in radioactive
particles while duly noting that their nuclear plant had not
exploded. A worldwide search for an exploded nuclear reactor quickly led to the Soviet Union, and Gorby finally confirmed eighteen days later, on television, that there had in
fact been a massive technical malfunction in Chernobyl. This
response, although extraordinarily belated, was at its most
basic an honest one. It was a watershed moment for the
regime.

Establishing a pattern of taking small, achievable steps
toward fantastically impossible goals, in 1986 Gorby allowed Andrei Sakharov, the Soviet intellectual hero and
father of the Soviet hydrogen bomb, to return after six years
of internal exile. This tiny step was the first tacit acknowl-
edgment of the seventy years of murder, terror, and other
errors of the regime.

In 1987 Gorby proposed multicandidate elections and
permitted the appointment of nonparty members to government posts. He also passed laws giving cooperative enter-
prises more independence, although curiously no provisions
were made to provide a functioning political, legal, financial,
or economic framework to support the cooperatives.

Gorby was inadvertently given a boost later in 1987 when
a young West German named Mathias Rust landed a small
plane just outside the Kremlin in Red Square. This embarrassment presented Gorby the opportunity to clean house at
the defense ministry. Gorby's new appointment, Dmitri
Yazov, a World War II veteran, seemed perfect for the dis-

mantling of the massive and inept Soviet army. Yazov later thanked Gorby by joining the coupsters.

Gorby had succeeded in opening a window to clean out the musty smell of Soviet history, but he now found himself subjected to an unending beat of criticism on the slow pace of reform, which came from the growing legion of citizens unsatisfied by their newfangled opportunity to complain in public without being hauled off to a Gulag. Gorby thought they would be thankful and it would spur them on to further reforms. It didn't quite work out that way.

Chief among these critics was Boris Yeltsin, the party leader of Sverdlovsk, an industrial area in the Urals Mountains, and one of Gorby's first political appointments to bite the hand that fed him. Yeltsin was different in that his betrayal began almost immediately, was pronounced publicly, and seemed to have been arrived at through the use of some sort of common sense. Yeltsin, despite an incautious, probing intelligence that had prodded him to disassemble a hand grenade as a youth, costing him two fingers, had risen steadily through the party.

Undaunted by the fact that his father had been tossed in a Gulag with a few million others by the Communists, Yeltsin had joined the party after obtaining his college degree in construction and rose through the ranks in Sverdlovsk to become party boss of the region. His practical achievements, such as demolishing the house where the tsar and his family had been killed by the founders of the party in 1917, were so impressive they brought him to Gorby's attention. Yeltsin was appointed an alternative Politburo member (the real seat of power in the Soviet Union) and the head of the Moscow party apparatchik apparatus in late 1985.

Yeltsin, who perhaps significantly was never given a cute nickname by the Western press, proved to be a master of showboating to a public impatient of the slow pace of reforms. This blatant politicking by Yeltsin annoyed Gorby so much that he found himself reverting to Communistic double-speak and criticized Yeltsin for "political immaturity." Gorby, establishing a pattern, neglected to toss him into the Gulag and soon found himself in the battle that was to define his career.

Yeltsin's criticisms of the glacial pace of reform continued, and by 1987 he so irritated Gorby that the leader stripped Yeltsin of his party job of running Moscow. Yeltsin, however, was handed a get-out-of-jail-free card by Gorby in 1989, when elections for the first and last. Congress of People's Deputies took place. These elections were revolutionary because they were competitive, people actually voted, and few if any candidates received more than 100 percent of the vote. Handily brushing aside a smear campaign intended to wound Yeltsin for being a fall-down drunk, it perhaps backfired and helped his cause. He won a seat to the Congress and was back in the game.

Despite the microscopic advances in democracy permitted by the party, to Gorby's annoyance the republics of the USSR that had been under forcible Soviet rule for decades were still unhappy and continued to press for their independence. In Tbilisi, Georgia, in April 1989, anti-Soviet demonstrations were put down by the Soviet army, resulting in twenty deaths and thousands of injured. The Soviet put-down troops were led by Gen. Alexander Lebed, a tough-as-nails commander who had made his bones putting down disturbances in the Crimea and who distinguished himself by claiming he was one of the few Russians who didn't drink. He was to play a key role in Gorby's coup.

In 1989 the Soviets also finally gave up trying to turn the people of Afghanistan into good Soviet citizens. They declared defeat and drove home. East Germany, also restive and sensing the winds of change in the air, allowed the Berlin

Wall to be torn down in November 1989, which quickly led in turn to Czechoslovakia, Poland, and Romania abandoning the Soviet's camp. The people of Eastern Europe had clearly lost all fear of the vaunted Red Army.

Gorby tried to play catch-up as the countries of the USSR began to willy-nilly declare independence, and he opened up the government to a multiparty system in February 1990. The Lithuanians, whose country had been annexed by the Soviets in the secret protocols to the Hitler-Stalin nonaggression pact during World War II, declared that November 7, the anniversary of the Bolshevik Revolution, would no longer be a national holiday. This was tantamount to giving the middle finger to the Soviet leaders, and Gorby now found his sense of propriety insulted. On January 12, 1991, the Soviets responded by attacking the Vilnius TV tower, led by black-bereted special troops with the James Bond–like name of OMON from their Interior Ministry. Thirteen Lithuanians died. Dmitri Yazov, the Soviet minister of defense and a coupster-in-training, accused the Lithuanians of provoking the army and on his own initiative attacked them. Gorby did nothing to punish Yazov. In March the Lithuanians proclaimed their independence. What had started as an attempt by Gorby to reform the Soviet Union had turned into the disintegration of the empire.

Gorby continued to work on his fantastical plan to rearrange the economy, called the "500-Day Plan," a command-economy answer to creating capitalism. It contained such gems of fantasy central planning as gutting the military-industrial complex, which happened to be the backbone of the economy and the last refuge of the hard-liners. On October 15, 1990, Gorby received the Nobel Peace Prize. With his plan certain to push the hard-liners over the edge, Gorby made the only move that would keep him in power: he withdrew his support for the obtuse plan.

Walking a tight line between true reformers like Yeltsin and the hard-line party men, Gorbachev had little wiggle room. These men were the princes of the Soviet otherworld, marching on inexorably, eyes fixed on the hazy, triumphant past, vacationing on the Black Sea, and enjoying the dubious fruits of the powerful Soviet oligarchs. They had climbed to the top of the gigantic criminal structure by constructing a nonstop barrage of bland, self-serving rhetoric that obfuscated the murderous, incompetent, and criminal actions of the government. They saw no reason to relinquish their grip on a world that gave them meaning.

The reformers saw clearly that Gorby was addicted to the insane logic of Soviet rule in which anything becomes permissible in order to stay in power. Gorby's faith in socialism led him to press on with those reforms that could end only in the dissolution of the empire. The danger was whether the streets would run with blood.

In June 1991 Gorby was informed by American authorities that there was a plot to oust him, which involved his top ministers. Gorby's response was to give the coup-minded ministers a tongue-lashing.

He pressed on, seemingly contemptuous of the dangers. He dotted the i's on the new Union Treaty that would shepherd the former Soviet Union into an absurd federation of independent republics with a single president and army. In a way, the disintegration of the Soviet Union had already begun as each republic had attained a certain autonomy. And when Yeltsin became president of the Russian republic in 1990 and left the Communist Party, he became Gorby's most significant opponent. On the eve of signing this treaty, which the hard-liners feared would radically reshape their world without them at the center, the coupsters made their move against Gorby.

The coupsters had everything going for them. At their fingertips was the institutional knowledge of seventy years of

maestro performances of ruthlessly crushing any and all opposition with brutal, organized efficiency. It was the one job
that their predecessors had always aced, staying in power by
any means necessary. It was truly the fruit of the system. But
the Soviet history of staggering incompetence had finally
caught up to them.

WHAT HAPPENED: OPERATION "COUP WHO?"

Gorby, desperate to pull off his balancing act, surrounded
himself with his betrayers. In August he took a vacation
to his luxurious villa in the Crimea. He had perfectly isolated
himself at a time when he was about to destroy the power
base of the hard-liners he was trying to coax toward democracy.

The coupsters finally made their decision to get rid of
Gorby while meeting at a KGB safe house in a scene more
like a drunken picnic than a devious plotters' den. They had
met before many times to grouse about their Gorby problems
but now, with the Union Treaty to be signed the next day, it
was time to act and for many of them to start drinking. They
arranged to "handle" Gorby, but like the central planning
for the glorious Communist future, which never required
much doing, everything else was left hazy and vague.

The coup, in official Soviet tradition, started with a lie.
The official Soviet News Agency TASS reported on the morning of August 19, 1991, that Gorbachev had resigned due to
an undisclosed illness and that a "state of emergency" committee had assumed power. In fact, Gorby had been confined
to his luxury dacha quite easily, as one of the coupsters,
Boldin, was his chief of staff. Another coupster told him, according to Gorby, "we'll do all the dirty work for you,"
hoping perhaps that Gorby would acquiesce and join them in
overthrowing himself. He told them to go to hell.

The hard-liners had finally acted, but no one had thought to neutralize Boris Yeltsin. Perhaps the coupsters were confused because Yeltsin seemed to be Gorby's enemy, and Gorby was *their* enemy. They didn't realize that the enemy of your enemy can also be your enemy. They also didn't realize how many enemies they actually had. Within hours of the announcement that Gorby had been replaced, Yeltsin evaded the feeble attempt to trap him and made it to the Russian "White House," the seat of power of the Russian republic, where he climbed atop a tank and boldly denounced the coup. Then he disappeared inside to organize the defense.

Down the road at the Kremlin, Vice President Yaneyev had to be bullied into signing the emergency decree giving him power by the rest of the emergency committee. He was a heavy drinker and seemed to be drunk that morning, which perhaps explained his surprising reluctance to sign a decree giving himself massive powers with a stroke of the pen, a chance that most dictators would give up a corner of their empire to win.

At the Russian White House, in the early afternoon, the first human chains were created as protesters grasped hands and faced down a column of small tanks clanking down one of the main avenues. People linked arms and barred the way. The tanks ground to a halt, obviously awaiting orders, as the hatches popped open and the young faces of the drivers appeared. Furious arguments ensued as angry citizens argued with the drivers, who seemed lackadaisical and inclined to neither argue nor attack.

The big battle tanks of the elite Taman Guard rolled in by the afternoon. They had been sent to attack the White House, but led by a general more sympathetic to Gorby than the coupsters; they swung their turrets around and positioned themselves to defend the White House instead. The huge tanks made a fearsome sound when they moved, chewing up the

ALEKSANDR YAKOVLEV

World War II veteran and one-time Russian ambassador to Canada, Yakovlev was plucked from this faraway post and made into Gorbachev's intellectual sidekick and chief advisor. Together they tried to reform the Soviet Union in order to save it. His full-throated promotion of democratic reform earned him the impressively cross-cultural nickname of "The Godfather of Glasnost." But as Gorby placated the hard-liners, the two friends parted ways, leading Yakovlev to bolt from the Communist Party just before the coup after warning Gorby that trouble was brewing. Later, they kissed and made up, and Yakovlev continued to push for democracy and press freedoms in Russia. His achievements were so widely recognized that on his death in 2005 politicians across the political spectrum in Russia praised him for pushing the country forward.

pavement, spewing exhaust, and lurching like bull elephants. The tank drivers, wearing padded leather helmets that made them look like 1920s footballers, chatted and smoked as people leisurely began to gather outside the building.

Slowly, barricades formed in front of the tanks. One man in a suit carried a briefcase in one hand and a long, thin steel rod in the other to add to the barricade. It was a measured and steady effort. People stood staring at the tanks, waiting for them to move, but they didn't. As the afternoon wore on more people sauntered in, although for most of the day the crowd behind the barricades around the White House seemed to be less than a thousand people. A few determined troopers could have sacked the place in fifteen minutes. It was a fantastic sight, though—dozens of tanks seemingly held off by a few hundred people.

The rest of the city didn't seem to be paying attention. Many people were apathetic, as if a coup happened every summer. Life went on as usual. At the Kremlin, where the party still held sway, the limousines came and went. The ceremonial guards stood outside Lenin's tomb, as they had for the last sixty-seven years. Just another day in the USSR.

That evening at around 5:00, desperate to reignite the stalled revolt, the coupsters made their TV debut at a press conference. Missing was Valentin Pavlov, who was too drunk to show up and stayed in bed where he remained for most of the coup. Holding a press conference is usually wrong for a coup. Properly done, a coup communicates with slashing violence and ruthless efficiency. Cramming vague explanations down the throats of testy journalists is the role of elected officials, not revolutionaries. Taking questions instead of shooting questioners revealed their inherent weakness.

It was obvious to everyone that the coupsters looked anxious, indecisive, and a bit preposterous as they sat around a table, hands shaking nervously, fielding questions from journalists. At one point Starodubtsev, the chief of Union of Collective Farm Chairmen, was asked why he was involved. "I was invited, so I came," he replied. Needless to say, rambling pap failed to strike fear into anyone.

As night fell over Moscow and a chilly, misty rain coated the city, the mood at the White House lightened. The barricades bulged as demonstrators pushed trolley cars across the avenues. The air crackled with nervous excitement. People knew they were involved in a grand affair whose outcome was unknown. The crowds had grown to thousands of people. Giant tricolor Russian flags flew. It was an outburst of long-suppressed political rebellion. A group of anarchists, dressed in black, wrapped in their flags, slumped against the building, sleeping. On state television that evening, a long report aired about Yeltsin's tank-top speech and on the growing resistance movement at the White House. A carnival atmosphere floated over the crowd. It was a crazy circus of democracy.

As the evening wore on, the fear of a night attack took hold. The Chinese military slaughter of the protesters in Tiananmen Square only a few years earlier lay fresh in people's minds. Around midnight on side streets, long lines of tanks waited in the darkness, soldiers milling around nervously. If an attack came it would be overwhelming.

The coupsters had given the orders to storm the White House but were refused outright or stalled by the generals, who faced a stark choice. They knew Gorby's regime no longer reflexively protected the men who did the dirty work. It was no longer possible to kill on command and not suffer blowback. Some were bitter about Afghanistan. The army had followed brutal orders from the politicians for a decade and, in the end, the defeat had ruined the army's reputation within the country itself.

Some soldiers had told their officers that they would refuse to attack Russians in Russia. Attacking Georgians in Tbilisi or other minorities far from the Russian center of power was one thing, but spilling Russian blood in Moscow was another. General Lebed, who had led the murderous attacks in Tbilisi, knew that by evening of the first night there were thousands of protesters surrounding the White House, and that any attack would kill hundreds if not thousands. Militarily, it would be an easy attack, but the blood would run in the streets and the ramifications could be catastrophic.

Divided, drunk, and—amazing as it sounds—unsure of how to finish off the coup, the cadre of would-be killers began looking like deer caught in the headlights. There was no brutal certainty in these men, no pistol shots into the back of the head for resisters as there had been for millions of others back in the good old days. Back then, the state-run media outlets like Pravda and Gostelradio had been silenced without hesitation by their mummified leaders who shared the same bleak future of the ossified institutions of the Soviet state.

PERSONAL ACCOUNT OF JUSTIN BURKE

Moscow-based journalist Justin Burke, in his memoirs, described the crowd the second night of the coup:

By this time, the White House crowd had formed a series of human chains surrounding the building. Everyone had been divided into companies of 100 people, each with a spontaneously appointed captain to lead it. The one-day transformation from a rabble into a cohesive and well-disciplined civilian defense force was awe inspiring. I never thought the Russians had it in them to potentially lay their lives on the line for an ideal—not necessarily democracy, but something better than what they had endured for the previous 70-plus years. I spoke with a lot of them that night, and most were admittedly scared. They truly believed that the tanks would be coming during the dark hours before dawn. It had only been a couple of years since the Chinese tragedy at Tiananmen Square, and people figured if the Chinese military could massacre their own people, so could the Russians.

But the new crop of media born during perestroika, Interfax news service, newspapers, radio stations, and satellite TV, continued to operate without interruption. Paper signs inviting citizens to come to the White House and help start a new republic were posted in subway stations and amazingly were not ripped down. The word got out. As people found their way to the White House, it became a giant Be-In. The coupsters had gambled that the massive state apparatus would submit to their dead hands on the levers as it had so many times before, but this time—finally—it wasn't happening.

In a way, it was ironic and somehow completely understandable that Soviet citizens were gaining their first great measure of new freedom in a long time by doing what they had been trained to do by their masters—nothing. Yeltsin's passive resistance was winning. It was nonviolent, a great nondoing. No one was doing anything really, except Yeltsin, and that was very little. A short speech. A raised fist. A refusal to move. But it was proving to be enough. The future of the Soviet Union was hanging by the thinnest of threads.

The people had been inspired, joined hands, stood shoulder to shoulder. It was enough to wilt the coupsters. Their plan had been based on the old Soviet world, and they never considered that anyone—especially not a powerful force such as Yeltsin—would oppose them. And once people blocked their plan, even the few thousands who stood outside the White House, the coupsters lacked the initiative and drive to come up with a backup strategy. They did nothing. Their coup simply melted.

That night there were three deaths, the only deaths during the coup. Someone had opened the hatch on a tank trying to leave town, and the tank drivers killed three people in their panicked reaction. They were the only martyrs that day. There was no river of blood.

During the afternoon of August 21, the third day, when it became clear that generals and troops would not attack Yeltsin, coupsters Yazov and Kryuchkov flew down to see Gorby. Even cut off from the world and surrounded by enemy troops, Gorby knew he was more powerful. He threw them all out and grabbed a plane back to Moscow. The visiting coupsters, unable to think of anything better to do, caught a ride with him. Just after midnight on August 22, Gorby landed in Moscow, stepped off the plane, and the coup ended.

But while Gorby had prevailed, Yeltsin had won. One day later, August 23, Yeltsin suspended the legal status of the Communist Party in Russia. Now it became clear who was really in charge. Yeltsin's move forced Gorby to abandon the position as head of the party. On November 6, Yeltsin banned the party completely in Russia. And on December 31, the USSR simply disappeared at the stroke of Gorby's pen.

The coupsters failed because they broke all the laws of a successful coup, as perfected by their hard-liner heroes of yore in Hungary, Czechoslovakia, and Afghanistan. They hadn't planned lightning strikes against their targets nor dealt ruthlessly with resistance. They hadn't smothered the media, corralled the intellectuals, and stonewalled the foreign press. Yeltsin was even able to speak to foreign leaders, including President George Bush. The coupsters had become trapped in the system just like all the victims they ruled.

In the end, the biggest mistake the coupsters made was that they had attacked the wrong man. It was Yeltsin who put the final spike into the heart of the system. His rise to power wasn't based on better ideas. He cared only about Russia, was honest enough to say it, and brave enough to stand up for it. He was a practical, impetuous man, very often drunk, who in his last years as the Russian president could be found dancing goofily onstage at political rallies, with the self-aggrandizing gusto and hearty irrelevance of a Boston-Irish city councilman. The coupsters lived for their system and wanted nothing more than to preserve it exactly as it had always existed. It was the only world they had ever known. But Yeltsin concerned himself only about Russia, not the whole diseased corpse of the USSR, and the coupsters could not grasp that concept. They, like Gorby, wanted to control the whole stinking system.

The coupsters never saw Yeltsin coming.

WHAT HAPPENED AFTER

The whole incident revealed that Gorby's small steps toward an impossible goal did create something good for the Soviet people. But Gorby himself resisted the inevitable changes he had brought about. After the coup he struggled to remain at center stage but found that Yeltsin had irretrievably replaced him. On the last day of 1991, Gorby signed off on the dissolution of the empire and became another faceless Eurocrat ranging the plains of Europe, his Nobel in tow.

In 1996 Yeltsin was reelected president of Russia and led the country through the chaotic devolution from superpower to a much poorer version of France but with lousy food. After almost ten years of increasingly corrupt governance, the Russian people came to hate Yeltsin for his many faults. He left office in 1999 and died in 2007, virtually forgotten. He had proved finally, alas, to be simply one of them. But for a few glorious days, he had been a democrat.

The coupsters, overall, fared pretty well. Most were rounded up after the coup collapsed. They were convicted for their roles; two years later they were given amnesty by the government. Perhaps it was the reformist nature of Soviet prisons, or maybe they saw the light, but most bought into the new system they opposed and became productive members of the new economic ruling class. Pugo, however, could not handle the strain of the defeat. Distraught over the coup's collapse, the next day, he and his wife committed suicide.

ACKNOWLEDGMENTS

The authors would like to acknowledge everyone who supported and encouraged us during the writing of this book.

SOURCES

CHAPTER 1

Baker, Simon. *Ancient Rome: The Rise and Fall of an Empire.* BBC Books, 2006.

Barbero, Alessandro. *The Day of the Barbarians; The Battle that Led to the Fall of the Roman Empire.* Walker and Co., 2007.

Lenski, Noel. *Failure of Empire, Valens and the Roman State in the Fourth Century, A.D.* University of California Press, 2002.

CHAPTER 2

Payne, Robert. *The Dream and the Tomb: A History of the Crusades.* Stein and Day, 1984.

Phillips, Jonathan. *The Fourth Crusade and the Sack of Constantinople.* Viking Penguin, 2004.

Robinson, John J. *Dungeon, Fire and Sword; The Knights Templar in the Crusades.* Brockhampton Press, 1999.

CHAPTER 3

Chernow, Ron. *Alexander Hamilton.* Penguin, 2004.

Ellis, Joseph J. *Founding Brothers.* Knopf, 2000.

Hogeland, William. *The Whiskey Rebellion.* Scribners, 2006.

Royster, Charles. *Lighthorse Harry Lee and the Legacy of the American Revolution.* Louisiana State University Press, 1981.

Slaughter, Thomas P. *The Whiskey Rebellion, Frontier Epilogue to the American Revolution.* Oxford University Press, 1986.

Sloan, Irving J. *Our Violent Past: An American Chronicle.* Random House, 1970.

CHAPTER 4

Brodsky, Alyn. *Madame Lynch & Friend.* Harper and Row, 1975.

Cawthorne, Nigel. *The Empress of South America.* Random House, 2003.

Gimlette, John. *At the Tomb of the Inflatable Pig: Travels through Paraguay.* Vintage Departure, 2003.

Leuchars, Chris. *To the Bitter End: Paraguay and the War of the Triple Alliance.* Greenwood Press, 2002.

Scheina, Robert L. *Latin America's Wars.* Vol. I. Brassey's Inc., 2003.

Whigham, Thomas. *The Paraguayan War.* University of Nebraska Press, 2002.

CHAPTER 5

Barton, Robert. *A Short History of Bolivia.* Werner Guttentag, 1968.

Farcau, Bruce W. *The Ten Cents War: Chile, Peru and Bolivia in the War of the Pacific, 1879–1884.* Praeger, 2000.

Hunefeldt, Christine. *A Brief History of Peru.* Facts on File, 2004.

Klein, Herbert S. *Bolivia: The Evolution of a Multi-Ethnic Society.* Oxford University Press, 1992.

Scheina, Robert L. *Latin America's Wars: The Age of the Caudillo, 1791–1899,* Brassey's Inc., 2003.

CHAPTER 6

Graves, William S. *America's Siberian Adventure.* Arno Press/New York Times, 1971. First published 1931 by Jonathan Cape and Harrison Smith.

Luckett, Richard. *The White Generals: An Account of the White Movement and the Russian Civil War.* Viking Press, 1971.

Maddox, Robert J. *The Unknown War with Russia: Wilson's Siberian Intervention.* Presidio Press, 1977.

Mead, Gary. *Doughboys: America and the First World War.* Overlook Press, 2000.

Unterberger, Betty Miller. *America's Siberian Expedition, 1918–1920.* Greenwood Press, 1956.

CHAPTER 7

Dornberg, John. *Munich 1923.* Harper and Row, 1982.

Jones, Nigel. *The Birth of the Nazis: How the Freikorps Blazed a Trail for Hitler.* Carroll and Graf, 2004.

Read, Anthony. *The Devil's Disciples: Hitler's Inner Circle.* Norton, 2003.

Shirer, William. *The Rise and Fall of the Third Reich.* Simon and Schuster, 1960.

CHAPTER 8

Farcau, Bruce W. *The Chaco War: Bolivia and Paraguay, 1932–1935.* Praeger Publishers, 1996.

Hughes, Matthew. "Logistics and the Chaco War: Bolivia versus Paraguay, 1932–1935." *Journal of Military History* (April 2005): 411–37.

Klein, Herbert S. *Parties and Political Change in Bolivia 1880–1952.* Cambridge University Press, 1969.

Time archives.

von Schey, Lida. *Estigarribia and the Chaco War.* University of St. Andrews, 1984.

Zook, David H. Jr., *The Conduct of the Chaco War.* Bookman Associates, 1960.

CHAPTER 9

Engle, Eloise, and Lauri Paananen.*The Winter War: The Russo-Finnish Conflict, 1939–40.* Charles Scribner's Sons, 1973.

Jakobson, Max. *The Diplomacy of the Winter War.* Harvard University Press, 1961.

Khrushchev, Nikita. *Memoirs of Nikita Khrushchev.* Edited by Sergei Khrushchev. Penn State University Press, 2004.

Trotter, William R. *A Frozen Hell: The Russo-Finnish Winter War of 1939–1940.* Algonquin Books, 1991.

CHAPTER 10

Ambrose, Stephen E. *The Wild Blue: The Men and Boys Who Flew the B–24s over Germany, 1944–1945,* Simon and Schuster, 2001.

Axworthy, Mark, Cornel Scafes, and Cristian Craciunoiu. *Third Axis, Fourth Ally, Romanian Armed Forces in the European War, 1941–1945.* Arms and Armour, 1995.

Filipescu, Mihai T. *Reluctant Axis: Romanian Army in Russia, 1941–1944.* FTM, 2006.

Sebastian, Mihail. *Journal 1935–1944.* Ivan R. Dee Inc., 2000.

Stout, Jay A. *Fortress Ploesti: The Campaign to Destroy Hitler's Oil.* Casemate, 2003.

CHAPTER 11

Brown, Anthony Cave. *Bodyguard of Lies.* Bantam Books, 1975.

Duffy, James, and Vincent Ricci. *Target Hitler.* Praeger Publishers, 1992.

Donhof, Marion. *Before the Storm.* Translated by Jean Steinberg. Alfred A. Knopf, 1990.

Hitler's Generals. Edited by Correlli Barnett. George Weidenfeld and Nicolson Ltd., 1989.

Moorhouse, Roger. *Killing Hitler: The Plots, the Assassins, and the Dictator Who Cheated Death*. Bantam Books, 2006.

CHAPTER 12

Lynch, Grayston L. *Decision for Disaster; The Battle of the Bay of Pigs*. Pocket Books, 1998.

Pavia, Peter. *The Cuba Project: Castro, Kennedy, and the FBI's Tamale Squad*. Palgrave Macmillan, 2006.

Schlesinger, Arthur M. Jr., *A Thousand Days: John F. Kennedy in the White House*. Houghton Mifflin Company, 1965.

Time archives.

Weiner, Tim. *Legacy of Ashes: The History of the Central Intelligence Agency*. Doubleday, 2007.

Wyden, Peter. *Bay of Pigs: The Untold Story*. Simon and Schuster, 1979.

CHAPTER 13

Borovik, Artyom. *The Hidden War: A Russian Journalist's Account of the Soviet War in Afghanistan*. Atlantic Monthly Press, 1990.

Coll, Steve. *Ghost Wars: the Secret History of the CIA, Afghanistan, and bin Laden, from the Soviet Invasion to September 10, 2001*. Penguin Books, 2004.

Service, Robert. *A History of Twentieth-Century Russia*. Harvard University Press, 1997.

Tamarov, Vladislav. *Afghanistan: A Russian Soldier's Story*. Ten Speed Press, 1992.

Tanner, Stephen. *Afghanistan: A Military History from Alexander the Great to the Fall of the Taliban*. Da Capo Press, 2002.

CHAPTER 14

Anderson, Duncan. *The Falklands War, 1982*. Osprey Publishing, 2002.

Middlebrook, Martin. *The Fight for the Malvinas*. Penguin, 1989.

Romero, Luis Alberto. *A History of Argentina in the Twentieth Century*. Pennsylvania State University Press, 2002.

Sunday *Times* (London) Insight Team. *War in the Falklands: The Full Story*. Harper and Row, 1982.

Thatcher, Margaret. *The Downing Street Years*. HarperCollins, 1993.

Winchester, Simon. *Outposts: Journeys to the Surviving Relics of the British Empire*. HarperCollins, 2003.

CHAPTER 15

Adkin, Mark. *Urgent Fury: The Battle for Grenada*. Lexington Books, 1989.

Sandford, Gregory, and Richard Vigilante. *Grenada: The Untold Story.*
    Madison Books, 1984.
Time archives.

CHAPTER 16

Burke, Justin. Personal memoir (former Moscow correspondent for the
    Christian Science Monitor).
Doder, Dusko. *Shadows and Whispers.* Random House, 1986.
Gorbachev, Mikhail. *Memoirs.* Doubleday, 1996.
New York Times archives on the Web.
Pozner, Vladimir. *Eyewitness.* Random House, 1992.
Remnick, David. *Lenin's Tomb.* Random House, 1993.
Time archives on the Web.

ABOUT THE AUTHORS

Michael Prince was born and raised in New Jersey and went to college and law school at Boston University. He chose to purse a career as a writer after graduating from the Columbia University Graduate School of Journalism. He currently spends his days as an attorney and writer, living in New York with his beautiful wife, Sheryl, and two great sons, Elias and Isaac. For more than 25 years he has been debating and laughing at the obscure and bizarre moments of history with **Ed Strosser**. A native of western Pennsylvania, Strosser also graduated from Boston University and currently resides in New York City with his two wonderful children. After working in book publishing, internet consulting, bartending, and as a handyman, it is with pride that he shares his passion for the dark recesses of history through the weighty yet amusing historical tome that you now hold in your hands.

INDEX

A

Abaroa, Eduardo, 88
Adams, John, 62
Adrianople, 12, 13, 16, 42
aerial combat. *See* aviation and
    aerial combat
Afghan Communist Party, 228
Afghanistan
    and collapse of the Soviet
        Union, 287, 294
    and coups, 297
    Soviet invasion of, xiv, 224–25,
        226–29, 230–40, 240–
        41, 261
Aide-Memoire, 102, 107
Al Qaeda, 241
Alabama Air National Guard,
    221–22
Alaric, 15, 16
alcohol, 47, 284. *See also* Whiskey
    Rebellion
Aleumes of Clari, 38
Alexander the Great, 3
Alexandria, Egypt, 24
Alexius Ducas ("Unibrow"), 32,
    34–39, 41
Alexius III (Alexius Angelos), 21–
    22, 29–32, 41
Alexius IV (Prince Alexius), 18,
    21–22, 27–32, 32–33, 33–
    36
Allegheny River, 46
Altiplano, 84, 97, 141
American Revolution, 47, 51

Amin, Hafizullah, 228
amphibious assaults
    Bay of Pigs invasion, 211, 214,
        215, 218–22
    and the Falkland Islands War,
        253–54
    and the Fourth Crusade, 29–30
    Grenada, 266, 269–71, 275
Andrew, Duke of York, 249
Andropov, Yuri, 227, 228
anti-Bolsheviks (White Russians),
    107, 109, 112, 113
anti-Communism, 258, 259, 264
Antofagasta, Chile, 85–86
Antonescu, Ion, 174–75, 177–79,
    183, 184–85, 187
Antonio López, Carlos, 65–66,
    66–67
Arabian Peninsula, 19
Arbitio, 6
Archangel, Russia, 107
Arctic Circle, 159–60
Arequipa, Peru, 99
Argentina
    and the Chaco War, 142, 151–
        52
    and the Falkland Islands War,
        xiv, 242–43, 245, 246–
        56, 256–57
    and the War of the Triple Alli-
        ance, 68, 69–70, 71–72,
        74, 79, 139
Arica, Peru, 96
Armenia, 7

Army Group Antonescu, 179–80
Ascension Island, 251
assassination plots
    Castro, 209–10
    Codreanu, 177
    Daza, 101
    and the Fourth Crusade, 34
    Hitler, xiii–xiv, 189–90, 191–
        94, 194–204
    Massoud, 241
    in Paraguay, 79
    and the Praetorian Guards, 2
"assumption" deal, 47
Astiz, Alfredo, 251–52, 255
Asunción, Paraguay, 66, 76, 78,
    144
Atacama desert, 83, 85
Athanaric, 6–7, 9
Atlantic Conveyor (cargo ship),
    253
Augustus, 1–2
Austin, Hudson, 263
Austria, 104–5, 106, 156, 176
aviation and aerial combat
    and Bay of Pigs invasion, 213,
        215–16, 217–18, 221–22
    and the Falkland Islands War,
        252–53, 254–55
    and Grenada, 271, 272–74,
        276–77, 277–78
    and Romania, 181–86
    and Russian invasion of Fin-
        land, 170
    and Stinger missiles, 236–37
Ayala, Eusebio, 147

B
B-24 bombers, 181–82, 186
Baldwin IV of Jerusalem, 40
Baldwin of Flanders, 22, 31, 40–
    42
Balkans, 5, 12
Barker, Bernard, 221
Batista, Fulgencio, 207, 208, 213
Battle of Belleau Wood, 111
Battle of Château-Thierry, 111
Battle of El Carmen, 150

Battle of Mount Longdon, 256
Battle of the Bulge, 184
Battle of Tuyuti, 74–75
Battle of Yorktown, 51, 58
Bavaria, 116–17, 123, 125, 126,
    129, 132
Bavarian State Police, 133–34, 135
Bay of Pigs invasion, xiv, 205–7,
    208–10, 210–22, 223, 230
Becerra, Busch, 148
Beck, Ludwig, 190–93, 195–99,
    201–2
Beer Hall Putsch, xii–xiii, 116–17,
    117–18, 118–24, 125–36, 148
Beirut, Lebanon, 261, 266
Benghazi, Libya, 182
Berlin, Germany, 125, 131, 134
Berlin Wall, 287–88
Bessarabia, Romania, 177, 180
Bhutto, Zulfikar Ali, 225
biathalon, 158–59, 172
"Big Oil" plan, 183
bin Laden, Osama, 236, 238, 241
Bird Drop Island, 211
Bishop, Maurice, 258–59, 260,
    261–63
Bismarck, Otto von, 119
Bissell, Richard, 206, 207–8, 209–
    10, 210–18, 220, 223
Black Buck Raids, 252
Black Hawk helicopters, 272,
    273–74, 278
Black Sea, 12
Blanco Encalada (battleship), 86
Blanco political party, 69–70, 71–
    72, 74
blitzkrieg warfare, 159, 180, 190
blockades, 89, 94, 97, 109–10. *See
    also* naval warfare
Bluff Cove, Falkland Islands, 254
Boldin, Valeri, 282, 290
Bolivia
    Chaco War, xiii, 79, 137–38,
        138–43, 144–52, 152–53
    War of the Pacific, xii, 81–83,
        83–86, 86–100, 101, 137,
        139

Bolsheviks, 103, 104–7, 107–10, 112–15, 122, 155, 288
Boniface I, Marquess of Montferrat, 24–25, 37, 39
Bosporus, 29
Brackenridge, Hugh, 54, 55–56, 57, 61
Braddock, Edward, 50, 55
Bradford, David, 54–55, 57, 62
Brandt, Heinz, 193, 197
Brazil
    and the Chaco War, 141, 151
    and the War of the Triple Alliance, 67, 69–70, 70–73, 75–78, 79, 139
Brezhnev Doctrine, 226, 240
Brigade 2506, 212, 213, 222
British Broadcasting Corporation (BBC), 253–54
British Empire, xiv. *See also* Great Britain
Brzezinski, Zbigniew, 230
Bucharest, Romania, 184
Buendia, Juan, 91–92
Bulgaria, 178
Bürgerbräukeller, 124, 125, 127
Burke, Arleigh A., 220
Burke, Justin, 295
Burr, Aaron, 61–62
Bush, George H. W., 297
Byzantine Empire, 19, 21, 27, 29, 43

C
Cáceres, Andrés, 98, 99, 101
Calama, Bolivia, 88
Calderón, Francisco García, 98–99
Callao, Peru, 89
Camarones River, 91
Camp Calivigny, 275, 277
Campero, Narciso, 94, 95–96
Canaris, Wilhelm Franz, 193
Cannae, 16
Carlisle, Pennsylvania, 58
Carol II, 175, 177, 178
Carreras, Enrique, 219

Carter, Jimmy, 230, 232
Carthaginians, 16
Casey, William, 225, 233–34, 235, 241
Castro, Fidel, 206–8, 217, 219–20, 262, 267–68, 270
Castro, Raul, 210
casualty rates
    and the Beer Hall Putsch, 135
    Chaco War, 145, 152–53
    Falkland Islands War, 248, 252, 254, 256, 257
    Fourth Crusade, 42
    Romanian invasion of Hungary, 186–87
    Romanian invasion of Russia, 180–81
    Soviet coup of 1991, 296
    Soviet invasion of Afghanistan, 235
    Soviet invasion of Finland, 163–66, 168, 170, 172–73
    U.S. invasion of Grenada, 276–77, 279
    U.S. invasion of Russia, 108, 114
    Valens's army, 14
    War of the Pacific, 92, 95
    War of the Triple Alliance, 73–74, 79
    World War II, 103, 187
Catholicism, 25, 42–43, 84, 121, 225, 233
cavalry, 13–14, 20, 23, 59, 60, 92
Central Asia, 229
Central Intelligence Agency (CIA)
    and Afghanistan, 228, 230–36, 238–40
    and the Bay of Pigs invasion, 205–6, 207–8, 208–10, 210–22, 223
    and Casey, 225
    and the Cold War, 261
    and Cuba, xiv
    and Grenada, 264
Cerro Cora, 77
Chaco region, 139, 145, 153

Chaco War, xiii, 79, 137–38, 138–43, 144–52, 152–53
Chamberlain, Neville, 193
Chernobyl nuclear accident, 285
Chile
    and the Chaco War, 138, 139–40, 151
    and the War of the Pacific, xii, 81–82, 83–86, 86–100, 101, 139
China, 233
Christianity, 19–20
Church of the Holy Sepulchre, 19
Churchill, Winston, 186
Coard, Bernard, 259, 260, 261–63, 267, 275, 278, 280
Cochrane (battleship), 86, 90
Codreanu, Cornelius, 177
Cold War
    and Afghanistan, 226, 230
    and Cuba, 209, 223
    and Grenada, 261
    Soviet invasion of Afghanistan, xiv, 224–25, 226–29, 230–40, 240–41, 261
Colorado political party, 69–70, 71, 87, 91, 94
Combat Control Teams (CCT), 268, 269, 278
Committee of Public Safety, 51
Commonwealth of Nations, 265. *See also* Great Britain
Communist Party (Russia), 282, 286, 296
Congress of People's Deputies, 282, 287
Conservative Party (Britain), 257
Constantine, 5, 21
Constantinople, xi, 6, 11, 17–19, 27–41
Contras, 261
Cook, James, 244
Corfu, Greece, 28
Corrientes, Argentina, 72, 73
Cossacks, 112, 113
Costa Rica, 212
coups

Argentina, 250–51
Bolivia, 82, 84–85, 87, 94, 138, 142–43, 149
Chile, 82
Constantinople, 29
Cuba, 208
Germany, xii–xiii, 116–17, 118–24, 125–36, 189–90, 191–94, 194–204
Grenada, 259, 262–63, 274, 280
Pakistan, 225
Paraguay, 79, 143, 153
Peru, 87
Roman Empire, 6
Romania, 179
Russia, 105
Soviet Union, xv, 237, 281, 282, 283–90, 290–97, 297–98
Covadonga (ship), 90
Crusades. *See specific crusades such as* Fourth Crusade.
Cuba
    and the Bay of Pigs invasion, xiv, 205–7, 208–10, 210–22, 223
    and the Cuban Missile Crisis, 223
    and Grenada, 259, 261, 264, 267–68, 270–71, 276, 277
Czechoslovakia
    and Beck, 190
    and coups, 297
    German invasion of, 156, 190, 193
    Romanian invasion of, 186, 188
    and the Soviet Union, 224, 228, 288
    and the U.S. invasion of Russia, 106, 108, 112, 113
    and Vladivostok, 108–9, 110

D
Dandolo, Enrico (Doge of Venice), 17–18, 23–30, 33–37, 40, 42

Danner, Jacob Ritter von, 127
Danube River, 9, 12
Daoud, Mohammed, 227
Daza, Hilarion, 82, 85–86, 88, 90–94, 101
Delta Force, 268, 273
democracy, xiv, 123–24, 156, 257, 285, 287
desertions, 6, 10, 14, 25, 90–91, 106, 150, 232
diplomacy, 98, 107, 140–41, 151, 158, 265
Dobrogea, 178
Doge of Venice. *See* Dandolo, Enrico
draft, 9, 74–75, 146, 150–51
Dubs, Adolph, 227

E
East Germany, 287–88
Eastern Orthodox Church, 21, 39–40, 43
Ebert, Friedrich, 120, 131
economics
  Afghanistan, 226
  Argentina, 246
  barter system, 47
  Bolivia, 141, 147
  and the Fourth Crusade, 17–18, 22–41
  Germany, 118–19, 123–24
  Gorbachev reforms, 284–85
  Grenada, 261–62
  Paraguay, 141
  Roman Empire, 5
  and sea-lanes, 86
  Soviet Union, 237, 288
  and the War of the Pacific, 97
  and the Whiskey Rebellion, 44–45, 47, 59
Edwards, Sheff, 209
Egypt, 181
Eighty-second Airborne, 266, 271–72, 276–77
Eisenhower, Dwight, 206, 209
El Salvador, 212
elections, 285, 287. *See also* democracy

England, 118. *See also* Great Britain
Escambray Mountains, 215
Esmeralda (ship), 89
Estigarribia, José Félix, 138, 143–45, 147–48, 150, 153
Europe, x, 66. *See also specific countries*
excise taxes, 45, 48
excommunication, 26, 43
Exocet missiles, 253, 256

F
Fahneneid, 192, 200
Falkland Islands War, xiv, 242–43, 244–45, 246–56, 256–57
federalism, 47, 58–59
Fellgiebel, Erich, 197–98
fertilizer, 81, 83
Fifteenth Air Force, 183
Finland, xiii, 154–56, 156–58, 158–72, 172–73
First Crusade, 20, 22
500-Day Plan, 288
Fort Ballivian, 149–50
Fort Boquerón, 145
Fort Frederick, Grenada, 267, 274, 276, 278
Fort Rupert, Grenada, 262–63
Forty-Fourth Division, 167
Fourteen Point Plan, 106
Fourth Crusade, xi, 17–18, 19–22, 22–41, 41–43
France
  and Astiz, 255
  and the Beer Hall Putsch, 131
  and the Chaco War, 138
  and the Falkland Islands, 244
  and the Fourth Crusade, 15, 22–23, 25, 39
  Franco-Prussian War, 119
  French Revolution, 51–52, 60
  Lynch exiled to, 78–79
  and Romania, 177, 179
  and Russian invasion of Finland, 160, 168–69, 171, 172

France (*cont.*)
St. Cyr academy, 94
and Vladivostok, 107–8, 109
and World War I, 104, 105,
106, 110–11, 118, 123
Francia, José Gaspar Rodriguez
de, 65
Franco, Francisco, 171
Freikorps, 119–20, 122–23, 126–
27, 129, 130
Fritigern, 9, 10, 12–13
Fritsch, Werner Freiherr von, 192–
93
Fromm, Friedrich, 191, 196, 197,
199, 201
Fuentes, Miguel Ydigoras, 211

G
Gairy, Eric, 259
Galatens, 8
Galtieri, Leopoldo, 243, 246–50,
255–57
Garmendia, Anibal Pinto, 82
Gaston, Comte d'Eu, 76
Gates, Robert, 239, 240
Gaulle, Charles de, 138
General Belgrano (ship), 252
Genuine Republican party, 150
Germany
and the Chaco War, 138
coup attempt, 189–90, 191–94,
194–204
economy, 118–19, 123–24
and Hitler's Beer Hall Putsch,
118–24
invasion of Poland, 159
and the League of Nations, 151
and Prussia, 203
and the Roman Empire, 6, 22
and Romania, xiii, 174–75,
176, 181, 185
and World War I, 104–5, 106
and World War II, xiii–xiv
Gestapo, 189, 195, 196
Giancana, Momo Salvatore, 209–10
glasnost, 239, 281, 283, 292
Godin, Michael von, 133

Goebbels, Josef, 199–200, 200–201
Goering, Hermann, 117, 121, 124,
125, 131–36
Golden Horn, 30, 32
"good wars," x
Goose Green, 254
Gorbachev, Mikhail, xv, 237,
239–40, 281–82, 283–90,
290–97, 297–98
Gostelradio, 294
Goths, 4–8, 9–15
Government House, 273–76
Graf, Ulrich, 135, 136
Gratian, 8, 11–12, 16
Grau Seminario, Miguel, 89, 90
Graves, William S., 102, 104, 109,
112–15
Great Britain
and Afghanistan, 229
and assassination plots against
Hitler, 193
and the Beer Hall Putsch, 131
and the Falkland Islands War,
xiv, 242–43, 244–45,
246–56, 256–57
and Jerusalem, 43
and Romania, 174, 177, 179,
181, 183
and Russian invasion of Finland, 160, 168–69, 172
and Vladivostok, 108, 109
and World War I, 104, 105,
106, 110, 111
World War II casualty rates,
187
Great Schism, 21, 27, 43
Greeks, x, 3, 21–22, 26–27, 29–
41, 42–43, 229
Grenada, xv, 258–59, 261–67,
267–79, 279–80
Greuthungi tribe, 10
Gromov, Boris, 239–40
guano, 81, 83, 101
Guarani Indians, 65
Guatemala, 211–12, 216
guerrilla warfare, 98, 162, 208,
210, 212, 215, 220, 236

Guggiari, José P, 144
Guzmán, Jacobo Arbenz, 210

H
Haase, Paul von, 198
Haeften, Werner von, 196–97
Hagia Sophia, 39–40, 42
Haig, Alexander, 248, 249, 251
Hall, Fawn, 260, 264, 279
Hamilton, Alexander, xi, 45, 47,
    49–52, 53–61, 61–62
Hayes, Rutherford B., 79
Heinrich, Wolf, 198
helicopters, 272, 273–74, 277–78
Himmler, Heinrich, 121–22, 127,
    134, 136, 179, 195
Hitler, Adolf
    background, 117–18
    and the Beer Hall Putsch, xii–
        xiii, 116–17, 118–24,
        125–36
    coup attempted against, xiii–
        xiv, 189–90, 191–94,
        194–204
    invasion of Czechoslovakia,
        156
    invasion of Poland, 156, 159
    in Munich, 120
    and the Nazi party, 123
    oath to, 192, 200
    and Röhm, 148
    and Romania, 177, 178–79, 183
    and Russian invasion of Fin-
        land, 155
HMS *Antelope*, 253
HMS *Ardent*, 253
HMS *Conqueror*, 252
HMS *Endurance*, 247
HMS *Glamorgan*, 256
HMS *Hermes*, 253
HMS *Sheffield*, 253
Holocaust, 175, 188
Huáscar (ship), 89, 90
Humaitá, Paraguay, 74–75
Human Rights Watch, 255
Hungary, 25–26, 177–78, 186,
    224, 228, 297

Huns, 4, 9, 15
Hunt, E. Howard, 221
Hunt, Rex, 247

I
Iglesias, Miguel, 99–100, 101
Ilo, Peru, 95
imperial guard, 2, 4, 15
imperialism, xv, 1–2, 58
Independencia (ship), 90
India, 229, 231
Infantry School, 126–27
Innocent III, 21, 22–23, 26, 28,
    42
Iquique, Peru, 89, 92
Iran, 228
Iran/Contra scandal, 264, 279
Iron Guard, 177–79
Isaac II, 21, 31–35
ISI (Pakistani intelligence), 232,
    233, 239
Islam, 19, 20–21, 23, 226–28,
    236, 238–39
Italy, 15, 111, 151, 181, 183

J
Jalalabad, Afghanistan, 229
Japan, 108, 109, 112–13, 114,
    151, 181
Jefferson, Thomas, 49, 51, 61–62
Jerusalem, 17, 19–20, 36, 40, 43
Jesus, 2, 18, 19, 22
Jewish populations, 120–21, 131
Johanitza of Bulgaria, 42
John Paul II, 43
Joint Chiefs of Staff, 216, 264,
    266
Jones, Herbert ("H" Jones), 254
Judaism, 19
Julian, 4

K
Kabul, Afghanistan, 229, 230,
    232, 234–35, 241
Kahr, Gustav von, 123–24, 125,
    127–33
Kannavos, Nicholas, 34–35

Kapp Putsch, 120
Karelian Isthmus, 157, 159, 161
Karmal, Babrak, 230, 232, 236
Keitel, Wilhelm, 196, 199, 202
Kennedy, John F., xiv, 205–6, 207,
        209, 212–14, 217, 219–21,
        222
Kentucky, 62
KGB, 227, 228, 290
Kluge, Günther von, 202–3
Knox, Henry, 56
Kolchak, Alexander, 104, 110,
        112–13, 114–15
Kollaa River, 166
Kollontay, Alexandra, 168
Kremlin, 292–93
Kryuchkov, Vladimir, 282, 296
Kundt, Hans, 138, 145–47, 147–
        49
Kuusinen, O. W., 162, 168

L
La Paz, Bolivia, 88, 96, 141, 144,
        145, 149
La Plata viceroyalty, 68
La Scala Opera House, 67–68
Lake Ladoga, 164, 166–67
Lamas, Carlos Saavedra, 152
land mines, 96
Landesberg prison, 136
Lascaris, Constantine, 38
Latin Empire, 41, 43
League of Nations, 147, 149, 151,
        152, 162
Lebed, Alexander, 287, 294
Lee, "Light-Horse" Harry, 58–59
Lee, Robert E., 58
Lenin, Vladimir, 103–4, 105, 115,
        157, 224
Lido Beach, 24–25
Lima, Peru, 92–93, 95, 97–98,
        100, 101
Lithuania, 288
López, Francisco Solano, xi–xii,
        63–64, 65–70, 70–78, 79–
        80, 139
Lossow, Otto von, 124, 127–32

Louis of Blois, 22, 42
Louis XVI, 51
Louisiana, 62
Löwenbräukeller, 127
Ludendorff, Erich
    and the Beer Hall Putsch, 117–
        18, 120, 124, 126, 128–
        30, 132–35
    and U.S. invasion of Russia,
        109–11
Lupicinus, 10
Lynch, Eliza, 63, 64, 66–70, 70–
        71, 73, 75–76, 78–80, 139
Lynch, Grayston, 218–19, 222

M
Maheu, Robert, 209
Malgarejo, Mariano, 84
Malvinas Islands, 245
Mannerheim, Carl Gustav, 155–
        56, 157–58, 160, 162, 164–
        66, 171, 172–73
Mannerheim Line, 158, 159, 163–
        65
Marcianople, 10
Marienplatz, 127, 135
Martinez, Eugenio Rolando, 221
Martínez de Irala, Domingo, 65
Marx, Karl, 224
Massoud, Ahmed Shah, 225–26,
        231, 234–35, 238, 240, 241
McCarthy, Joseph, 103
McWilliams, Ed, 239
media, 133–34, 294–95, 297
Mein Kampf (Hitler), 136
Mesopotamia, 11
Miami Herald, 212
Middle Ages, 20
Middle East, 229
Mihai of Romania, 175–76, 184–
        85, 187
Militia Act, 49–50, 53, 54, 56
Mingo Creek Association, 48, 52,
        54
Mississippi River, 62
Mitre, Bartolomé, 72, 74
modernization, 67

Molotov, Vyacheslav, 158, 171, 185
Molotov cocktails, 162–63, 171
monarchism, 52, 124, 126, 132
Mongols, 229
Monongahela River, 46
Monroe, Marilyn, 207
Monroe Doctrine, 248
Montero, Lizardo, 92, 93–94, 96, 99
Morales, Agustín, 84
Mount Potosi, 84
Muhammad, 19
mujahideen, 225, 230, 233, 235, 238, 240, 261
Munich, Germany, 116–17, 122–24, 126–27, 134–35
Murmansk, Russia, 107

N
Najibullah, Mohammed, 236, 239, 240
National Gazette, 49, 52
National Reorganization Process, 243, 246
National Security Council (NSC), 264
nationalism, 58, 101, 174, 242, 258, 279
Native Americans, 44, 46, 55
naval warfare
    and Bay of Pigs invasion, 215–16
    and the Chaco War, 142
    and the Falkland Islands War, 252, 255–56
    and the Fourth Crusade, 17, 23, 30, 37
    and Grenada invasion, 269–70, 271
    and U.S. invasion of Russia, 109–10
    and the War of the Pacific, xii, 86–90, 97
Nazi party
    and the Beer Hall Putsch, 119–20, 122–23, 124, 126–28, 131, 134–35

    and coup attempt, 198
    and Finland, 172–73
    and the German military, 192–94, 195
    and Hitler, 117
    and Röhm, 148
    and Romania, 177
    and Von Godin, 133
Nazi-Soviet Nonagression Pact, 156, 288
Neville, John, 49, 50, 52, 53–54
New Jersey horse troop, 60
New Jewel Movement, 258–59
New York City, 47
New York Times, 134, 212
Nicaragua, 216–17, 261
Nixon, Richard, 206, 208, 209, 221
Nobel Peace Prize, 152, 282, 288
North, Oliver, 260, 264, 265–66, 268, 276, 279
North Africa, 181–82
North Atlantic Treaty Organization (NATO), 248
Northern Alliance, 241
Northern Bukovina, Romania, 177, 180
Norway, 168
nuclear weapons, 175, 188, 209, 223, 232, 285

O
Oberkommando der Wehrmacht (OKW), 192
Oberkommando des Heeres (OKH), 192
O'Connell, James, 209
Odeonplatz, 135, 136
Odessa, Russia, 180
Office of Strategic Services (OSS), 206, 233
Ohio River, 46, 52, 54, 60, 62
oil, 179, 180–86, 188
Olbricht, Friedrich, 195–99, 201
Omsk, Russia, 108, 112, 113
Operation Corporate, 251
Operation Dirty Boots, 211

Operation Valkyrie, 195, 197–99
Order of the Red Banner of Labor, 284
Organization of Eastern Caribbean States, 264–65
Ostrogoths, 15

P
Pajari, Aaro, 164
Pakistan, 225, 227, 231–32, 233, 235, 238–41
Panjshir Valley, 234
Panzers, 183
Paraguay
  and the Chaco War, xiii, 79, 137–38, 138–43, 144–52, 152–53
  and the War of the Triple Alliance, xi–xii, 63–64, 64–70, 70–78, 78–80
Paraguay River, 70, 74, 75, 153
Paraná River, 71–72
Paris, France, 110–11
Parkinson's Ferry, 57
Pavlov, Valentin, 282, 293
Pearl Harbor, 181
Pedro II, 67
Pennsylvania, 47–48, 50, 52, 58, 62
perestroika, 281, 283, 295
Persians, 4, 7, 8, 11, 229
Peru
  and the Chaco War, 141, 151
  and the War of the Pacific, xii, 81–83, 83–86, 86–100, 101
Philadelphia, Pennsylvania, 47–48, 54–56
Pierola, Nicolas, 93, 97–99
Pinto, Anibal, 86–87, 95
Pittsburgh, Pennsylvania, 46, 54, 55, 61
Ploesti oil fields, 181–86
Point Salines, Grenada, 269, 271, 277–78
Poland, 109, 156, 177, 203, 288
Port Stanley, Falkland Islands, 254–56

Portugal, 178
Potomac Company, 52, 59
Potomac River, 52
Prado, Mariano Ignacio, 85, 92–93
Praetorian Guards, 2
Prat, Arturo, 89
Pravda, 294
Procopius, 6, 11
propaganda, 133, 199–200, 211, 216, 217, 222
Prussia, 119, 192, 202, 203
Prussian General Staff, 189, 201
Puerto Suarez, Bolivia, 141
Pugo, Boris, 282, 298

Q
Quirnheim, Mertz von, 201

R
Rastenburg, Poland, 196, 197–99, 202
Reagan, Ronald, 225, 232–33, 235, 243, 248, 258–60, 263–64, 266–67, 279
Remer, Adolf, 199–200, 201
Replacement Army, 191
Revolutionary Military Council (RMC), 263, 265, 267, 268, 274, 276
Richard the Lionhearted, 21
Richmond Hill prison, 273
Robespierre, Maximilien, 51, 55
Röhm, Ernst, 122, 124, 127–28, 129–30, 134, 136, 148
Roman Catholic Church, 20–21
Roman Empire, x–xi, 1–2, 3–8, 9–15, 15–16, 27
Romania, xiii, 174–76, 176–79, 179–87, 187–88, 288
Roosevelt, Franklin Delano, 186
Roosevelt, Theodore, 205
Roselli, Johnny, 209
Rossbach, Gerhard, 126–27, 128, 129–30, 130
Royal Marines, 247, 248
Ruhr valley, 123

Rusk, Dean, 218
Russia
  after Soviet collapse, 298
  and Bay of Pigs invasion, 217
  coup attempt on Gorbachev,
    xv, 237, 281, 282, 283–
    90, 290–97, 297–98
  failed invasions of, xiii
  and Grenada, 277
  Romanian attack on, xiii, 174
  U.S. invasion of, xii, 102–3,
    104–7, 107–14, 114–15
  winter war with Finland, xiii,
    154–56, 156–58, 158–
    72, 172–73
Rust, Mathias, 285

S
Sakharov, Andrei, 239, 285
Saladin, 21, 40
Salamanca, Daniel, 142–43, 144–
  45, 146, 149–50
Salang Highway, 234
Samnite War, 16
San Juan Hill, 205
San Roman, Pepe, 222
Sandanistas, 261
Saudi Arabia, 233, 236
Scandinavians, 29
Schwarze Kapelle (Black Orches-
  tra), 193, 194
Schwarzkopf, Norman, 276
Scoon, Paul, 273
Second Crusade, 20
Seeckt, Hans von, 131
Seisser, Hans Ritter von, 124,
  125–26, 128–32
Semenov, Grigori, 112–13
September 11 terrorist attacks,
  241
Shevardnadze, Eduard, 238
Shultz, George, 238
Siberia, 111–12
Silva, Luís Alves de Lima e (Duke
  of Caxias), 76
silver mines, 84
Sima, Horia, 179

Sixth Army (German), 182
slavery
  and the Roman Empire, 2, 4,
    9–10, 15
  and the Turks, 19–20
  and the War of the Pacific, 84
  and the War of the Triple Alli-
    ance, 71
  and the Whiskey Rebellion, 44,
    50
Social Democrats (Germany), 120
Somoza, Luis, 217
Sotomayor, Rafeal, 82, 87, 88–89,
  95
South America, 68. *See also specific countries*
South Georgia Island, 247, 251,
  255
Soviet News Agency (TASS), 290
Soviet Union
  and Afghanistan, xiv, 224–25,
    226–29, 230–40, 240–
    41, 261
  collapse of, 287, 294, 297, 298
  coup attempt against Gor-
    bachev, 281, 283–90,
    290–97, 297–98
  and Cuba, 207, 223
  economy, 237, 288
  and Prussia, 203
  and Romania, 176, 179–87
  winter war with Finland, xiii,
    154–56, 156–58, 158–
    72, 172–73
  World War II casualty rates,
    187
Spaatz, Carl A. "Tooey," 175,
  181–83, 187–88
Spain
  and the Falkland Islands, 244–
    45
  and the Goths, 15
  and Paraguay, 65, 68
  and the War of the Pacific, 81–
    82, 83, 84, 85, 98, 101
Spanish American War, 205
Spanish Civil War, 171

Spanish influenza, 111
Special Forces
    British commandos, 251–52,
        253
    and the Fourth Crusade, 38
    and Grenada invasion, xv, 268,
        269–70, 272, 277, 279
    and Soviet invasion of Afghani-
        stan, 235
Spectre gunships, 273
SS troops, 189, 195–98, 202–3
St. George's University, Grenada,
    259, 261, 263
Stalin, Josef
    background, 155
    and collectivization, 284
    and Lenin's death, 115
    and the Nazi-Soviet Nonagres-
        sion Pact, 156
    and Russian invasion of Fin-
        land, 154, 156–58, 159–
        61, 165–66, 168–72,
        172–73
Stalingrad, Russia, 182, 185
Stanley, Falkland Islands, 248,
    252
Starodubtsev, Vasily A., 293
Stauffenberg, Klaus Schenk Graf
    von, 191, 194–99, 201, 204
Stevenson, Adlai, 217
Stinger missiles, 236–37
Stroessner, Alfredo, 80
Stülpnagel, Karl-Heinrich von,
    202, 203
Sturmabteilung (SA), 121, 122,
    124, 126–27, 129, 131–33,
    148
Sugerman, Danny, 279
supply issues
    and the Chaco War, 140–43,
        145, 150–51, 152
    and CIA support in Afghani-
        stan, 225, 231–32, 235
    and Falkland Islands War,
        252–53, 254
    and the Fourth Crusade, 25,
        29–30, 32–33, 35

and Romanian oil, 180–86
and Russian invasion of Fin-
    land, 160–62, 166
and U.S. invasion of Grenada,
    xv
and U.S. invasion of Russia,
    112–13
and Valens, 12
and the War of the Pacific, 88
and the Whiskey Rebellion, 58,
    59–60
and World War I, 110–11
Swan Island, 211, 216
Sweden, 159, 168–69
Swedish Kingdom, 157
Switzerland, 173, 187

T
Tacna, Peru, 95
Tajikistan, 241
Taliban, 241
Taman Guard, 291
Taraki, Nur Mohammed, 227–28
Tarapacá desert, 83, 85, 92, 95
taxation, 44–45, 49–50, 62
Tbilisi, Georgia, 287, 294
Tejada Sorzano, Luis, 143, 150–51
Temple of Solomon, 19
Ten Commandments, 19
Termez Bridge, 239
terrorism, 241, 266
Tervingi Goths, 6–7
Teutonic knights, 15, 121–22,
    192, 203
Thatcher, Margaret, xiv, 243, 246,
    248–50, 252, 255–57
Theodosius, 16
Thibault of Champagne, 22, 24
Third Crusade, 21
Thrace, 12
Tiananmen Square, 294, 295
Trafficante, Santos, 209–10
Trans-Siberian Railroad, 106–7,
    108, 110, 112
Transylvania, 174–76, 178–79,
    188
Treaty of Brest Litovsk, 106

Treaty of the Triple Alliance, 72
trench warfare, 147
Trotsky, Leon, 105
Turkey, 19, 43, 105

U
Union Treaty, 289, 290
United Kingdom, 248
United Nations, 217
United States
    and Afghanistan, 227, 228
    and the Bay of Pigs invasion,
        xiv, 205–7, 208–10, 210–
        22, 223
    and the Chaco War, 151
    and the Falkland Islands War,
        248
    and the invasion of Grenada,
        xv, 258–59, 261–67,
        267–79, 279–80
    and the invasion of Russia, xii,
        102–4, 104–7, 107–14,
        114–15
    and Romania, 174, 180–86
    and the War of the Pacific, 98
    and the War of the Triple Alli-
        ance, 76
    World War II casualties, 187
Upper Peru, 84
Urban II, 20
Uruguay, 68–70, 70–73, 139, 151
U.S. Army Rangers, 266, 268,
    270, 273, 276–78
U.S. Congress, 49, 53
U.S. Department of State, 217
U.S. Marines, 266, 268, 271, 275–
    76, 277
U.S. Navy, 266, 268–69, 272–76,
    277
U.S. Supreme Court, 49, 56
USS *Essex,* 220, 221
USS *Guam,* 271, 275, 276
USS *Independence,* 266

V
Valens, x–xi, 1–2, 3, 4–8, 9–15,
    15–16

Valentinian I, 3, 4–5, 6, 7–8
Valentinian II, 8
Vandals, 4
Varangians, 29
Varona, Antonio de, 213
Venice, 17–18, 23–25
Versailles Treaty, 121
Victoria I, 176
Vietnam War, 209, 231, 232, 268
Virginia, 47, 50–52, 58, 59
Visigoths, 15
Vladivostok, Russia, 106–7, 107–
    14
Voroshilov, Kliment, 165

W
War of 1812, 59
War of the Pacific, xii, 81–82, 83–
    86, 86–100, 101, 137
War of the Triple Alliance
    aftermath, 78–80
    background, 64–70
    and the Chaco War, 137, 139,
        140, 144
    and dictatorship, xi–xii
    events of, 70–78
    overview, 63
Washington, George, 45–46, 47,
    50–52, 53–54, 57–58, 61–
    62
Watergate scandal, 221
Weddell, Alexander Wilbourne,
    151–52
Weimar Republic, 118, 120
Wells, Benjamin, 51–53
Whiskey Rebellion, xi, 44–45,
    53–61
White House (Russian), 291–96
White Russians (anti-Bolsheviks),
    107, 109, 112, 113
Wilhelm II, 103, 111, 126, 138
Williams Rebolledo, Juan, 88–89
Wilson, Charlie, 235
Wilson, Woodrow, xii, 102–3,
    106–7, 112, 114, 151
Wittelsbach family, 123
World War I

World War I (*cont.*)
  and explosives, 101
  and Himmler, 121–22
  and Hitler, 117, 118, 191
  impact on Germany, 192
  and Ludendorff, 120
  and machine guns, 147
  and Romania, 176
  and U.S. invasion of Russia,
      xii, 102–3, 104–7, 107–
      14, 114–15
World War II
  and Afghanistan, 226, 233
  and the Beer Hall Putsch, xii–
      xiii
  and Casey, 225
  and Czechoslovakia, 110
  as "good war," x
  and the League of Nations, 151
  Nazi-Soviet Nonagression Pact,
      156, 288
  and plot against Hitler, xiii–
      xiv, 189–90, 191–94,

      194–204
  and Romania, xiii, 174–76,
      176–79, 179–87, 187–88
  and Russian invasion of Fin-
      land, 168–69
Wuolijoki, Hella, 168

Y
Yakovlev, Aleksandr, 292
Yalta Conference, 186
Yaneyev, Gennadi, 282, 291
Yazov, Dmitri, 282, 285–86, 288,
    296
yellow fever, 52
Yeltsin, Boris, 282, 286–87, 289,
    291, 293, 296–97

Z
Zahir Shah, Muhammad, 226–27
Zara, Hungary, 25–28
Zia-ul-Haq, Mohammed, 225,
    232, 233–34, 235, 239,
    240–41